BOREDOM

AF083827

Documents of Contemporary Art

Co-published by Whitechapel Gallery
and The MIT Press

First published 2017
© 2017 Whitechapel Gallery Ventures Limited
All texts © the authors or the estates of the authors,
unless otherwise stated

All rights reserved. No part of this publication
may be reproduced, stored in a retrieval system
or transmitted in any form or by any means,
electronic, mechanical, photocopying or otherwise,
without the written permission of the publisher

ISBN 978-0-85488-252-6 (Whitechapel Gallery)
ISBN 978-0-262-53344-7 (The MIT Press)

A catalogue record for this book is available from
the British Library

Library of Congress Cataloging-in-Publication Data

Names: McDonough, Tom, 1969- editor.
Title: Boredom / edited by Tom McDonough.
Description: Cambridge, MA : The MIT Press, 2017. |
Series: Whitechapel: documents of contemporary
art | Includes bibliographical references.
Identifiers: LCCN 2016036120 | ISBN
9780262533447 (pbk. : alk. paper)
Subjects: LCSH: Emotions in art. | Boredom.
Classification: LCC NX650.E46 B67 2017 | DDC
700/.453--dc23 LC record available at https://lccn.
loc.gov/2016036120

Whitechapel Gallery   10 9 8 7 6 5 4 3 2 1
The MIT Press   10 9 8 7 6 5 4 3 2 1

Series Editor: Iwona Blazwick
Commissioning Editor: Ian Farr
Project Editor: Francesca Vinter
Design by SMITH
Allon Kaye, Justine Schuster
Printed and bound in China

Cover, John Pilson, from the series *Interregna*
(1998–2000). Gelatin silver print, dimensions
variable. Courtesy of the artist.

Whitechapel Gallery Ventures Limited
77–82 Whitechapel High Street
London E1 7QX
whitechapelgallery.org
Distributed to the book trade (UK and Europe only)
by Central Books
centralbooks.com

The MIT Press
Cambridge, MA 02142
mitpress.mit.edu

Simone de Beauvoir//Walter Benjamin//Bernadette Corporation//Maurice Blanchot//Ina Blom//Nicolas Bourriaud//Stefan Brüggemann//John Cage//Ivan Chtcheglov//Critical Art Ensemble//Jennifer Doyle//Alla Efimova//Mikhail Epstein//Peter Fischli//Jonathan Flatley//Claire Fontaine//Dominic Fox//Betty Friedan//Elizabeth S. Goodstein//Dan Graham//Boris Groys//Julian Jason Haladyn//Dick Hebdige//Richard Hell//Dick Higgins//The Invisible Committee//Ilya Kabakov//Jonathan D. Katz//Siegfried Kracauer//Chris Kraus//Henri Lefebvre//Tan Lin//Sven Lütticken//Greil Marcus//Ivone Margulies//Jonas Mekas//John Miller//Robert Morris//Agne Narusyte//Sianne Ngai//Peter Osborne//Georges Perec//Patrice Petro//Sadie Plant//Yvonne Rainer//Barbara Rose//Christine Ross//Moira Roth//Jon Savage//Situationist International//Valerie Solanas//Susan Sontag//Georges Teyssot//Mierle Laderman Ukeles//Raoul Vaneigem//Geoff Waite//David Foster Wallace//Andy Warhol//Faith Wilding//Aleksandr Zinoviev

Boredom

Whitechapel Gallery
London
The MIT Press
Cambridge, Massachusetts

Edited by Tom McDonough

Documents of Contemporary Art

In recent decades artists have progressively expanded the boundaries of art as they have sought to engage with an increasingly pluralistic environment. Teaching, curating and understanding of art and visual culture are likewise no longer grounded in traditional aesthetics but centred on significant ideas, topics and themes ranging from the everyday to the uncanny, the psychoanalytical to the political.

The Documents of Contemporary Art series emerges from this context. Each volume focuses on a specific subject or body of writing that has been of key influence in contemporary art internationally. Edited and introduced by a scholar, artist, critic or curator, each of these source books provides access to a plurality of voices and perspectives defining a significant theme or tendency.

For over a century the Whitechapel Gallery has offered a public platform for art and ideas. In the same spirit, each guest editor represents a distinct yet diverse approach – rather than one institutional position or school of thought – and has conceived each volume to address not only a professional audience but all interested readers.

Series Editor: Iwona Blazwick; Commissioning Editor: Ian Farr; Project Editor: Francesca Vinter; Editorial Advisory Board: Roger Conover, Sean Cubitt, Neil Cummings, Gabriela Salgado, Sven Spieker, Gilane Tawadros, Sofia Victorino

Boredom *like stupidity* contains its own treasures

Bernadette Corporation, *Reena Spaulings*, 2004

INTRODUCTION//12

MODERNITY'S EMPTY MOMENTS//24
THE WILL TO BOREDOM//44
INDIFFERENCE//70
SILENCE//92
NOTHING HAPPENS//124
NO FUTURE//146
BLOCS OF THE MIND//172
DISENGAGE!//194

BIOGRAPHICAL NOTES//226
BIBLIOGRAPHY//228
INDEX//232
ACKNOWLEDGEMENTS//239

MODERNITY'S EMPTY MOMENTS
Elizabeth S. Goodstein Experience without Qualities, 2005//26
Walter Benjamin The Arcades Project, 1927–40//28
Julian Jason Haladyn Boredom and Art, 2015//30
Siegfried Kracauer Boredom, 1924//34
Georges Teyssot Boredom and Bedroom: The Suppression of the Habitual, 1996//37
Patrice Petro Aftershocks of the New: Feminism and Film History, 2002//40

THE WILL TO BOREDOM
Ivan Chtcheglov Formulary for a New Urbanism, 1953//46
Situationist International The Adventure, 1960//47
Henri Lefebvre Critique of Everyday Life, 1961//49
Maurice Blanchot Everyday Speech, 1962//53
Georges Perec Things: A Story of the Sixties, 1965//58
Raoul Vaneigem The Revolution of Everyday Life, 1967//60
Sadie Plant Now, the SI, 1992//64

INDIFFERENCE
John Cage Silence, 1961//72
Moira Roth The Aesthetic of Indifference, 1977//73
Jonathan D. Katz Identification, 1998//77
Dick Higgins Boredom and Danger, 1968//81
Ina Blom Boredom and Oblivion, 1998//84
Andy Warhol In Conversation with Joseph Gelmis, 1969//87
Jonas Mekas Notes after Reseeing the Movies of Andy Warhol, 1970//88
Tan Lin Warhol's Aura and the Language of Writing, 2001//90

SILENCE

Yvonne Rainer On *Parts of Some Sextets*, 1965//**94**
Robert Morris Three Folds in the Fabric and Four Autobiographical Asides as Allegories (or Interruptions), 1989//**97**
Barbara Rose ABC Art, 1965//**98**
Susan Sontag The Aesthetics of Silence, 1967//**103**
Nicolas Bourriaud The Legacy of Indifference, 1987//**110**
Jonathan Flatley Allegories of Boredom, 2004//**112**
John Miller No More Boring Art, 2001//**118**

NOTHING HAPPENS

Betty Friedan The Feminine Mystique, 1963//**126**
Simone de Beauvoir Les Belles Images, 1966//**129**
Mierle Laderman Ukeles MANIFESTO! MAINTENANCE ART – Proposal for an Exhibition 'CARE', 1969//**129**
Faith Wilding Waiting, 1971//**133**
Ivone Margulies On *Jeanne Dielmann*, 1996//**136**
Jennifer Doyle I Must Be Boring Someone, 2006//**138**
Valerie Solanas S.C.U.M. Manifesto, 1967//**144**

NO FUTURE

Peter Fischli Sigmar Polke – A Contemporary Visionary: In Conversation with Mark Godfrey, 2014//**148**
Jon Savage England's Dreaming: Anarchy, Sex Pistols, Punk Rock and Beyond, 1991//**149**
Dan Graham The Producer as Artist, 1988//**150**
Greil Marcus The Last Sex Pistols Concert ..., 1989//**152**
Dick Hebdige Bleached Roots: Punks and White Ethnicity, 1979//**157**
Richard Hell CBGB as a Physical Space, 2006//**161**
Geoff Waite On the Politics of Boredom (A Communist Pastiche), 1992//**162**

BLOCS OF THE MIND
Aleksandr Zinoviev Homo Sovieticus, 1982//**174**
Agne Narusyte The Aesthetics of Boredom: Lithuanian
   Photography 1980–1990, 2010//**177**
Alla Efimova Photographic Ethics in the Work of Boris
   Mikhailov, 1994//**181**
Ilya Kabakov On Emptiness, 1990//**183**
Mikhail Epstein Negative Emptiness, 1999//**186**
Boris Groys Comrades of Time, 2009//**189**

DISENGAGE!
Critical Art Ensemble Case History and Clinical Report
   on the Pastiche of Boredom, 1992//**196**
David Foster Wallace The Pale King, 2011//**197**
Sianne Ngai Stuplimity, 2005//**199**
Christine Ross The Performance-Management Model
   of Performative Subjectivity, 2006//**203**
Dominic Fox The Cold World, 2009//**207**
Bernadette Corporation Bedrooms Boredoms (Short
   Escapes in New York City), 2004//**209**
Claire Fontaine Dear R., 2007//**211**
The Invisible Committee The Coming Insurrection,
   2007//**213**
Sven Lütticken Lazy Labour: Chronopolitical Remarks,
   2014/16//**216**
Peter Osborne Art Time, 2013//**220**
Stefan Brüggemann In Conversation with Malcolm
   McLaren, 2006//**222**
Chris Kraus Twelve Words, Nine Days, 2011//**224**

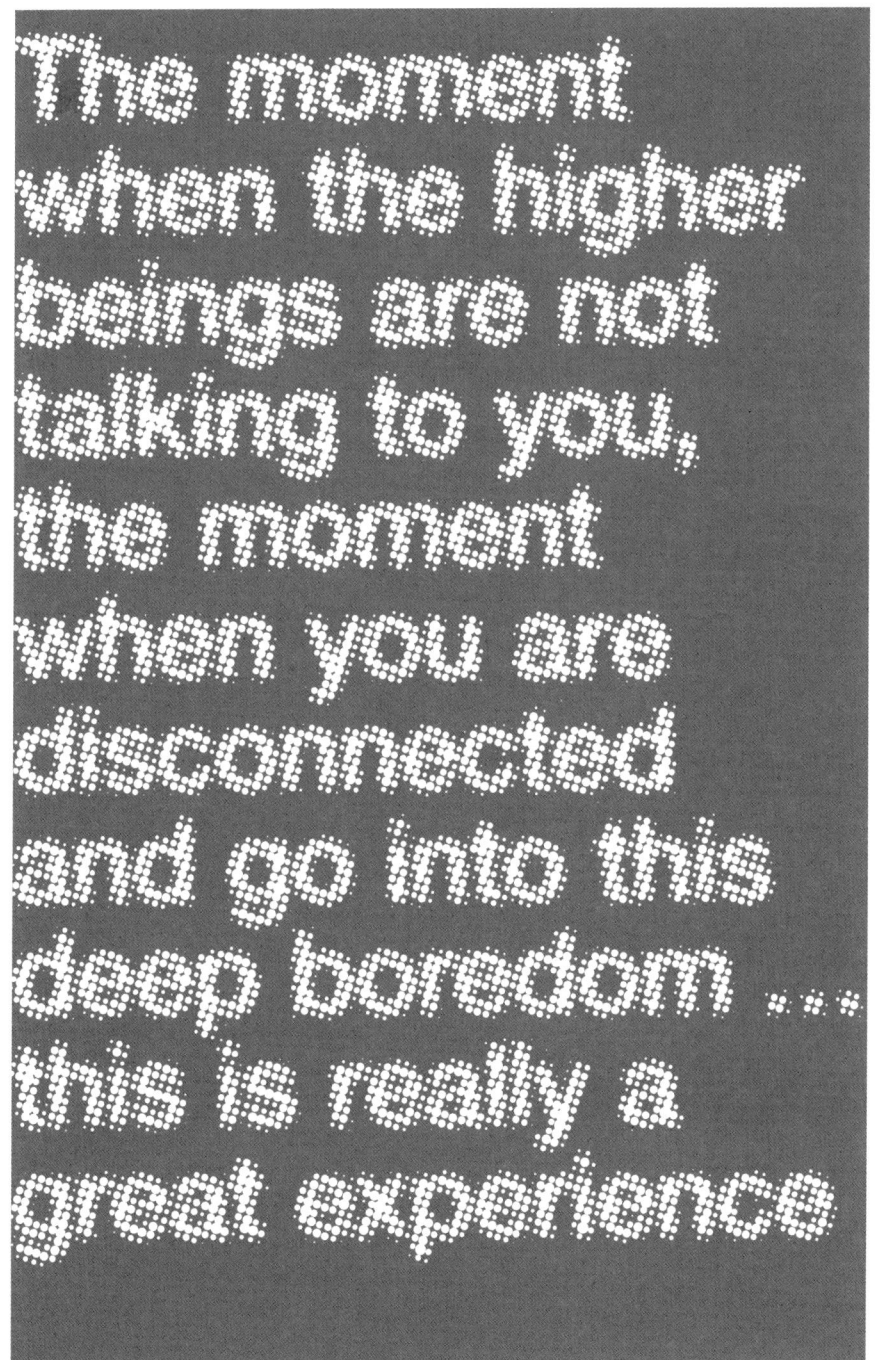

Peter Fischli, 'Peter Fischli on Sigmar Polke', *Tate Etc.*, Autumn 2014

Tom McDonough
Introduction//An Aesthetics of Impoverishment

Contemporary life is lived, more and more frequently, in spaces defined by their anonymity, their blandness, their ordinariness, even their dullness. Such spaces – typified by transport infrastructure such as highways, train stations or airports – aim to go unnoticed the better to accommodate the accelerated circulation of people and goods through them; our means of transportation themselves – cars, trains or planes – similarly seek to disappear for their users into pure functionality. So too do large hotel chains, with their interchangeable rooms, or supermarkets. What all these characteristic sites of late modernity share is a resistance to our identification, to our desire to develop an empathetic relation with the spaces we interact with daily.[1] In the early 1990s, anthropologist Marc Augé famously called them *non-lieux*, 'non-places', to insist on their opposition to what is connoted by terms like abode or residence – 'places' in its common sense meaning, or what, philosophically, is meant by the word 'dwelling'.[2] Isolated even as we are reduced to the same serial condition as everyone else, we users of these non-places maintain with them purely contractual relations, symbolized by the train or plane ticket, by the pass scanned at the tollbooth, or even by the cart pushed through the aisles of the big-box store. The non-place is, we could say, the very locus of our everyday experience of *boredom*.

A generation ago, Henri Lefebvre had already suggested something similar when he described the *everyday* as 'the ethics underlying routine and the aesthetics of familiar settings', as 'what is taken for granted and that of which all the parts follow each other in such a regular, unvarying succession that those concerned have no call to question their sequence'.[3] Whether in work or consumption, the relations of production or the reproduction of those relations, a repetitive monotony had come to characterize the quotidian experience of modernity; the years separating Lefebvre's diagnosis from that of Augé simply saw the further expansion of this anonymous routine into our surroundings and our social life, along with the gradual eradication of those zones in which some other, affectively charged relation to the world could be consistently maintained. For many, at least in those parts of the world where the question of survival has been resolved, today's dominant social experience could be expressed as boredom … tedium … monotony – our vocabulary is rich in terms for this anti-feeling.

Boredom, as many cultural historians have noted, is a peculiarly modern sentiment. Earlier periods might have known *acedia*, the withdrawal of a sense of the divine from the world, or *melancholia*, a disturbance of the humours, but only with the dawn of our own era does a recognizable sense of *boredom* emerge. This feeling, oddly combining weariness and restlessness, in which the world around us fails to provoke any spark of interest, arises at the very same moment of the mid nineteenth century when modernity itself was birthed from the combined forces of urbanization, industrialization and the rise of mass politics and consumerism. There was a boredom experienced at work, whether on the rationalized factory floor or at the desks of an increasingly bureaucratized administrative labour; there was a boredom encountered amidst the ever more standardized pursuits of a leisure time defined by the acquisition of mass-produced commodities. And there was the boredom circumscribed by the repetitive tasks of domestic labour, an age-old imposition that appeared as such only now that women began to demand their right to a place in the public sphere. It was an experience captured in literature by Charles Baudelaire, Gustave Flaubert and Charlotte Perkins Gilman. Karl Marx inventoried its social origins on the assembly line; Søren Kierkegaard plumbed the depths of its toll on the human spirit; Sigmund Freud parsed its psychic origins in the unconscious.

  Simultaneously boredom, as opposed to aristocratic idleness, appears in visual art for the first time, most famously perhaps etched into the features of the barmaid in Édouard Manet's *A Bar at the Folies-Bergère* (1882), where, as T. J. Clark describes it, her look – 'public, outward, "blasé"' – fails to register '*any* identity', foregoing even 'identity in general'.[4] Boredom, unlike joy or anger, lacks positive attributes – it is an *absence* or withdrawal of affect, and is as such peculiarly well-suited to the service role she performs, in which she appears, in Carol Armstrong's words, 'more as a commodity similar in shape and objective appearance to the bottle on the counter' than as a fellow human subject.[5] We could be more specific by noting that boredom is tied, not simply to the commodity, but to commodity exchange and the objectification of social relations: the reduction of human experience to 'contractual relations' in which we seem to become mere appendages serving the needs of the objects around us. It would be little exaggeration to claim that from this moment on, whenever art addressed the conditions of everyday life within modernity, a confrontation with boredom was inevitable. But even when modern art retreated from this world and ensconced itself in a realm of pure abstraction, monotony might remain present, now in the form of the viewer's encounter with an artwork from which so much aesthetic richness had been revoked. Tedium, dullness and ennui haunt the modern like a ghost of our impoverished experience.

  Contemporary art has inherited that condition, and this anthology of artists' writings, critical texts and literary excerpts surveys the contours of what we might properly call our *boredoms* over the last half-century. For boredom can no longer be considered a singular experience, but one that is articulated in widely divergent forms depending on class, gender and cultural position; moreover, we find a great split between those who suffer boredom as a burden to be lifted and those who face boredom as itself an aesthetic experience with critical and transformative potential – an aesthetics of impoverishment that must then be understood in this dual sense, both as the artistic transcription of our world of social privation and as its possible redemption. The remainder of the introduction explores the categories – at once roughly chronological and thematic – into which the anthology is organized.

Modernity's Empty Moments
This introductory section lays out a brief survey of the emergence of boredom within the experience of modernity, with an emphasis on the social, psychic and philosophical responses developed in the early twentieth century. If the expression of boredom as a social and individual response to modern life may be found across a wide range of literary and critical texts from the mid nineteenth century forward, it was only in the decades following the First World War that a truly *theoretical* approach to boredom was articulated. This task largely fell to those Marxist scholars associated with the Frankfurt School, most notably Walter Benjamin, as they sought to excavate the origins of modernity at the moment of its crisis, threatened on one hand by fascist atavism and on the other by proletarian revolution. While their sympathies clearly lay with the latter, these authors nevertheless felt compelled to diagnose the contradictions within bourgeois society in order to better chart the means of undoing them.

For the poets, as for much of the rest of society, boredom seemed to be nothing less than a curse, an indelible part of the nature of the times. It inhered in the long, straight new boulevards driven through the capital cities, in the monotony of the newspaper, in the grand, mirrored cafes with their noise and smoke. What they could not see, and what the Frankfurt School writers would insist upon, was the dialectical relation of this upper-class boredom with the tedium of modern labour. In one of his notes for the *Arcades Project*, Benjamin describes workers' repetitive labour as the 'economic infrastructure of the ideological boredom of the upper classes', provocatively drawing together the two separated arenas of factory and salon.[6] Boredom, he insisted, was a thoroughly historical category, and one whose origins lay in the counter-revolutionary suppression of humanity's march toward liberation:

> The upper classes do not know, and do not wish to know, that the objective source of boredom is because history is languishing – and the moment of their own overthrow is delayed. They are addicted to boredom, as they are to remaining asleep. The average man – and the poet – blames boredom on the weather. But for

the working class, industrial labour shatters the illusion that nature rather than society is to blame.⁷

The work of the Frankfurt School would be brutally interrupted by the rise of Nazism and the outbreak of war, but its insights would fundamentally shape how we understand the experience of boredom. These writings provide the context against which distinctly contemporary approaches to this topic have been articulated since the early 1960s.

The Will to Boredom

Ivan Chtcheglov's 'Formulary for a New Urbanism', written in obscurity in Paris in the early 1950s, opens with a repeated assertion: 'We are bored in the city, there is no longer any Temple of the Sun. […] We are bored in the city, we really have to strain to still discover mysteries on the sidewalk billboards, the latest state of humour and poetry[.]'⁸ For the Surrealists a generation earlier, the street could yet be the site of the marvellous – the surprising encounter that shattered the narrow rationality of the bourgeois world – but for those coming of age in the postwar city, such possibilities seemed foreclosed. What Chtcheglov expressed poetically would be explored further in a series of texts, written in France and appearing for the most part in the 1960s, that in many ways return to the themes of earlier critiques of boredom developed within the Marxist tradition. But now those critiques had developed an added urgency and a rootedness in a new conceptual category, 'the everyday', whose study was pioneered by Henri Lefebvre. Alienation and boredom were no longer to be met solely within the realm of labour or upper-class idleness, but were now perceived as integral to mass leisure, long considered a space of freedom; the city as much as the factory had been rationalized and become monotonous and dull.

And yet the everyday as a category of experience was, as Lefebvre and his fellow philosopher Maurice Blanchot found, everywhere denied, derided as a topic too trivial for serious consideration. Situationist Guy Debord, writing in the context of the former's 'Group for Research on Everyday Life' in the early 1960s, explained why this should be the case:

> […] if people censor the question of their own everyday life, it is both because they are aware of its unbearable impoverishment and because sooner or later they sense – whether they admit it or not – that all the real possibilities, all the desires that have been frustrated by the functioning of social life, are focused there […] Awareness of the profound richness and energy abandoned in everyday life is inseparable from awareness of the poverty of the dominant organization of this life.⁹

Boredom, then, is a symptom of repression: it both masks and marks all the potentialities and desires whose realization class society frustrates. As such, it is both the site of our greatest alienation and the site of that alienation's potential overcoming since, as Blanchot insists, boredom at least makes that alienation visible, perceptible: 'Boredom is the everyday become manifest: as a consequence of having lost its essential – constitutive – trait of being *unperceived*.'[10] In this rich strain of social and political symptomatology of boredom, we find a return to and updating of that properly dialectical understanding of its experience first outlined by the German scholars of the 1920s.

Indifference / Silence

While the French were advancing a critique of boredom in the early 1960s, in New York artists and critics were developing an aesthetics that privileged this experience. 'If, on seeing some of the new paintings, sculpture, dances or films, you are bored', wrote critic Barbara Rose in 1965, 'probably you were intended to be. Boring the public is one way of testing its commitment.'[11] Minimalist sculptors worked with repetitive structures and uninflected surfaces; Andy Warhol, in his art but especially in his experimental films, pushed repetition and duration to barely endurable limits. In the context of an ever more strident media environment, the very inexpressiveness and lack of interest found in Minimalism and Pop could be construed as critical strategies, refusals or negations of the alienated plenitude on offer among the culture industries. They were also, as Susan Sontag argued, means of frustrating the sensibilities of a privileged audience that had come to expect complexity and differentiation as hallmarks of 'high art': 'There is, in a sense, no such thing as boredom. Boredom is only another name for a certain species of frustration. And the new languages which the interesting art of our time speaks are frustrating to the sensibilities of educated people.'[12] But for a new generation, boredom and its seeming opposite, interest, proved to be curiously linked; we hear this novel sensibility articulated in Henry Geldzahler's description of watching Warhol's 320-minute-long film *Sleep* (1963):

> what appears boring is the elimination of incident, accident, story, sound and the moving camera. [...] As less and less happens on the screen, we become satisfied with almost nothing and find the slightest shift in the body of the sleeper or the least movement of the camera interesting enough.[13]

John Cage, with his Zen embrace of a non-hierarchical conception of sound, was the key reference point for these new configurations of the aesthetics of boredom. As composer and teacher, he encouraged attention to what had previously been considered unworthy of our notice, fundamentally calling into question established aesthetic canons and notions of taste and discrimination. And yet, in comparison to the militant rejection of boredom among Parisian intellectuals, the American postwar avant-garde's embrace of this 'aesthetic of indifference' in the wake of Cage seemed to represent a retreat in the face of – if not acquiescence to – the hysterical anti-communism of the McCarthy era that then typified public, political life. The silence and absence that marked all these works would appear, in this light, a kind of blank-face refusal to take up sides in a society that was demanding steadfast, patriotic loyalty; whether such a retreat was a viable position would be a question posed by scholars at a moment of renewed activism in the early 1970s, and reassessed again a generation later in light of the necessity of strategies of disguise and obliquity on the part of queer artists such as Cage during that era of intolerance.

Nothing Happens
Even as boredom was being viewed through simultaneous political and aesthetic lenses, a third perspective opened up with the advent of the contemporary feminist movement. In 1963 Betty Friedan's *Feminine Mystique* diagnosed a malaise among American housewives trapped in suburban lives devoted to marriage and motherhood. Her critique of postwar domesticity and the condition of femininity within the society of consumption, what Friedan called 'the comfortable concentration camp', radically reoriented our understanding of boredom by recognizing the gendered specificity of this experience. It was also a rejoinder to those who conceived of boredom as merely a reaction to external circumstance – of boring objects or monotonous environments. For an American, and soon global, feminist audience, Friedan insisted on its origins in blocked energies, thus seeing the question of boredom for the first time as belonging at once to the realm of the political and that of the individual psyche. In boredom's malaise, its borderline anxiety, its feeling of emptiness, these blockages manifest themselves as alienation from one's own doing and being; it is, as one cultural historian has written, 'a quotidian crisis of subjectivity'.[14] Kristin Ross described it as an ambient fear of one's own fictiveness, of being effaced or absorbed into a level of abstraction that was reshaping not only the urban and periurban landscape but the very topography of the self. The anxiety manifested by Laurence, the protagonist of Simone de Beauvoir's novel *Les belles images*, written in the mid 1960s, is rooted in her suspicion that she has become as unreal as the advertisements she designs, what Ross calls 'the fear that she has passed through to the other side of the mirror, become the reification of a reification, been subsumed into an image'.[15]

From these positions we can trace the rise of a feminist consciousness and aesthetics of boredom, particularly as it plays out in performance cultures of the 1970s. If women were particularly marginalized through repetitive cultural practices that were devalued as inherently monotonous – domestic maintenance and other reproductive labour such as food preparation and childcare – then these would become precisely the sites of critical intervention.[16] Some artists, such as Faith Wilding, developed performances that made this monotony visible, while others, such as Mierle Laderman Ukeles, hoped to valorize activities of 'maintenance' that the dominant, masculinist culture failed to recognize. In each instance, boredom is taken up as a confrontation with the everyday of patriarchy, presenting the mundane details of a 'woman's world' that had previously been belittled, when it had been represented at all. Chantal Akerman's film *Jeanne Dielman, 23 quai du Commerce, 1080 Bruxelles* (1975) did not merely figure this monotony within its narrative, but integrated it into its very form:

> fixed, symmetrical framing and long shot duration clear the scene, and magnify the focus on single characters as they speak. Along with the fixed perspective, there are no reverse or point-of-view shots; the characters are always seen from the outside […] Akerman's dialogue-as-monologue structure displaces response onto the audience. With no reversal of perspective, she establishes a non-complicit relation with her audience.[17]

Here boredom is explicitly cultivated in the viewer, not in the name of a renewed sense of 'interest', as in the Warholian aesthetics of the 1960s, but in order to exacerbate our anxiety and unpleasure, asking us to confront the very routineness of feminine tedium.

No Future

A very different attack on some of the same forms of social conditioning and their attendant oppressions was directed against boredom by punk, beginning in the mid 1970s. From the Ramones sniffing glue ('Now I wanna have somethin' to do'), to the Sex Pistols' vacancy ('There's no point in asking, you'll get no reply / Oh just remember I don't decide'), to the Clash's stifling cities ('London's burning with boredom now / London's burning dial 999'), boredom in all its inflections was a key term. Influenced by the Situationist critiques of the 1960s, British punk set its sights on the banality and conformity of contemporary daily life in the regimented West – and thereby has enjoyed a lingering influence on subsequent art, as well as theorizations of the postmodern.

Both Malcolm McLaren, manager of the Sex Pistols, and Jamie Reid, designer at the Suburban Press responsible for their most famous graphics, had absorbed the French Situationist theories of spectacle and alienation as well as their practices of *détournement* – the subversive appropriation of texts and images – while in art school at the end of the 1960s; determined to bring these concepts into popular culture, McLaren saw fashion and music as key realms in which to probe 'the politics of boredom' – to quote the banner he once strung across the stage at a New York Dolls concert. That ambition was met by a groundswell of youth in London and other cities who had had enough of the grandiosity and pretensions of post-Sixties mainstream rock and roll. Johnny Rotten summed it up neatly when he remarked, early in the Sex Pistols' history: 'The great ignorant public don't know why we're in a band. It's because we're bored with all that old crap. Like every decent human being should be.' Steve Jones, the band's guitarist, concluded, 'we're not into music, we're into chaos.'[18]

Cultural studies theorist Dick Hebdige, writing in the immediate wake of the initial wave of punk in 1977, would restate its position as follows: 'Clothed in chaos, they produced Noise in the calmly orchestrated Crisis of everyday life in the late 1970s – noise which made (no)sense in exactly the same way and to exactly the same extent as a piece of *avant-garde* music.'[19] Just as Dada's mimetic strategies had aped the alternately armoured and fragmented bodies of the First World War, punk's sartorial and musical anti-styles were intended to mirror the emptiness and monotony of the late-capitalist lifeworld.[20] If the disappearance of our importance and autonomy in economic life had been paralleled by the severe diminishment of an entire sector of our intellectual and affective life, then punk proposed to exacerbate precisely those qualities of indifference and estrangement cultivated by a society of consumption.[21]

Blocs of the Mind
In the early 1980s, Aleksandr Zinoviev's *Homo Sovieticus* provided a description of a peculiarly Soviet form of boredom enforced not through the compulsory leisure of capitalist democracies but the strictures of statist bureaucracy. All the tedium, hypocrisy and cynicism that characterized a 'postmodern' West were found to have their counterparts in the so-called workers' states. By the end of that decade, there was widespread recognition of a form of ennui particular to the Eastern bloc, and of the ways that artists there had given form to it. And yet this should not be reduced to a cliché of the drabness of Soviet society, of the lack of variety in the environment, of the scarcity of commodities. Fredric Jameson, reflecting on the postmodern politics of boredom, cautions that boredom is not the result of such environmental factors; rather, its roots lie in something more profound – the obstruction of libidinal and social drives: 'in both the Freudian and Marxist traditions … "boredom" is taken not so much as an objective property of things and works but rather as a response to the blockage of energies (whether those be grasped in terms of desire or of praxis).'[22] Soviet boredom was

the product of those blockages peculiar to the East, to its own forms of historical stagnation and frozen time.

But within this system, boredom could also possess a critical force: in a society whose proclaimed 'socialism' compelled individual participation, the withdrawal and malaise of boredom offered a form of passive non-cooperation that potentially eluded the state apparatus. We find it in Ilya Kabakov's albums of the early 1970s, collections of drawings and texts recounting the joyless lives of the inhabitants of Moscow's communal apartments, such as the boy, Primakov, who retreats to the back of a dark closet. We find it in the anti-heroic photographs of Boris Mikhailov, which captured the underside of Soviet and, later, post-Soviet everyday life. In a society defined by what Boris Groys has called 'metanoia', a state-mandated condition of permanent change and constant transition, boredom could provide a means to step out of this accelerated time, this exacerbated dialectic – it could create a subversive form of belatedness.[23] But with the collapse of the Soviet project and the concomitant abandonment of a utopian 'infinite future', our relation to the triangulation of time, change and boredom has shifted. 'Today', Groys writes, 'we are stuck in the present as it reproduces itself without leading to any future. We simply lose our time […].' Temporality becomes 'unproductive, wasted' – or perhaps, more positively, 'excessive', the possible site of a quasi-Heideggerian boredom through which we might begin to feel our own presence in the world: as 'time that attests to our life as pure being-in-time, beyond its use within the framework of modern economic and political projects'.[24]

Disengage!
Boredom and the unproductive as figures of resistance are hardly unique to the Eastern bloc; Jean Baudrillard had already characterized them as forms of opposition to late capitalism in the immediate aftermath of the revolts of '68, pushing the earlier Situationist analysis of boredom onto new terrain and aligning it with emergent categories of working-class and youth struggle. In *The Consumer Society*, he writes:

> Fatigue (or 'asthenia') will […] be interpreted as a response on the part of modern man – a response in the form of a passive refusal – to his conditions of existence. […] The fatigue of the citizen of post-industrial society is not far removed from the 'go-slow' or 'slowdown' of factory workers, or the schoolchild's 'boredom'. These are all forms of passive resistance; they are 'ingrowing' in the way one speaks of an 'ingrowing toenail', turning back in towards the flesh, towards the inside.[25]

However, if in the East the passivity of boredom was set against the accelerated time of the state's utopian project, in the West fatigue becomes '*the only form of activity* which can, in certain conditions, be set against the constraint of general passivity which applies in current social relations'.[26] True passivity is the domain of those who willingly participate in neoliberalism's call to 'invest in the self', to become an entrepreneur of one's own intellectual and 'biopolitical' capital. Fatigue, depression and various neuroses are, by contrast, disguised forms of protest that, as Baudrillard remarks, 'grow into' our minds and bodies because these are the only things on which we, in our dispossession, can take out our frustration.

We live in a moment when work is everywhere and anytime, when the forces of production are no longer concentrated in the punctual site of the factory but have been dispersed among the most various locales, when the deadening reach of the exchange relation extends ever farther into subjective experience. Fatigue, boredom and their cognates are passive refusals of the demands of this regime of contemporary capital. They are updated forms of the rebuff first articulated by Herman Melville's legendary scrivener: 'I would prefer not to.'[27] But such refusals can become conscious or active as well – in which case, we might call them, adopting a term first developed among the post-Situationist militants and theorists of Tiqqun in the later 1990s, a 'human strike'. 'The human strike', they write, 'corresponds to an era when the borders between work and life have become blurred. […] [It] never attacks the relations of production without attacking at the same time the affective relations that sustain it.'[28] Contemporary art, to the extent it is able to confront and address the neoliberal economy, recognizes the peculiar forms of boredom and servitude specific to it. The disengagement of the human strike provides a model; here, it is less a matter of an external cleavage between classes than one that operates within the individual herself, dividing us internally between what is dead – what belongs to capital – and what belongs to life.

1   For an early architectural defence of such spaces, see Robert Venturi, Denise Scott Brown and Steven Izenour, *Learning from Las Vegas* (Cambridge, Massachusetts: The MIT Press, 1972); for a more jaundiced view, see Martin Pawley, *Terminal Architecture* (London: Reaktion Books, 1998).

2   See Marc Augé, *Non-Places: Introduction to an Anthropology of Supermodernity*, trans. John Howe (London and New York: Verso, 1995).

3   Henri Lefebvre, *Everyday Life in the Modern World*, trans. Sacha Rabinovitch (London: Allen Lane, 1971) 24. See also his 'The Everyday and Everydayness', trans. Christine Levich, *Yale French Studies*, no. 73 ('Everyday Life') (1987) 7–11.

4   T. J. Clark, *The Painting of Modern Life: Paris in the Art of Manet and His Followers* (New York: Knopf, 1985) 285.

5   Carol Armstrong, *Manet Manette* (New Haven and London: Yale University Press, 2002) 290.

6   Walter Benjamin, *The Arcades Project*, trans. Howard Eiland and Kevin McLaughlin (Cambridge,

Massachusetts: The Belknap Press of Harvard University Press, 1999) 106.
7   Susan Buck-Morss, *The Dialectics of Seeing: Walter Benjamin and the Arcades Project* (Cambridge, Massachusetts: The MIT Press, 1989) 105.
8   Gilles Ivain [Ivan Chtcheglov], 'Formulary for a New Urbanism', in *Situationist International Anthology*, ed. and trans. Ken Knabb (Berkeley: Bureau of Public Secrets, 1981) 1.
9   Guy Debord, 'Perspectives for Conscious Changes in Everyday Life', in *Situationist International Anthology*, op. cit., 71.
10 Maurice Blanchot, 'Everyday Speech', trans. Susan Hanson, *Yale French Studies*, no. 73 ('Everyday Life') (1987) 16.
11 Barbara Rose, 'ABC Art', *Art in America*, vol. 53, no. 5 (October/November 1965) 65.
12 Susan Sontag, 'One Culture and the New Sensibility', in *Against Interpretation and Other Essays* (New York: Dell, 1966) 303.
13 Henry Geldzahler, 'Some Notes on Sleep', in *Film Culture Reader*, ed. P. Adams Sitney (New York: Praeger, 1970) 300–301.
14 Elizabeth S. Goodstein, *Experience without Qualities: Boredom and Modernity* (Stanford: Stanford University Press, 2005) 10.
15 Kristin Ross, *Fast Cars, Clean Bodies* (Cambridge, Massachusetts: The MIT Press, 1995) 148.
16 Lefebvre himself had recognized something like an 'uneven development' of boredom, noting that a generalized passivity in our society was 'distributed unequally': 'It weighs more heavily on women, who are sentenced to everyday life, on the working class, on employees who are not technocrats, on youth […].' Lefebvre, 'The Everyday and Everydayness', op. cit., 10. See also his *Everyday Life in the Modern World*, op. cit., 35, where he notes the ways in which 'the conditions of everyday life bear heaviest' upon women.
17 Ivone Margulies, *Nothing Happens: Chantal Akerman's Hyperrealist Everyday* (Durham, North Carolina: Duke University Press, 1996) 156–7.
18 Quoted in the Sex Pistols inductees page at the Rock & Roll Hall of Fame, accessible at https://www.rockhall.com/inductees/sex-pistols.
19 Dick Hebdige, *Subculture: The Meaning of Style* (London and New York: Routledge, 1994) 114–15.
20 On those strategies, see Hal Foster, 'Dada Mime', *October*, no. 105 ('Dada') (Summer 2003) 166–76.
21 Here I echo the observations of Lucien Goldmann, developing Lukacs's idea of *Verdinglichung* (reification), whose essence is the repression of the fact that the world and society are made by human activity. See Goldmann, *Cultural Creation in Modern Society*, trans. Bart Grahl (Candor, New York: Telos Press, 1976) 84–5.
22 Fredric Jameson, *Postmodernism, or The Cultural Logic of Late Capitalism* (Durham, North Carolina: Duke University Press, 1991) 71.
23 On 'metanoia', see Boris Groys, *The Communist Postscript*, trans. Thomas H. Ford (London and New York: Verso, 2009).
24 Groys, 'Comrades of Time', *e-flux journal*, no. 11 (December 2009) 4.
25 Jean Baudrillard, *The Consumer Society: Myths and Structures* (London and Thousand Oaks, California: Sage, 1998) 182–3.

26 Ibid., 183.

27 On Bartleby see, among others, Gilles Deleuze, 'Bartleby; or, The Formula', in *Essays Critical and Clinical*, trans. Daniel W. Smith and Michael A. Greco (Minneapolis: University of Minnesota Press, 1997) 68–90.

28 Tiqqun, *Introduction to Civil War*, trans. Alexander R. Galloway and Jason E. Smith (Los Angeles: Semiotext[e], 2010), 220–21.

Boredom

is a warm grey fabric lined on the inside with the most lustrous and colourful of silks. In this fabric we wrap ourselves when we dream

Walter Benjamin, *The Arcades Project*, 1927–40

MODERNITY'S EMPTY MOMENTS

Elizabeth S. Goodstein
Experience without Qualities//2005

[…] In the course of the eighteenth and early nineteenth century, an aristocratic, worldly mode of resignation yielded to bourgeois withdrawal into the 'interior' – literally, of the home and, figuratively, of the self. Through this discursive shift from public mourning to private suffering, from collective to individual forms of malaise, itself borne along by a revolutionary resignification of temporality, a modern conception of subjectivity came into being. The new discourse of reflection on subjective malaise, the language of interiority in which the modern conception of boredom has its place, bears within itself the scars of historical struggle. The melancholic longing for wholeness that animates Romantic literature is already forsaken in what Friedrich Schiller christened the 'sentimental' consciousness of the modern artist who knows that 'naïve' unity with nature is ineffably lost. The interiority of the cultivated self becomes the only refuge in a world 'fragmented' by the emergence of modern modes of social organization.[1] The Romantic exploration of the depths of the self could not restore what had disappeared from the disenchanted real world, and in the course of the nineteenth century, subjective malaise grew ever less worldly, ever more overshadowed by renunciation in the face of metaphysical loss. As all that was solid melted into air in the ever-busy hands of the bourgeoisie, the modern experience of boredom as a radically isolating 'encounter with nothingness' became possible.

In other words, the democratization of leisure that conditions the emergence of modern subjectivity was accompanied by a *democratization of scepticism*. Among the fruits of bourgeois industry were the processes of industrialization and urbanization that transformed the sociological conditions of everyday life. As people moved from the intimacy and inter-generational continuity of rural and village life into the anonymity of urban populations, the traditional parameters of identity and community were undermined with such rapidity and thoroughness that it is not too much to speak of a collective 'loss of cultural self-evidence'. As the bourgeois reinterpretation of the ends of human existence via a revaluation of labour and worldly accomplishment gained sway, so did a pragmatic and rationalistic attitude toward questions of meaning. 'Modernity' was valorized; scientific progress converged with social transformations, and traditional modes of thinking came to seem outdated on a hitherto unheard-of scale. Religious institutions began to lose their sway over the mass of the population. With the rise of modern technology and the successes of science –in themselves transformations that democratized leisure – the sceptical attitudes of the Enlightenment were also popularized.

The corollary to this process was a democratization of boredom. As the conditions of mass leisure emerged, an initially elitist discourse of subjective disaffection gradually took hold in popular culture, so that by the early twentieth century the experience of ennui had become truly universal. While a century earlier, melancholy had been cultivated as a sign of spiritual distinction, this modern boredom signified, if anything, the lack of an inner life, the failure to find meaning in anything at all. Such boredom was the reflex of a culture in which time had become money, for from the outset the democratization of leisure was allied with the marketing of pastimes. True, the bourgeois condemnation of ennui as a moral failure – the Enlightenment's secularized formulation of the religious proscription against the sin of *acedia* [listlessness] – persists in the contemporary world where eighty-hour work weeks are a status symbol. Nonetheless, the very frenzy of the 'successful' attests to the ultimate inefficacy of activity as such in alleviating subjective malaise. The democratization of leisure has bred a culture of frenetic amusement, one in which Siegfried Kracauer's 1920 remark that 'The form of free-time busy-ness necessarily corresponds to the form of business' is truer than ever.[2] The contemporary terror of boredom, which testifies to its apparent inevitability, is saturated with the post-Romantic resignation to a world in which neither work nor leisure can bring happiness to subjects who no longer hope for divine restitution in the next.

Modern boredom, which masquerades as a universal feature of the human condition, is a democratized form of the disaffection that plagued the nineteenth-century outsiders, ineffectual protestors against an order ineluctably on the rise. […] Baudelaire's poetry of urban despair excavated the foundations of the youthful malaise that has been discovered and rediscovered in every generation since. In it, the modern subject's nihilistic vacillation between desires for total renewal (and their accompanying political expressions) and bitter acceptance of an inhuman order (and the flight into the self) is represented as a product of ennui, that 'delicate monster' who 'would happily destroy the earth and swallow the world in a yawn'. In the very movement by which it effaces its own historicity, such ennui also raises profound questions about the meaning of existence and the significance of action. Its nihilistic dynamic captures the fundamental dilemma of the modern subject, for whom the loss of cultural self-evidence has inaugurated both the radical transcendence of absolute freedom and the radical immanence of a lonely and meaningless death. […]

1 [footnote 30 in source] See Friedrich Schiller, *Über naïve und sentimentalische Dichtung* [On Naïve

and Sentimental Poetry, 1795]; the reference to fragmentation is in the sixth of the letters *Über die aesthetische Erziehung des Menschen* [On the Aesthetic Education of Man, 1794]. [...]

2   [31] Siegfried Kracauer, 'Kult der Zerstreuung', *Das Ornament der Masse* (Frankfurt am Main: Suhrkamp, 1977) 314.

Elizabeth S. Goodstein, extract from *Experience without Qualities: Boredom and Modernity* (Stanford: Stanford University Press, 2005) 98–100.

Walter Benjamin
The Arcades Project//1927–40

'This dull, glib sadness called ennui.' Louis Veuillot, *Les Odeurs de Paris* (Paris, 1914) 177. [D2,5] [...]

We are bored when we don't know what we are waiting for. That we do know, or think we know, is nearly always the expression of our superficiality or inattention. Boredom is the threshold to great deeds. – Now, it would be important to know: What is the dialectical antithesis to boredom? [D2,7]

The quite humorous book by Émile Tardieu, *L'Ennui* (Paris, 1903), whose main thesis is that life is purposeless and groundless and that all striving after happiness and equanimity is futile, names the weather as one among many factors supposedly causing boredom. – This work can be considered a sort of breviary for the twentieth century. [D2,8]

Boredom is a warm grey fabric lined on the inside with the most lustrous and colourful of silks. In this fabric we wrap ourselves when we dream. We are at home then in the arabesques of its lining. But the sleeper looks bored and grey within his sheath. And when he later wakes and wants to tell of what he dreamed, he communicates by and large only this boredom. For who would be able at one stroke to turn the lining of time to the outside? Yet to narrate dreams signifies nothing else. And in no other way can one deal with the arcades – structures in which we relive, as in a dream, the life of our parents and grandparents, as the embryo in the womb relives the life of animals. Existence in these spaces flows then without accent, like the events in dreams. Flânerie is the rhythmics of this slumber. In 1839, a rage for tortoises overcame Paris. One can well imagine the elegant set mimicking the pace of this creature more easily in the arcades than on the boulevards. | Flâneur | [D2a,1]

Boredom is always the external surface of unconscious events. For this reason, it has appeared to the great dandies as a mark of distinction. Ornament and boredom. [D2a,2] […]

Factory labour as economic infrastructure of the ideological boredom of the upper classes. 'The miserable routine of endless drudgery and toil in which the same mechanical process is repeated over and over again is like the labour of Sisyphus. The burden of labour, like the rock, always keeps falling back on the worn-out labourer.' Friedrich Engels, *Die Lage der arbeitenden Klasse in England* (2nd ed. [Leipzig, 1848]) 217; cited in Marx, *Kapital*, vol. 1 (Hamburg, 1922) 388. [D2a,4]

The feeling of an 'incurable imperfection in the very essence of the present' (see *Les Plaisirs et les jours*, cited in Gide's homage) was perhaps, for Proust, the main motive for getting to know fashionable society in its innermost recesses, and it is an underlying motive perhaps for the social gatherings of all human beings. [D2a,5]

On the salons: 'All faces evinced the unmistakable traces of boredom, and conversations were in general scarce, quiet and serious. Most of these people viewed dancing as drudgery, to which you had to submit because it was supposed to be good form to dance.' Further on, the proposition that 'no other city in Europe, perhaps, displays such a dearth of satisfied, cheerful, lively faces at its soirées as Paris does in its salons … Moreover, in no other society so much as in this one, and by reason of fashion no less than real conviction, is the unbearable boredom so roundly lamented.' 'A natural consequence of this is that social affairs are marked by silence and reserve, of a sort that at larger gatherings in other cities would most certainly be the exception.' Ferdinand von Gall, *Paris und seine Salons*, vol. 1 (Oldenburg, 1844) 151–3, 158. [D2a,6]

The following lines provide an occasion for meditating on timepieces in apartments: 'A certain blitheness, a casual and even careless regard for the hurrying time, an indifferent expenditure of the all too quickly passing hours – these are qualities that favour the superficial salon life!' Ferdinand von Gall, *Paris und seine Salons*, vol. 2 (Oldenburg, 1845) 171. [D2a,7] […]

Rather than pass the time, one must invite it in. To pass the time (to kill time, expel it): the gambler. Time spills from his every pore. – To store time as a battery stores energy: the flâneur. Finally, the third type: he who waits. He takes in the time and renders it up in altered form – that of expectation. [D3,4] […]

Boredom – as index to participation in the sleep of the collective. Is this the reason it seems distinguished, so that the dandy makes a show of it? [D3,7] […]

'Happy the man who is an observer! Boredom, for him, is a word devoid of sense.' Victor Fournel, *Ce qu'on voit dans les rues de Paris* (Paris, 1858) 271. [D3a,1]

Boredom began to be experienced in epidemic proportions during the 1840s. Lamartine is said to be the first to have given expression to the malady. It plays a role in a little story about the famous comic Deburau. A distinguished Paris neurologist was consulted one day by a patient whom he had not seen before. The patient complained of the typical illness of the times – weariness with life, deep depressions, boredom. 'There's nothing wrong with you', said the doctor after a thorough examination. 'Just try to relax – find something to entertain you. Go to see Deburau some evening, and life will look different to you.' 'Ah, dear sir', answered the patient, 'I *am* Deburau.' [D3a,4] […]

Walter Benjamin, extracts from *Das Passagen-Werk* (1927–40), ed. Rolf Tiedemann (Frankfurt am Main: Suhrkamp, 1982); trans. Howard Eiland and Kevin McLaughlin, *The Arcades Project* (Cambridge, Massachusetts: Belknap Press of Harvard University Press, 1999) 105–8.

Julian Jason Haladyn
Boredom and Art//2015

The modern conception of boredom develops at the end of the eighteenth and beginning of the nineteenth century, within the same time period as the establishment of the nation state and the growth of industrialization and consumerism. Unlike previous social afflictions associated with select groups and individuals within cultures or even as a phenomenon of privilege typically restricted to people of specific classes – such as *horror loci*, *taedium vitae*, *acedia* and *melancholy*[1] – boredom is an experience open to all citizens of modernity. In her important study *Experience without Qualities: Boredom and Modernity* (2005), Elizabeth Goodstein convincingly argues for what she calls the 'democratization of boredom', in which the conditions of mass leisure allowed 'an initially elitist discourse of subjective disaffection' gradually to take 'hold in popular culture, so that by the early twentieth century the experience of ennui had become truly universal'.[2] The succession of affections or conditions that ends with modern boredom arguably forms a genealogy of human malaise, with each registering deficiencies of social experience within a particular historical period, be it from a moral or psychological, mundane or philosophical perspective.

From this point of view, being 'bored' is just our way of naming the present manifestation of this discontent. Quite distinct from any early malady of this kind, however, is what Walter Benjamin describes as the *epidemic* proportions of boredom as a specifically modern phenomenon directly related to mass culture. It is not simply a matter of immediacy that distinguishes this condition from others of its kind, but the fact that people of all classes, races and genders within modern cultures can share in this experience without substantive difference. The boredom of a housewife or factory worker is no less significant than that of a politician or philosopher. In fact, the most compelling attributes of this condition are precisely those that give it such a democratizing affect, to which every individual is susceptible, and inevitably experiences it as a consistent and often unavoidable part of life in the modern world.

As such, studies of boredom are faced with the inescapable problem of attempting to differentiate and even reconcile individualized attributes of this affliction with those that are more collective or social. Being bored is regarded primarily as the private experience of a given person, yet it is one shared generally by a multitude of people – so many in fact that it can be viewed as an assumed response indicative of anyone who is not fully engaged or, more precisely, *entertained* at a given moment or by a given object or event. On the one hand, it would be a misnomer to claim that such an experience is completely subjective, raising the question of why boredom is so culturally diffuse. On the other hand, to believe that a subject's boring encounter with an object or situation remains entirely external appears equally absurd, particularly considering the profoundly personal affects and effects of this condition. 'As a discursively articulated phenomenon', Goodstein explains, 'boredom is at once objective and subjective, emotion and intellectualization – not just a response to the modern world but also an historically constituted strategy for coping with its discontents'.[3] This borderland of discontented experience that the term *boredom* attempts to communicate resides firmly in the back-and-forth relationship between the subject and the world: it exists as a corollary or by-product of the specifically modern visions of human existence. In this capacity, the bored subject is one driven to seek a level of personal and cultural engagement that is not present, one whose interactions with the world are, or at least continually are made to feel, historically and culturally absent or nullified, in which life appears without purpose or meaning as a result of fixed, ready-made ways of living and thinking.

We see instantly a correlation between the emergence of modernization, most notably the mass-production of the industrial revolution, and the onset of boredom in modernity. Much of the literature on boredom highlights the relationship between our consumer-based culture and the apparent decrease in people's attention spans, which in all likelihood is the result of the promotion of disposable objects and constantly changing interests (often treated positively by referring to them as 'trends'). As a result, our desires are typically satiated only temporarily when treated to new forms of stimuli. We expect to be constantly entertained, so much so that we judge every aspect of our daily lives in terms of how it holds our *interests* – experiences that do not promise immediate engagement are quickly labelled 'boring'. Arthur Schopenhauer articulated this sentiment in *The World as Will and Representation* (1818) when he described life as a pendulum swinging 'to and fro between pain and boredom', between the suffering caused by our inability to accomplish or hold onto our desire and the boredom of lacking any accomplishable desire.[4] It is our desire or will that is the target of consumerism, which aims to make us *want* what we do not have and reciprocally to not want what we already have.

It is important to note that the concept of 'boredom' comes into existence with its doppelgänger term 'interest' – these two affective states, in a sense, representing the two key poles of the modern subject. To be bored or interested, boring or interesting, registers the functioning of this will in and through acts of perceiving the world from an increasingly individualized perspective. The preoccupation with the subject or self is an early precept of modernity, particularly in the shift from the Enlightenment into Romanticism [...].

It is in relation to the overwhelming demands placed on the individual within modern culture through, most notably, the rise of industrialization and consumerism that the *epidemic* of boredom must be understood. In its most affirmative and wilful state, the experience of being bored goes beyond this act of (personal) retreat and becomes an active position of (aesthetic) refusal that approaches boredom as a form of will. It is the creative and passionately affective potential of subjectivity enacted through this will to boredom that challenges the perceived meaninglessness of lived existence within modernity. We must therefore consider boredom not in opposition to interest, as is the common-sense interpretation, but instead as a possible source for subjectively creating interest where previously none existed. Stated differently, it is the *interest* of boredom that compels us to question our existing vision of the world and to recognize – through the experience of an absent or missed experience – the limitations we impose on ourselves through our conceptions and definitions of *reality*. The problem of boredom is not the experience of a lack of interest, which speaks to one's failed ability to be fascinated or feel a connection with one's life; boredom in its affirmative state functions to establish just such a link. Rather, it is through a profound lack of fulfilment that subjective will is confronted with its own limit, forced to extend itself – beyond mere interest, yet dependent upon a passionate interest – to the extremity of its power.

The 'boredom' we are discussing is clearly more than its common or colloquial usage, the term defining not just a minor personal problem but also and more importantly a subject's experiential lack of meaning within modern life. It defines a borderland of affective experiences that confronts us with, rather than distracting us from, the crisis of meaning in modern culture. As such, what boredom in fact describes is the subjective lack that is at once the cause and result of being bored. Boredom calls upon us, inciting us to look into this meaninglessness that refuses to give a purpose or a final goal to life, leaving us at the mercy of our own subjective causality – Rodolphe Gasché explains the 'subjective' as 'the understanding's reappropriation of what happens when it is at a loss, and reason becomes animated, but the objects still have to be accounted for '[5] – as we futilely attempt to avoid feeling the loss of our very being. […] Seen in this way the experience of being bored can no longer be understood as an aberration within an otherwise *interesting* life, passed over as a trivial or inconsequential moment of detachment. Instead, boredom functions as an integral component in the very fabric of human life and knowledge within modernity – a condition that is fundamentally connected to the question of will.

While many initial responses to boredom were negative, we see among the artists, writers and philosophers associated with the modernist avant-garde an active attempt to use this lack of interest to challenge people. Instead of accepting the prescribed meanings of life given to us by consumer or mass culture, one based on the perpetual need for the ever-new, boredom represents the possibility of creating meaning: a *threshold of great deeds* in Benjamin's memorable wording. At its most affirmative, this subjective stance is the will to boredom: an aesthetic condition of modernity by which the subject, knowingly or unknowingly, consciously or unconsciously, judges the relationship of self and world through a question of will – understood in the Nietzschean sense of willing as *creating*. […]

1   Discussions of these terms and the manner in which each differs from modern boredom can be found in a number of studies, most notably Reinhard Kuhn, *The Demon of Noontide: Ennui in Western Literature* (Princeton: Princeton University Press, 1976).

2   Elizabeth Goodstein, *Experience without Qualities: Boredom and Modernity* (Stanford: Stanford University Press, 2005) 99.

3   [footnote 4 in source] Ibid., 3.

4 [5] Arthur Schopenhauer, *The World as Will and Representation*, vol. 1, trans. E.F.J. Payne (New York: Dover, 1969) 312.
5 [6] Rodolphe Gasché, *The Idea of Form: Rethinking Kant's Aesthetics* (Stanford: Stanford University Press, 2003) 33.

Julian Jason Haladyn, extract from *Boredom and Art: Passions of the Will to Boredom* (Alresford, England, and Washington, DC: Zero Books, 2015) 1–5. (www.zerobooks.net)

Siegfried Kracauer
Boredom//1924

People today who still have time for boredom and yet are not bored are certainly just as boring as those who never get around to being bored. For their self has vanished – the self whose presence, particularly in this so bustling world, would necessarily compel them to tarry[1] for a while without a goal, neither here nor there.

Most people, of course, do not have much leisure time. They pursue a livelihood on which they expend all their energies, simply to earn enough for the bare necessities. To make this tiresome obligation more tolerable, they have invented a work ethic that provides a moral veil for their occupation and at least affords them a certain moral satisfaction. It would be exaggerated to claim that the pride in considering oneself an ethical being dispels every type of boredom. Yet the vulgar boredom of daily drudgery is not actually what is at issue here, since it neither kills people nor awakens them to new life, but merely expresses a dissatisfaction that would immediately disappear if an occupation more pleasant than the morally sanctioned one became available. Nevertheless, people whose duties occasionally make them yawn may be less boring than those who do their business by inclination. The latter, unhappy types, are pushed deeper and deeper into the hustle and bustle until eventually they no longer know where their head is, and the extraordinary, radical boredom that might be able to reunite them with their heads remains eternally distant for them.

There is no one, however, who has no leisure time at all. The office is not a permanent sanctuary, and Sundays are an institution. Thus, in principle, during those beautiful hours of free time everyone would have the opportunity to rouse himself into real boredom. But although one wants to do nothing, things are done to one: the world makes sure that one does not find oneself. And even if one perhaps isn't interested in it, the world itself is much too interested for one to find the peace and quiet necessary to be as thoroughly bored with the world as it ultimately deserves.

In the evening one saunters through the streets, replete with an unfulfilment from which a fullness could sprout. Illuminated words glide by on the rooftops, and already one is banished from one's own emptiness into the alien *advertisement*. One's body takes root in the asphalt, and, together with the enlightening revelations of the illuminations, one's spirit – which is no longer one's own – roams ceaselessly out of the night and into the night. If only it were allowed to disappear! But, like Pegasus prancing on a carousel, this spirit must run in circles and may never tire of praising to high heaven the glory of a liqueur and the merits of the best five-cent cigarette. Some sort of magic spurs that spirit relentlessly amid the thousand electric bulbs, out of which it constitutes and reconstitutes itself into glittering sentences.

Should the spirit by chance return at some point, it soon takes its leave in order to allow itself to be cranked away in various guises in a *movie theatre*. It squats as a fake Chinaman in a fake opium den, transforms itself into a trained dog that performs ludicrously clever tricks to please a film diva, gathers up into a storm amid towering mountain peaks, and turns into both a circus artist and a lion at the same time. How could it resist these metamorphoses? The posters swoop into the empty space that the spirit itself would not mind pervading; they drag it in front of the silver screen, which is as barren as an emptied-out palazzo. And once the images begin to emerge one after another, there is nothing left in the world besides their evanescence. One forgets oneself in the process of gawking, and the huge dark hole is animated with the illusion of a life that belongs to no one and exhausts everyone.

Radio likewise vaporizes beings, even before they have intercepted a single spark.[2] Since many people feel compelled to broadcast, one finds oneself in a state of permanent receptivity,[3] constantly pregnant with London, the Eiffel Tower, and Berlin. Who would want to resist the invitation of those dainty headphones? They gleam in living rooms and entwine themselves around heads all by themselves; and instead of fostering cultivated conversation (which certainly can be a bore), one becomes a playground for worldwide noises that, regardless of their own potentially objective boredom, do not even grant one's modest right to personal boredom. Silent and lifeless, people sit side by side as if their souls were wandering about far away. But these souls are not wandering according to their own preference; they are badgered by the news hounds, and soon no one can tell any more who is the hunter and who is the hunted. Even in the cafe, where one wants to roll up into a ball like a porcupine and become aware of one's insignificance, an imposing loudspeaker effaces every trace of private existence. The announcements it blares forth dominate the space of the concert intermissions, and the waiters (who are listening to it themselves) indignantly refuse the unreasonable requests to get rid of this gramophonic mimicry.

As one is enduring this species of antennal fate, the five *continents* are drawing ever closer. In truth, it is not we who extend ourselves out toward them; rather, it is their cultures that appropriate us in their boundless imperialism. It is as if one were having one of those dreams provoked by an empty stomach: a tiny ball rolls toward you from very far away, expands into a close-up, and finally roars right over you. You can neither stop it nor escape it, but lie there chained, a helpless little doll swept away by the giant colossus in whose ambit it expires. Flight is impossible. Should the Chinese imbroglio be tactfully disembroiled, one is sure to be harried by an American boxing match: the Occident remains omnipresent, whether one acknowledges it or not. All the world-historical events on this planet – not only the current ones but also past events, whose love of life knows no shame – have only one desire: to set up a rendezvous wherever they suppose us to be present. But the masters are not to be found in their quarters. They've gone on a trip and cannot be located, having long since ceded the empty chambers to the 'surprise party' that occupies the rooms, pretending to be the masters.

But what if one refuses to allow oneself to be chased away? Then boredom becomes the only proper occupation, since it provides a kind of guarantee that one is, so to speak, still in control of one's own existence. If one were never bored, one would presumably not really be present at all and would thus be merely one more object of boredom, as was claimed at the outset. One would light up on the rooftops or spool by as a filmstrip. But if indeed one is present, one would have no choice but to be bored by the ubiquitous abstract racket that does not allow one to exist, and, at the same time, to find oneself boring for existing in it.

On a sunny afternoon when everyone is outside, one would do best to hang about in the train station or, better yet, stay at home, draw the curtains, and surrender oneself to one's boredom on the sofa. Shrouded in *tristezza*, one flirts with ideas that even become quite respectable in the process, and one considers various projects that, for no reason, pretend to be serious. Eventually one becomes content to do nothing more than be with oneself, without knowing what one actually should be doing – sympathetically touched by the mere glass grasshopper on the tabletop that cannot jump because it is made of glass and by the silliness of a little cactus plant that thinks nothing of its own whimsicality. Frivolous, like these decorative creations, one harbours only an inner restlessness without a goal, a longing that is pushed aside, and a weariness with that which exists without really being.

If, however, one has the patience, the sort of patience specific to legitimate boredom, then one experiences a kind of bliss that is almost unearthly. A landscape appears in which colourful peacocks strut about, and images of people suffused with soul come into view. And look – your own soul is likewise swelling, and in ecstasy you name what you have always lacked: the great *passion*. Were this passion – which shimmers like a comet – to descend, were it to envelop you, the others, and the world – oh, then boredom would come to an end, and everything that exists would be …

Yet people remain distant images, and the great passion fizzles out on the horizon. And in the boredom that refuses to abate, one hatches bagatelles that are as boring as this one.

1   Kracauer here plays with the resonance between *langweilen* ('to bore') and *Lange (ver)weilen* ('to tarry' or 'to linger').
2   [translator's footnote 3 in source] Kracauer here plays on the resonance between *Funk*, which means 'radio', and *Funke*, which means 'spark' or 'flicker'.
3   [4] The semantic fulcrum of this sentence is provided by the ambiguity of *Empfängnis*, which can mean both 'reception' (as in a radio broadcast) and 'conception' (the result of a sexual – as opposed to radiophonic – dissemination).

Siegfried Kracauer, 'Boredom' (1924), in Kracauer, *The Mass Ornament: Weimar Essays*, ed. and trans. Thomas Y. Levin (Cambridge, Massachusetts: Harvard University Press, 1995) 331–4.

Georges Teyssot
Boredom and Bedroom: The Suppression of the Habitual//1996

Sensory Deprivation
Ennui, it has been said, is a 'domestic demon'. This remark by the philosopher Arthur Schopenhauer reveals that within the space of the house and the time of everyday life, something happens that has to do with ennui: boredom belongs to a sort of demonology, or actually, a 'eudaemonics', in an Aristotelian sense.[1] Another philosopher, Vladimir Jankélévitch, has made a study of what he distinguishes as 'adventure', 'seriousness' and 'ennui'.[2] Life is absorbing when it

is condensed, that is, when time passes very quickly. The most interesting moments in one's life are related to beginnings: embarking on an adventure, whether in relation to a love affair or a voyage, one experiences the advent of the future within the present. Hence, one lives a condensation of duration: everything seems to collapse into an instant. At another level, someone who is serious considers the possibility of a future by extending the present time forward. He organizes his own activity according to a 'project' and projects (literally, throws himself forward) into the future. It is this that a serious person does when 'designing', 'projecting', a family, a house, or any other building. Someone who is bored, however, lives exclusively in the present: he is totally immersed in the *interval* of duration. For him, the future is too far away to be interesting or to offer any possibility of hope. Thus ennui is neither directed toward the past, as in nostalgia, nor to the future, as in the adventure, but to an exclusive present.

Jankélévitch has likewise established a distinction between anxiety and ennui. The anxious person waits with fear for the deadline of the instant. Each instance of life, at any moment, carries for the anxious some sort of danger. By contrast, the bored person, the *ennuyé*, exists *between* two instants; his is the state of mind defined as the unhappiness of being too happy. This form of ennui, 'from plenty', is the 'sickness of happy people', the 'rotten fruit of civilization and pleasure', according to Émile Tardieu's *L'Ennui: Étude psychologique* of 1903.[3] Ennui was also for Tardieu a 'disease of nothingness', a condemnation by the 'sense of the nothingness of life.' The poet Giacomo Leopardi has described ennui, in Italian *la noia*, as 'figlia delle nullità, madre del nulla': daughter of null things, mother of the void.[4] The notion of ennui was invented to explain this perception of a void, a void usually recognized in the circumstances of everyday life. It appears as a pure possibility and is characterized as an indifference to form. Indeed, boredom denies any form: it induces the uniform, the shapeless. At the same time, it is also multiform: a mishap, the effect of the 'misshapen'. Boredom may dictate a kind of polymorphism, an excess of ornament; or, as in the nineteenth-century bourgeois apartment, it may induce effects of exaggerated polychromy.

Ennui must also be understood in a kind of paradoxical causality, for it is not very clear what produces what. There seem to be general causes: inaction or idleness, solitude or loneliness, monotony or dullness, fatigue or weariness. But do these, in fact, generate ennui? Jankélévitch suggests that ennui produces these effects, which then re-establish ennui itself, in a cycle of cause and effect. One might conclude that ennui isolates the bored, homogenizing things around him and increasing his disposition to inertia. Inaction, solitude, monotony, fatigue: borne out of ennui, they reinforce ennui. […]

In the nineteenth and twentieth centuries, ennui would become a favourite subject of psychology and sociology. The psychoanalyst Otto Fenichel, in 'On the Psychology of Boredom' of 1934, defined boredom as the self-evident 'unpleasurable experience of a lack of impulse'.[5] Basing his diagnosis on the 'classical' distinction between the 'pathological' and the 'innocent' (equivalent to the 'normal'), Fenichel attempted to establish the following distinction: 'The first type of boredom is the orgiastically impotent individual who is in a state of longing because he is unable to enjoy pleasure. The second type is the "Sunday neurotic" mentioned above [Sandor Ferenczi's symptom of one who is bored on Sundays or during vacations]. We believe that in both cases boredom has a physiological foundation, namely, that of the damning up of the libido.'[6] American behaviouralist scientists such as Mihaly Csikszentmihalyi would look for 'theoretical models for enjoyment' in various games or sports, including 'Chess, Rock Climbing, Rock Dancing'.[7] And the American sociologist Orrin E. Klapp would attempt to establish, with the help of 'science', the connection between boredom and the phenomenon of entropy in information theory: to show 'how communication could fail to deliver information (surprise) from extremes either of redundancy or variety. One cannot be surprised if things are all the same or all different. Entropy, as loss of meaning, always lurks at both ends of the continuum from banality to noise.'[8] Redundancy and variety alike spell boredom.

In Jankélévitch's opinion, ennui is neither an economic nor a medical nor a socio-psychological phenomenon: to attribute physiological or psychological causes to boredom would be like trying to cure nostalgia with pills. Ennui is to be bored by variety, not monotony. Ennui is to be bored by rest, not weariness. Ennui is to be bored by idleness, not work. Ennui is to be bored by happiness, not sadness. Probably the best representation in literature of an *ennuyé* is the dressing-gown existence of Ivan Goncharov's character in the novel of 1859 that bears his name, Ilya Ilyitch Oblomov, who could not rise from his bed and dress. One might say that ennui is a disease of luxury, a luxurious disease. Its nature is paradoxical, equivocal, contradictory, ambiguous. It has been suggested that ennui is the opposite of masochism, since it consists not of the pleasure of suffering, but rather, of the pain of enjoying. Ennui is a failure of happiness, the result of a decay, a slovenliness of the instant in the interval of duration. Happiness is lived and experienced in the flash of an instant; it is a high condensation of time. Any attempt to maintain this instant of happiness within the flow of duration creates a confusion between the instant and the interval. This confusion induces a strong disappointment that may, in turn, engender ennui. Thus when one proposes a stabilization of pleasure – as in the late eighteenth and nineteenth centuries many philosophers did through theories of utilitarianism and positivism – one only provokes ennui. […]

1   [footnote 13 in source] Arthur Schopenhauer, quoted by Vladimir Jankélévitch, *L'Aventure, l'ennui, le sérieux* (Paris: Montaigne/Aubier, 1963) 136. [...]
2   [14] Vladimir Jankélévitch, op. cit. [...]
3   [15] Émile Tardieu, *L'Ennui: étude psychologique*, 2nd ed. (Paris: Alcan, 1913) 136.
4   [16] Giacomo Leopardi, *Zibaldoni*, frag. 1815, 13 September 1821. [...]
5   [21] Otto Fenichel, 'On the Psychology of Boredom', in *The Collected Papers of Otto Fenichel* (New York: W.W. Norton, 1953) 292. [...]
6   [22] Otto Fenichel, quoted by Donald Moss in *Documents*, no. 1–2 (Fall/Winter 1992) 84. [...]
7   [23] Mihaly Csikszentmihalyi, *Beyond Boredom and Anxiety* (San Francisco: Jossey-Bass, 1975).
8   [24] Orrin E. Klapp, *Overload and Boredom: Essays on the Quality of Life in the Information Society* (New York: Greenwood Press, 1986) 82.

Georges Teyssot, extract from 'Boredom and Bedroom: The Suppression of the Habitual', trans. Catherine Seavitt, *Assemblage*, no. 30 (August 1996) 48–50.

Patrice Petro
Aftershocks of the New: Feminism and Film History//2002

Boredom, Distraction, Shock

[...] In his 1903 essay 'The Metropolis and Mental Life' [...], Georg Simmel describes the effects of transportation and industrial production on the human sensorium and explains how overstimulation produces a peculiarly modern form of boredom in what he calls the 'blasé attitude' or 'outlook':

> There is perhaps no psychic phenomenon which is so unconditionally reserved to the city as the blasé outlook ... [For] just as an immoderately sensuous life makes one blasé because it stimulates the nerves to their utmost reactivity until they finally can no longer produce any reaction at all, so, less harmful stimuli ... force the nerves to make such violent responses, tear them about so brutally that they exhaust their last reserves of strength and, remaining in the same milieu, do not have time for new reserves to form ... This psychic mood is the correct subjective reflection of a complete money economy to the extent that money takes the place of all the manifoldness of things and expresses all qualitative distinctions between them in the distinction of 'how much'.[1]

Although Simmel never uses the term *distraction* in this essay, the violent sense impressions he describes are clearly the equivalent of distraction – an experience of sensory stimulation as sensory overload that leads to boredom, exhaustion and indifference – the perception of a universal equality of things. Significantly, Simmel suggests that boredom is no longer the sole possession of a particular class (as it was thought to have been in the eighteenth and nineteenth centuries, especially in the attitudes and practices of those who pursued 'an immoderately sensual life'). Instead, he argues, by the turn of the century, boredom had become available to all through the levelling effects of a money economy, which had permeated leisure as well as labour time.

These ideas had a tremendous impact on the writings of Siegfried Kracauer and Walter Benjamin, two of the most important theorists of film in the twentieth century. It is well known, for example, that Kracauer and Benjamin extend the notions of distraction, sensory stimulation and shock, initially elaborated by Simmel, to describe the aesthetics and reception conditions of photography and film. According to both theorists, film and photography rehearse in the realm of reception what Taylorism and industrial management impose on the human body in the realm of production; these media are, in Kracauer's words, 'the aesthetic reflex of the rationality aspired to by the prevailing economic system'.[2] Importantly neither Kracauer nor Benjamin sees film and photography as symptom of a general cultural or historical decline; instead, they celebrate the cultural negativity of the new media for subverting the bourgeois cult of art and its aesthetic of illusionist absorption. Reception in a state of distraction, they argue, allows for a complex kind of training, sharpening the senses and enabling the subject to parry the shocks of a new, and often antagonistic, reality.

While Kracauer and Benjamin are best known for their theories of modernity based on shock and distraction, what is less known, and less remarked upon, is their central preoccupation with boredom. As Heide Schlüpmann has argued in an extremely influential essay on early German film theory: 'The relation between film and the end of bourgeois culture is not so much captured in the term *distraction* [*Zerstreuung*], in which, after all, capitalism protects itself from its loss of metaphysical elevation. It is captured rather in what are interruptions in the production process: in a boredom that protects itself against organization, in a form of leisure as waiting.'[3] For Benjamin and Kracauer, boredom becomes a key concept for exploring subjectivity in modernity, not least of all because, in its German formulation (*Langeweile*, literally, 'a long whiling away of time'), boredom captures the modern experience of time as both empty and full, concentrated and distracted. Whereas Benjamin tends to theorize boredom in relation to emptiness and ennui (typical of nineteenth-century formulations), Kracauer emphasizes the distracted fullness of a leisure time become empty (a twentieth-century view). The differences between these views on boredom are perhaps best illuminated by the images of modernity that emerge from their work: in Benjamin, the empty streets of Eugène Atget's Paris; in Kracauer, the crowded stadiums and picture palaces of 1920s Berlin.

Both theorists nonetheless agree that boredom retains a radical edge – not unlike that which is attributed elsewhere to distraction and the sensation of shock – in that it helps to sustain subjectivity rather than simply contribute to its loss. 'Monotony nourishes the new', writes Benjamin in the note to his unfinished Arcades project, where he also remarks that 'boredom is the threshold of great deeds'.[4] Similarly, in a 1924 essay devoted to boredom, Kracauer criticizes the restless pursuit of novelty in modernity and extols the virtues of boredom as perhaps 'the only activity that may be called proper, since it offers a certain guarantee that one will have, so to speak, an existence at one's disposal'.[5] *Boredom* and *distraction*, in other words, are complementary rather than opposing terms, whose relationship might be stated as follows: reception in a state of distraction reveals cultural disorder and increasing abstraction; the cultivation of boredom, however, discloses the logic of distraction, in which newness becomes a fetish, and shock itself a manifestation of the commodity form. To reverse the slogan of the Russian formalists, *boredom habitualizes renewed perception*, opening up the potential to see differences that make a difference, and to refuse the ceaseless repetition of the new as the always-the-same.

In this regard, the relationship between boredom and waiting becomes especially important, for it is in a waiting without aim or purpose that the possibility of change might be sighted. 'The more life is regulated administratively', writes Benjamin, 'the more people must learn waiting.' Or, as Kracauer put it, 'He who decides to wait neither closes himself off from the possibilities of faith like the stubborn disciples of total emptiness, nor does he force this faith like the soul searchers who have lost all restraint in their longing.' Otherwise expressed, hidden in the innovation of distraction and shock is a despair that nothing further will happen. Hidden in the negativity of boredom and waiting, however, is the anticipation that something (different) might occur.[6]

This becomes especially apparent when boredom, as a peculiarly twentieth-century experience, is refracted through the lens of sexual difference. It is not insignificant, for example, that Kracauer describes boredom in relation to Taylorized labour and rationalized leisure and chooses a twentieth-century female figure – a middle-aged, working-class woman, who stops outside a movie theatre, to stand for 'those who wait'. Benjamin, by contrast, describes boredom primarily as a form of leisure and embodies this figure in a variety of heroic nineteenth-century male types: 'the gambler just killing time, the flâneur, who charges time with power like a battery, and finally, a third type, he who charges time and gives its power out again in changed form – that of expectation'.[7] If we recall that, for many intellectuals at this time, the boredoms of modern life included 'the spread of democracy to women and the lower classes, the replacement of governmental authority by popular votes, [and] the liberation of sexual activity from state and church dictates', then we might reformulate the relationship between boredom and shock, and boredom and anxiety, along the lines of both historical and gender difference.[8] As Jean-François Lyotard has written, 'Shock is, par excellence, the evidence of (something) happening, rather than nothing at all.'[9] Boredom, in this view, might be seen as evidence of nothing happening – a nothingness that accounts for women's experiences of modernity (particularly in relation to the promises and failures of social change), and for men's perceptions of feminine excess and lack typical of nineteenth-century discourses on ennui.

Boredom, in other words, helps to describe a post-shock economy – that moment after the shock of the new described by Simmel – when exhaustion and indifference are no longer the preserve of a particular class (or, indeed, the sole prerogative of men). This is a moment when the new ceases to be new and ceases to be shocking; when leisure as well as labour time becomes routinized, fetishized, commodified; and when the extraordinary, the unusual and the unfamiliar are inextricably linked to the boring, the prosaic and the everyday. […]

1   [footnote 19 in source] Georg Simmel, 'The Metropolis and Mental Life', in *Georg Simmel: On Individuality and Social Forms*, ed. Donald N. Levine (Chicago: University of Chicago Press, 1971) 329–30.
2   [20] Siegfried Kracauer, 'The Mass Ornament', trans. Barbara Correll and Jack Zipes, *New German Critique*, no. 5 (1975) 70.
3   [21] Heide Schlüpmann, 'Kinosucht', *Frauen und Film*, no. 33 (October 1982) 50.
4   [22] Walter Benjamin, *Das Passagen-Werk* (1927–40), ed. Rolf Tiedemann (Frankfurt am Main: Suhrkamp, 1982) 962, 162.
5   [23] Siegfried Kracauer, 'Langeweile', in *Das Ornament der Masse* (Frankfurt am Main: Suhrkamp, 1977) 324.
6   [24] Walter Benjamin, *Das Passagen-Werk*, op. cit., 178; Kracauer, 'Die Wartenden', in *Das Ornament der Masse*, op. cit., 116.
7   [25] Walter Benjamin, *Das Passagen-Werk*, op. cit., 164.
8   [26] Gregory Jay, 'Postmodernism and The Waste Land: Women, Mass Culture and Others', in *Re-reading the New*, ed. Kevin Dettmar (Ann Arbor: University of Michigan Press, 1992) 238.
9   [27] Jean-François Lyotard, 'The Sublime and the Avant-Garde', trans. Linda Liebmann, *Artforum*, vol. 22, no. 8 (April 1984) 40.

Patrice Petro, extract from *Aftershocks of the New: Feminism and Film History* (New Brunswick: Rutgers University Press, 2002) 64–7.

THIS EMPTY CULTURE IS AT THE HEART OF AN EMPTY EXISTENCE, AND THE REINVENTION OF A PROJECT OF GENERALLY TRANSFORMING THE WORLD MUST ALSO AND FIRST OF ALL BE POSED ON THIS TERRAIN

Situationist International, 'The Adventure', 1960

THE WILL TO BOREDOM

Ivan Chtcheglov
Formulary for a New Urbanism//1953

SIRE, I AM FROM THE OTHER COUNTRY

We are bored in the city, there is no longer any Temple of the Sun. Between the legs of the women walking by, the dadaists imagined a monkey wrench and the surrealists a crystal cup. That's lost. We know how to read every promise in faces – the latest stage of morphology. The poetry of the billboards lasted twenty years. We are bored in the city, we really have to strain to still discover mysteries on the sidewalk billboards, the latest state of humour and poetry:

Shower-Bath of the Patriarchs
Meat Cutting Machines
Notre-Dame Zoo
Sports Pharmacy
Martyrs Provisions
Translucent Concrete
Golden Touch Sawmill
Centre for Functional Recuperation
Sainte-Anne Ambulance
Café Fifth Avenue
Prolonged Volunteers Street
Family Boarding House in the Garden
Hotel of Strangers
Wild Street

And the swimming pool on the Street of Little Girls. And the police station on Rendezvous Street. The medical-surgical clinic and the free placement centre on the Quai des Orfèvres. The artificial flowers on Sun Street. The Castle Cellars Hotel, the Ocean Bar and the Coming and Going Cafe. The Hotel of the Epoch.

And the strange statue of Dr Philippe Pinel, benefactor of the insane, in the last evenings of summer. To explore Paris.

And you, forgotten, your memories ravaged by all the consternations of two hemispheres, stranded in the Red Cellars of Pali-Kao, without music and without geography, no longer setting out for the hacienda *where the roots think of the child and where the wine is finished off with fables from an old almanac*. Now that's finished. You'll never see the hacienda. It doesn't exist.

The hacienda must be built. […]

Ivan Chtcheglov (under the pseudonym Gilles Ivain), extract from 'Formulary for a New Urbanism', *Internationale Situationniste*, no. 1 (Paris, October 1953); in *Situationist International Anthology*, ed. and trans. Ken Knabb, (Berkeley: Bureau of Public Secrets, 1981) 1.

Situationist International
The Adventure//1960

The conditions of the SI's activity explain both its discipline and the forms of hostility it encounters. The SI is interested not in finding a niche in the present artistic edifice, but in undermining it. The situationists are in the catacombs of visible culture.

Anyone who is at all familiar with the social milieu of those with special status in cultural affairs is well aware of how everyone there despises and is bored by almost everyone else. This situation is not even hidden, they are all quite aware of it; it is even the first thing they talk about. What is their resignation due to? Clearly to the fact that they are incapable of being bearers of a common project. Each one thus recognizes in the others his own insignificance and conditioning: the resignation he had to subscribe to in order to participate in this separate milieu and its established aims.

Within such a community people have neither the need nor the objective possibility for any sort of collective discipline. Everyone always politely agrees about the same things and nothing ever changes. Personal or ideological disagreements remain secondary in comparison with what they have in common. But for the SI and the struggle it sets for itself, exclusion is a possible and necessary weapon.

It is the only weapon of any group based on complete freedom of individuals. None of us likes to control or judge; if we do so it is for a practical purpose, not as a moral punishment. The 'terrorism' of the SI's exclusions can in no way be compared to the same practices in political movements by bureaucracies holding some power. It is, on the contrary, the extreme ambiguity of the situation of artists, who are constantly tempted to integrate themselves into the modest sphere of social power reserved for them, that makes some discipline necessary in order clearly to define an incorruptible platform. Otherwise there would be a rapid and irremediable osmosis between this platform and the dominant cultural milieu because of the number of people going back and forth. It seems to us that the present-day cultural avant-garde question can only be posed at an integral level, a level not only of collective works but of collectively interacting problems. This is why certain people have been excluded from the SI. Some of them have rejoined the world they previously fought; others merely console themselves in a pitiful community with each other, although they have nothing in common but the fact that we broke with them – often for opposite reasons. Others retain a certain dignity in isolation, and we have been in a good position to recognize their talents. Do we think that in leaving the SI they have broken with the avant-garde? Yes, we do. There is, for the moment, no other organization constituted for a task of this scope.

The sentimental objections to these breaks seem to us to reflect the greatest mystification. The entire socio-economic structure tends to make the past dominate, to freeze living man, to reify him as a commodity. A sentimental world in which the same sorts of tastes and relations are constantly *repeated* is the direct product of the economic and social world in which *gestures must be repeated* every day in the slavery of capitalist production. The taste for false novelty expresses its unhappy nostalgia.

The violent reactions against the SI, especially those coming from people who were previously excluded from its collective activity, are first of all a measure of the personal passion that this enterprise has been able to bring into play. Reversed into a boundless hostility, this passion has spread it about that we are loafers, Stalinists, imposters and a hundred other clever characterizations. One had it that the SI was a cunningly organized economic association for dealing in modern art; others have suggested that it was rather for the purpose of dealing in drugs. Still others have declared that we have never sold any drugs since we have too great a propensity for taking them ourselves. Others go into detail about our sexual vices. Others have gotten so carried away as to denounce us as social climbers.

These attacks have long been whispered around us by the same people who publicly pretend to be unaware of our existence. […]

To the question, Why have we promoted such an impassioned regrouping in this cultural sphere whose present reality we reject? the answer is: Because culture is the centre of meaning of a society without meaning. This empty culture is at the heart of an empty existence, and the reinvention of a project of generally transforming the world must also and first of all be posed on this terrain. To give up demanding power in culture would be to leave that power to those who now have it. […]

Situationist International, extracts from 'L'aventure', *Internationale Situationniste*, no. 5 (Paris,

December 1960); in *Situationist International Anthology*, ed. and trans. Ken Knabb (Berkeley: Bureau of Public Secrets, 1981) 60–61.

Henri Lefebvre
Critique of Everyday Life//1961

[…] Only partially technicized, everyday life has not created its own specific style or rhythm. Unconnected objects (vacuum cleaners, washing machines, radio or television sets, refrigerators, cars, etc.) determine a series of disjointed actions. Small technical actions intervene in the old rhythms rather like fragmented labour in productive activity in general. The equipment of everyday life finds itself more or less in the same situation as industrial mechanization in its early stages, in the period when specific tools had unique and exclusive functions. If these gestures increase effectiveness – productivity – they also split things up; they truncate, they make mincemeat of everyday life; they leave margins and empty spaces. They increase the proportion of passivity. Dialectically, progress consists of gaps and partial regressions. What is more, a reduction in the time devoted to productive actions and gestures which are now carried out by technical objects has raised the question of time itself, and already this is a very urgent problem. If we examine time as it is experienced by many of today's men and women, we will see that it is chock-a-block full and completely empty. On the horizon of the modern world dawns the black sun of boredom, and critique of everyday life has a sociology of boredom as part of its agenda. […]

Could we not say that of all new phenomena the 'reprivatization' of life is the strangest, and that to a certain extent it encompasses all the previous ones? To use a certain philosophical language which explains nothing and which would demonstrate the need for a deeper theoretical development of these concepts as well as of the facts themselves, the point of view of totality bears witness to a 'detotalization'.

Let us look at these facts more closely. They are paradoxical. The 'reprivatization' of everyday life, which both modified and confirmed the everyday in the modern world, started from 1950 onwards. It consisted of an escape from the nuclear threat and from the setbacks of history. It evaded civic tasks while at the same time suffering the mystifications of official public-mindedness. However, we cannot explain reprivatization by these historical conditions alone, nor as a simple reaction to certain setbacks. At the same time needs were being aroused, some new, some existing potentially as mass phenomena and only crystallized by advertising, by the mediation of which they were connected to their objects. What was most striking, and still is, was the isolated nature of these needs and of the ways they were stimulated. Each one of them has its objects and its slogans. Therefore each has its own distinct satisfaction which does not become part of a coherent totality. The satisfaction of contingent needs by objects which are themselves external and contingent defines one of the characteristics of the new 'private life', where general economic and social necessity is expressed by a series of chances (needs experienced, needs satisfied). Once need becomes for *this* or for *that* it loses its fundamental spontaneity, while failing to individualize desire. This does not make the process any the less irreversible. Options have been taken (for example, as regards the role and importance of the motor car!). *Growth of needs, alienation of desire* is how we expressed it previously. We can now formulate it more precisely: *the external necessity of needs and the randomness of satisfactions*, with private life continuing to be the arena of these disjointed needs and satisfactions, and the link which joins them together. [...]

'Reprivatization' has its pleasant advantages; it creates a certain taste and a certain skill in the use of everyday objects. At the same time, its end product is submission to an impersonal, encyclopaedic and vulgarized culture; like the feminine press, it introduces moral order through innuendo; it facilitates all the rigging and fixing that goes on in mass information. It is the world as an entity passively perceived, and without effective participation, and processes unfold within it which are visible but inaccessible: technology, space exploration, political strategies. Under the socialized gaze which substitutes for the active consciousness of social practice, these processes vanish into the distance at breakneck speed.

So the word 'private' has not lost its main meaning: privation. Private life remains privation. The 'world' is there to plug up the holes, fill in the cracks, paper over the gaps, camouflage the frustrations. Time is crammed full and life seems fit to burst. Or else it is empty. 'Chock-a-block full and completely empty.'

At the same time as life was being 'reprivatized', power and wealth were being personalized, and by the same means. Public and political life became laden with images borrowed from private life. For a long time, perhaps from the start, 'public' men and women – in other words, powerful or famous people – were commonplaces. They belonged (apparently) to everyone. This illusion was part of the way politics operated. It was part of the essence of the state and of the culture which had been established above society while appearing to remain part of it. It was not incompatible with democracy as a political system. It was one of the more honourable and relatively profound contradictions of a democracy which had been relatively successfully established.

Using modern means, this illusion deploys itself in a vast representation of real and practical social life. We are spared no detail of the everyday lives of princes and queens, of stars and millionaires, since 'great men' and 'bosses' and even 'heroes' have an everyday life on a par with our own. We 'know' their bathrooms almost as well as we know our own, we 'know' their mansions almost as well as we know our own flat, we 'know' their bodies almost as well as we know our own. This 'knowledge', if we can call it that, is spread throughout the world by means of images, and helps to create the attraction or powerful influence these celebrities exert. They are slaves to this knowledge. They cannot do without it. They know this, and submit to the demands of the public and of publicity, even if it means that they too must find refuge elsewhere. In short, seen from this angle, grandeur and the sublime are restored to the everyday. The public becomes private and the private becomes public, but in appearance only, since power retains its properties and wealth its possibilities. The humblest citizen knows his prince. He has been able to see him close up, almost as if he could touch him; but once he accepts this illusion, he has stopped being a citizen. The humblest farm-hand 'knows' queens, princesses and film stars. But if he really believes he has attained a 'knowledge' of something, he is being trapped by one of modernity's strangest and most disturbing alienations. The rift between the private and the public has been overcome in appearance only. The supersession of these two aspects of social practice is nothing more than an illusion.

The social appears more open and more transparent than ever before. The *socialization of society* has adopted new forms, more extensive than previous ones, and on a truly 'world' scale, but mystification, alienation and privation have also adopted a world dimension. However, it is curiously 'worldly minded', and turns the world into a caricature of itself.

The world carries on its business beneath a gaze which has become social. But what happens in people's homes, in the enclosure of their private lives and behind the wall that is their forehead? Viewed from outside, private life appears opaque. From the warm and damp intimacy within, it is what is outside which appears threatening, storm-tossed and opaque. Inside, we do not know what is happening outside, where events come from or what causes tensions. The most petty side of the everyday becomes reassuring. There, in private life, we think we are sure of being loved or hated (or both at once), of being protected and smothered, of being taken care of and pushed towards morbid states of mind. We are given the assurance that however insignificant we may be, at least we exist. This is one nucleus of the everyday, and one of its polarities.

It is the place where significations rise and then fall away into insignificance. (Let us take a photo album. Every face and every scene contains an episode or sums up a period in someone's life; each age is loaded with significations. Very quickly, these faces and scenes fade away; they become forgotten, dying their own social death, and are dead for ever; dramas lose their cutting edge and things lose their halo of meaning …)

Thus 'reprivatization' is prolonging and replacing the individualism of the earlier period, by substituting the small family group in place of the individual. Our society harbours profound contradictions, which mark the necessary and inevitable 'socialization of society'. While not making it completely problematic, these contradictions do raise many problems. Groups are getting larger (cities, businesses, classes) while at the same time the differentiations at the heart of these groups are becoming more strongly asserted. Information is increasing while direct contacts are in decline. Relations are becoming more numerous while their intensity and authenticity are diminishing. Along with segregations come diversities, and with possibilities of initiative and freedom come stricter conditionings.

Withdrawal into the self is passive in relation to an overcomplex social reality which oscillates between innuendo and brutal explicitness, but it appears to be a solution of sorts. It is as difficult to assess it is to understand. It cannot be said that 'reprivatization' has not been *actively chosen*. There has been an *option*, and a general one (social options, group choices, socially accepted and adopted proposals for choice). Nor can it be said that it has been chosen freely. However, the choice itself is imposed and the solution is indicated or countermanded. This constraint operates within a fairly narrow margin of freedom; the weight from outside and from the 'world' becomes increasingly oppressive for an intimacy which has been metamorphosed into a mass phenomenon.

Is this a lifestyle, or is it life unequivocally stripped of all style? Although we would tend towards the second of these hypotheses, it is still too early to reach a decision; scrutiny of these hypotheses and this problem is part of the *sociology of boredom* … […]

Henri Lefebvre, extracts from *Critique de la vie quotidienne, II: Fondements d'une sociologie de la quotidienneté* (Paris: L'Arche, 1961); trans. John Moore, *Critique of Everyday Life*, vol. II (London and New York: Verso, 2002) 75, 87–8, 90, 91–3.

Maurice Blanchot
Everyday Speech//1962

[…] The everyday is no longer the average, statistically established existence of a given society at a given moment; it is a category, a utopia and an Idea, without which one would not know how to get at either the hidden present, or the discoverable future of manifest beings. Man (the individual of today, of our modern societies) is at the same time engulfed within and deprived of, the everyday. And – a third definition – the everyday is also the ambiguity of these two movements, the one and the other hardly discernible.

From here, one can better understand the diverse directions in which the study of the everyday might be oriented (bearing now upon sociology, now upon ontology, at another moment upon psychoanalysis, politics, linguistics, literature). To approach such a movement one must contradict oneself. The everyday is platitude (what lags and falls back, the residual life with which our trash cans and cemeteries are filled: scrap and refuse); but this banality is also what is most important, if it brings us back to existence in its very spontaneity and as it is lived – in the moment when, lived, it escapes every speculative formulation, perhaps all coherence, all regularity. Now we evoke the poetry of Chekhov or even Kafka, and affirm the depth of the superficial, the tragedy of nullity. Always the two sides meet: the daily with its tedious side, painful and sordid (the amorphous, the stagnant), and the inexhaustible, irrecusable, always unfinished daily that always escapes forms or structures (particularly those of political society: bureaucracy, the wheels of government, parties). And that there may be a certain relation of identity between these two opposites is shown by the slight displacement of emphasis that permits passage from one to the other; as when the spontaneous, the informal – that is, what escapes forms – becomes the amorphous and when, perhaps, the stagnant merges with the *current* of life, which is also the very movement of society.

Whatever its other aspects, the everyday has this essential trait: it allows no hold. It escapes. It belongs to insignificance, and the insignificant is without truth, without reality, without secret, but perhaps also the site of all possible signification. The everyday escapes. This makes its strangeness – the familiar showing itself (but already dispersing) in the guise of the astonishing. It is the unperceived, first in the sense that one has always looked past it; nor can it be introduced into a whole or 'reviewed', that is to say, enclosed within a panoramic vision; for, by another trait, the everyday is what we never see for a first time, but only see again, having always already seen it by an illusion that is, as it happens, constitutive of the everyday.

[...] We believe we know things immediately, without images and without words, and in reality we are dealing with no more than an insistent prolixity that says and shows nothing. How many people turn on the radio and leave the room, satisfied with this distant and sufficient noise? Is this absurd? Not in the least. What is essential is not that one particular person speak and another hear, but that, with no one in particular speaking and no one in particular listening, there should nonetheless be speech, and a kind of undefined promise to communicate, guaranteed by the incessant coming and going of solitary words. One can say that in this attempt to recapture it at its own level, the everyday loses any power to reach us; it is no longer what is lived, but what can be seen or what shows itself, spectacle and description, without any active relation whatsoever. The whole world is offered to us, but by way of a look. We are no longer burdened by events, as soon as we behold their image with an interested, then simply curious, then empty but fascinated look. What good is it taking part in a street demonstration, since at the same moment, secure and at rest, we are at the demonstration itself, thanks to a television set? Here, produced-reproduced, offering itself to our view in its totality, it allows us to believe that it takes place only so that we might be its superior witness. Substituted for practice is the pseudo-acquaintance of an irresponsible gaze; substituted for the movement of the concept – a task and a work – is the diversion of a superficial, uncaring and satisfied contemplation. Man, well protected within the four walls of his familial existence, lets the world come to him without peril, certain of being in no way changed by what he sees and hears. 'Depoliticization' is linked to this movement. And the man of government who fears the street – because the man in the street is always on the verge of becoming political man – is delighted to be no more than an entrepreneur of spectacle, skilled at putting the citizen in us to sleep, the better to keep awake, in the half-light of a half-sleep, only the tireless voyeur of images.

Despite massive development of the means of communication, the everyday escapes. This is its definition. We cannot help but miss it if we seek it through knowledge, for it belongs to a region where there is still nothing to know, just as it is prior to all relation in so far as it has always already been said, even while remaining unformulated, that is to say, not yet information. It is not the implicit (of which phenomenology has made broad use); to be sure, it is always already there, but that it may be there does not guarantee its actualization. On the contrary, the everyday is always unrealized in its very actualization which no event, however important or however insignificant, can ever produce. Nothing happens; this is the everyday. But what is the meaning of this stationary movement? At what level is this 'nothing happens' situated? For whom does 'nothing happen' if, for me, something is necessarily always happening? In other words, what corresponds to the 'who?' of the everyday? And, at the same time, why, in this 'nothing happens', is there the affirmation that something essential might be allowed to happen?

What questions these are! We must at least try to hold onto them. Pascal gives a first approach, which is taken up again by the young Lukàcs and by certain philosophies of ambiguity. The everyday is life in its equivocal dissimulation, and 'life is an anarchy of clair-obscur. … Nothing is ever completely realized and nothing proceeds to its ultimate possibilities … Everything interpenetrates, without discretion, in an impure mix, everything is destroyed and broken, nothing blossoms into real life … It can only be described through negations …' This is Pascalian diversion, the movement of turning this way and that; it is the perpetual alibi of an ambiguous existence that uses contradictions to escape problems, remaining undecided in a restless quietude. Such is quotidian confusion. Seeming to take up all of life, it is without limit and it strikes all other life with unreality. But there arises here a sudden clarity. 'Something lights up, appears as a flash on the paths of banality … it is chance, the great instant, the miracle.' And the miracle 'penetrates life in an unforeseeable manner … without relation to the rest, transforming the whole into a clear and simple account.'[1] By its flash, the miracle separates the indistinct moments of day-to-day life, suspends nuance, interrupts uncertainties, and reveals to us the tragic truth, that absolute and absolutely divided truth, whose two parts solicit us without pause, and from each side, each of them requiring everything of us and at every instant.

Against this movement of thought nothing can be said, except that it misses the everyday. For the ordinary of each day is not such by contrast with some extraordinary; this is not the '*nul moment*' that would await the 'splendid moment' so that the latter would give it a meaning, suppress or suspend it. What is proper to the everyday is that it designates for us a region, or a level of speech, where the determinations true and false, like the opposition yes and no, do not apply – it being always before what affirms it and yet incessantly reconstituting itself beyond all that negates it. An unserious seriousness from which nothing can divert us, even when it is lived in the mode of diversion; so we experience it through the boredom that seems to be indeed the sudden, the insensible apprehension of the quotidian into which one slides in the levelling of a steady slack time, feeling oneself forever sucked in, though feeling at the same time that one has already lost it, and is henceforth incapable of deciding if there is a lack of the everyday, or if one has too much of it. Thus is one maintained in boredom by boredom, which develops, says Friedrich Schlegel, as carbon dioxide accumulates in a closed space when too many people find themselves together there.

Boredom is the everyday become manifest: as a consequence of having lost its essential – constitutive – trait of being *unperceived*. Thus the daily always sends us back to that inapparent and nonetheless unhidden part of existence: insignificant because always before what signifies it; silent, but with a silence that has already dissipated as soon as we keep still in order to hear it, and that we hear better in idle chatter, in that unspeaking speech that is the soft human murmuring in us and around us.

The everyday is the movement by which the individual is held, as though without knowing it, in human anonymity. In the everyday we have no name, little personal reality, scarcely a face, just as we have no social determination to sustain or enclose us. To be sure, I work daily, but in the day-to-day I am not a worker belonging to the class of those who work. The everyday of work tends to keep me apart from this belonging to the collectivity of work that founds its truth; the everyday breaks down structures and undoes forms, even while ceaselessly regathering itself behind the form whose ruin it has insensibly brought about. […]

The street, [Lefebvre] notes, has the paradoxical character of having more importance than the places it connects, more living reality than the things it reflects. The street renders public. 'The street tears from obscurity what is hidden, publishes what happens elsewhere, in secret; it deforms it, but inserts it in the social text.' And yet what is published in the street is not really divulged; it is said, but this 'is said' is borne by no word ever really pronounced, just as rumours are reported without anyone transmitting them and because the one who transmits them accepts being no one. There results from this a perilous irresponsibility. The everyday, where one lives as though outside the true and the false, is a level of life where what reigns is the refusal to be different, a yet undetermined stir: without responsibility and without authority, without direction and without decision, a storehouse of anarchy, since casting aside all beginning and dismissing all end. This is the everyday. And the man in the street is fundamentally irresponsible; while having always seen everything, he is witness to nothing. He knows all, but cannot answer for it, not through cowardice, but because he takes it all lightly and because he is not really there. Who is there when the man in the street is there? At the most a 'who?', an interrogation that settles upon no one. In the same way indifferent and curious, busy and unoccupied, unstable, immobile. So he is; these opposing but juxtaposed traits do not seek reconciliation, nor do they, on the other hand, counter one another, all the while still not merging; it is the *vicissitude* itself that escapes all dialectical recovery. […]

[T]he everyday does not belong to the objective realm. To live it as what might be lived through a series of separate technical acts (represented by the vacuum cleaner, the washing machine, the refrigerator, the radio, the car), is to substitute a number of compartmentalized actions for this indefinite presence, this connected movement (which is however not a whole) by which we are *continually*, though in the mode of discontinuity, in relation with the indeterminate totality of human possibilities. Of course the everyday, since it cannot be assumed by a true subject (even putting in question the notion of subject), tends unendingly to weigh down into things. This anyone presents himself as the common man for whom all is appraised in terms of good sense. The everyday is then the medium in which, as Lefebvre notes, alienations, fetishisms, reifications produce their effects. He who, working, has no other life than everyday life, is also he for whom the everyday is the heaviest; but as soon as he complains of this, complains of the burden of the everyday in existence, the response comes back: 'The everyday is the same for everyone' and even adds, like Büchner's Danton: 'There is scarcely any hope that this will ever change.'

There must be no doubt about the dangerous essence of the everyday, nor about this uneasiness that seizes us each time that, by an unforeseeable leap, we stand back from it and, facing it, we discover that precisely nothing faces us: 'What?' 'Is this my everyday life?' Not only must one not doubt it, but one must not dread it; rather one ought to seek to recapture the secret destructive capacity that is in play in it, the corrosive force of human anonymity, the infinite wearing away. The hero, while still a man of courage, is he who fears the everyday; fears it not because he is afraid of living in it with too much ease, but because he dreads meeting in it what is most fearful: a power of dissolution. The everyday challenges heroic values, but even more it impugns all values and the very idea of value, disproving always anew the unjustifiable difference between authenticity and inauthenticity. Day-to-day indifference is situated on a level at which the question of value is not posed: 'il y a du quotidien' [there is everydayness], without subject, without object, and while it is there, the 'he' ['il'] of the everyday does not have to be of account, and, if value nevertheless claims to step in, then 'he' is worth 'nothing' and 'nothing' is worth anything through contact with him. To experience everydayness is to be tested by the radical nihilism that is as if its essence, and by which, in the void that animates it, it does not cease to hold the principle of its own critique. [...]

1   [footnote 4 in source] Georg Lukács, *L'Âme et les formes* (Paris: Gallimard, 1974), as cited by Lucien Goldmann in *Recherches dialectiques* (Paris: Gallimard, 1959); Georg Lukács, *Soul and Form*, trans. Anna Bostock (London: Merlin Press, 1971, 1974).

Maurice Blanchot, extracts from 'La Parole quotidienne' (1962); revised in *L'Entretien infini* (Paris: Gallimard, 1969); trans. Susan Hanson, in *Yale French Studies*, no. 73 ('Everyday Life') (1987) 13–14, 15, 16–17, 19.

Georges Perec
Things: A Story of the Sixties//1965

They could not have said exactly what it was that changed when the war ended. For a long time it was as if the only impression they could feel was the sense of an ending, of something completed or concluded. Not a happy ending, not a dramatic resolution, but quite the opposite, a melancholy, dying fall, which left behind it feelings of emptiness, of bitterness, memories clouded over by darkness. Time had passed, time had fled; an era was over; peace had returned, a peace they had never known; the war came to an end. At a stroke, seven years tipped into history: their student years, their years of making friends, the best years of their lives.

Maybe nothing had changed. They would still sometimes stand at their window, looking at the courtyard, the tiny gardens, the chestnut tree, listening to the birds singing. Other books, other records were now piled up on their rickety bookshelves. The gramophone needle was beginning to wear out.

Their work had stayed the same. They were doing the same surveys as three years before. What do you shave with? Do you put polish on your shoes? They had seen films, and seen films again, they had travelled, and discovered other restaurants. They had bought shirts and shoes, jumpers and skirts, plates, sheets and trinkets.

What was new was terribly insidious, terribly vague, terribly bound up with their own unique story, with their dreams. They were weary. They had aged; yes, they had. Some days they felt as if they still hadn't begun to live. But the life they were leading came more and more to seem to them a precarious and ephemeral thing; and they felt drained of strength; as if their waiting, their hardships, their pinched budgets had worn them out, as if all of it – unsatisfied desires, imperfect pleasures, wasted time – had been in the natural order of things.

On occasions they wished everything would stay the same, not ever move. Then they would be able just to drift. Their life would keep them warm: it would stretch ahead through the months and years without – or almost without – altering, without ever hampering them. It would be but the harmonious sequence of their days and nights, the one almost imperceptibly modulating the other, a never-ending reprise of the same themes, a continuous happiness, a perpetuated enjoyment which no upset, no tragic event, no twist or turn of fate would ever bring into question.

At other times they could not stand it a moment longer. They wanted to fight, and to win. But how could they fight? Whom would they fight? What should they fight? They lived in a strange and shimmering world, the bedazzling universe of a market culture, in prisons of plenty, in the bewitching traps of comfort and happiness.

Where were the dangers? Where were the threats? In the past men fought in their millions, and millions still do fight, for their crust of bread. Jérôme and Sylvie did not quite believe you could go into battle for a chesterfield settee. But that was all the same the banner under which they would have enlisted most readily. There was nothing, they thought, that concerned them in party manifestos or in government plans: they would sneer at early retirement pension schemes, increased holiday entitlements, free lunches, the thirty-hour week. They wanted superabundance – Garrard turntables, empty beaches for their eyes only, round-the-world trips, grand hotels.

The enemy was unseen. Or, rather, the enemy was within them, it had rotted them, infected them, eaten them away. They were the hollow men, the turkey round the stuffing. Tame pets, faithfully reflecting a world which taunted them. They were up to their necks in a cream cake from which they would only ever be able to nibble crumbs.

For years the crises they had encountered had scarcely dented their good humour. They hadn't taken them as inevitable or terminal affairs; they were crises in which nothing was at stake. They often reflected that friendship was protecting them. The group held together, reliably, cohesively, it was a firm guarantee of their stability, a force they could count on. They were sure they were right because they knew they would stick together, and they liked nothing more than to be together at one or another's flat towards the end of an especially awkward month, sitting around a tureen of potatoes and bacon, sharing their last cigarettes as fraternally as it was possible to do.

But friendships, too, began to fray. Some evenings, within the finite fields of their unspacious rooms, the couples that had come together crossed swords by word and eye. Some evenings, they finally grasped that their fine friendships, their almost hermetic language, their private jokes, this shared world, shared language, the common gestures they had made up, were based on nothing: theirs was a shrunken universe, a world running out of steam, opening onto nothing. Their lives were not conquests, but slow collapses, dispersions. That was when they realized how deeply they were condemned to habit, to sluggishness. They were bored in each other's company as if all there had ever been between them was a void. Puns, boozing, walks in the woods, dinner parties, endless discussions about films, plans, gossip had long stood in for adventure, history and truth. But the words were hollow, the gestures empty, without substance, without consequence, without a future, words repeated a thousand times, hands shaken a thousand times, ritual actions which no longer afforded them any protection.

At that time they would spend an hour trying to agree about which film they would go to see. They would talk just for the sake of talking, play at riddles or at guessing games. Each couple, when alone, would speak harshly of the others and sometimes of themselves; they would harp on their lost youth; they would recall having once been enthusiastic, spontaneous, brim-full of real plans, of images of wealth, of desires. They would dream of new friendships; but they could barely manage to picture them.

Slowly but with inexorable obviousness, the group fell apart. With sometimes brutal suddenness, in the space of barely a few weeks, it became obvious to some of them that the life of old would never again be on. Their weariness was too great. The outside world too demanding. People who had lived in rooms with no running water, who had dined on a quarter of a stick-loaf, who had believed they were living as they pleased, who had burnt the candle at both ends without running out of wick, such people, one fine day, settled down. They were swayed, almost naturally, almost objectively, by the temptation of a steady job, a staff appointment, bonus payments, and an extra salary cheque at Christmas.

One after another almost all their friends gave in. The age of rootless living gave way to the age of security. […]

Georges Perec, extract from *Les Choses: Une histoire des années soixante* (Paris: Éditions Julliard, 1965); in Perec, *Things: A Story of the Sixties/A Man Asleep*, trans. David Bellos and Andrew Leak (Boston: David R. Godine, 1990) 76–8.

Raoul Vaneigem
The Revolution of Everyday Life//1967

Like the crowd, like drugs or love, drink has the special power to bewitch the most lucid mind. It can make the concrete wall of isolation seem like the kind of paper curtain that actors can tear open at will, for alcohol places everything on the stage of a private theatre. A generous illusion – and all the more deadly for that.

In a gloomy bar where everyone is bored to tears, a drunken young man breaks his glass, then picks up a bottle and smashes it against the wall. Nobody gets excited; disappointed in his expectations, the young man lets himself be thrown out. Yet everyone there was in silent sympathy with his gesture. He alone made the thought concrete, crossing the first radioactive belt of isolation, namely inner isolation, the inward-looking separation between self and outside world.

Nobody responded to a sign which he thought was explicit. He remained alone like the hooligan who burns down a church or kills a policeman, at one with himself but condemned to exile as long as other people remain exiled from their own existence. He has not escaped from the magnetic field of isolation; he is suspended in a zone of zero gravity. All the same, the indifference which greets him allows him to hear the sound of his own cry; and even if this revelation torments him, he knows that he will have to start again in another register, more loudly – more *coherently*.

A common doom will be the only thing people share so long as isolated human beings refuse to understand that a free gesture, however weak and clumsy, always embodies an authentic communication, an adequate personal message. The repression that comes down on the anarchist comes down on everyone: the blood of all flows with the blood of a murdered Durruti. When freedom retreats an inch, there is a hundredfold increase in the weight of the order of *things*. Excluded from authentic participation, human actions are waylaid either by the fragile illusion of being together, or else by its opposite, a brutal, total refusal of all social life. They swing from one to the other like a pendulum turning the hands on the clock-face of death.

As for love, it too fertilizes the illusion of unity. In general it miscarries or sinks into triviality. Fear of taking the well-trodden and only too familiar path to solitude, whether as a couple or as a small group, casts a chilling pall over love's symphonies. What drives us to despair is not the immensity of our unsatisfied desires, but the moment when our fledgling passion discovers its own emptiness. Insatiable desire for passionate knowledge of one pretty girl after another stems from anxiety and from fear of love, so afraid are we of never encountering anything but *objects*. The dawn when lovers leave each other's arms is the same dawn that breaks on the execution of revolutionaries without a revolution. Isolation *à deux* cannot prevail over the isolation of all. Pleasure is broken off prematurely and lovers find themselves naked in the world, their actions suddenly ridiculous and feeble. No love is possible in an unhappy world.

The boat of love breaks up on the reefs of ordinary life (Mayakovsky). Are we ready, so that our desire may never come to grief – are we ready to breach the reefs of the old world? Lovers must love their pleasure with more earnestness, and with more poetry. It is said that Prince Shekur captured a city and presented it to his favourite in exchange for a smile. A few of us at least have fallen in love with the pleasure of loving without reservations – passionately enough to offer love the sumptuous bed of a revolution.

Adapting to the world is a trick coin-toss where heads always comes up: it is decided a priori that the negative is positive and that the impossibility of living is a prerequisite of life. Alienation never takes such firm root as when it passes itself off as an inalienable good. In its positive disguise, the consciousness of isolation is simply the private consciousness, the unforsakable shard of individualism that respectable people drag around like a piece of cumbersome but cherished property. A sort of pleasure-anxiety prevents us from settling thoroughly into the illusion of community yet keeps us locked up in the dungeons of isolation.

The no-man's-land of neutral relations is the territory between the blissful acceptance of bogus communities and the total rejection of society. Its moral principles are those of the shopkeeper: 'One hand washes the other'; 'There are good people everywhere'; 'Things are not too bad. Not too good either. It's up to us.' In short, politeness – the art-for-art's-sake of non-communication.

Let's face it: human relationships being what social hierarchy has made of them, neutrality is the least tiring form of contempt. It allows us to pass without needless friction through the hopper of daily contacts. But it does not prevent us from dreaming – far from it –of such superior forms of civility as the courtliness of Lacenaire, on the eve of his execution, urging a friend: 'Above all, please convey my gratitude to Monsieur Scribe. Tell him that one day, suffering from the pangs of hunger, I presented myself at his house to worm some money out of him. He complied with my request with admirable deference; I am sure he will recall. Tell him that he acted wisely, for I had in my pocket, ready to hand, the means of depriving France of a dramatist.'

The innocuousness of neutral relations, however, offers no more than a moment of dead time in the ceaseless battle against isolation, a brief stopping-place on the road that seems to lead towards communication but that in fact leads far more often to the illusion of community. Which probably explains my reluctance to stop a stranger for the time of day, for directions, or simply to exchange of couple of words, for I am loath to seek contact in this dubious fashion. The pleasantness of neutral relations is built on sand, and empty time never does me any good.

Living is made impossible with such cynicism that even the balanced pleasure-anxiety of neutral relations may function as a cog in the machinery that destroys people. It seems better in the end to go straight to a radical and tactically worked-out rejection rather than knock politely on every door looking to swap one kind of survival for another.

'It would irk me to die so young,' wrote Jacques Vaché two years before his suicide. If the desperation of survival fails to join forces with a new consciousness and transform the years ahead, only two 'options' will be left for the isolated individual: the potty-chair of political parties and pataphysico-religious sects, or immediate death with *Umour*. A sixteen year-old murderer recently explained: 'I did it because I was bored.' Anyone who has felt the drive to self-destruction welling up inside him knows with what jaded insouciance he might just happen to kill the organizers of his boredom. One day. If he was in the mood.

After all, if individuals refuse either to adapt to the violence of the world or to embrace the violence of the maladapted, what path is still open to them? Unless they elevate their will to achieve perfect union with the world and with themselves to the level of consistent theory and practice, the vast silence of social space will surely confine them to a palace of solipsism and delusion.

From the depths of their prisons those who have been convicted of mental illness add the screams of their strangled revolt to the sum of negativity. What a Fourier in potentia was consciously destroyed in a patient described by the psychiatrist Volnat: 'He began to lose all capacity to distinguish between himself and the external world. Everything that happened in the world also happened in his body. He could not put a bottle between two shelves in a cupboard because the shelves might come together and break the bottle. And that would hurt inside his head, as if his head was wedged between the shelves. He could not shut a suitcase, because pressing the effects in the case would exert pressure inside his head. If he walked into the street after closing all the doors and windows of his house, he felt uncomfortable, because his brain was compressed by the air, and he had to go back home to open a door or a window. 'For me to be at ease', he would say, 'I must have wide open space in front of me ... I have to be *free in my space*. It's a battle with the *things* around me.'

The Consul paused, turning. He read the inscription: 'No se puede vivir sin amar' (Lowry, *Under the Volcano*).

Raoul Vaneigem, extract from *Traité de savoir-vivre à l'usage des jeunes générations* (Paris: Gallimard, 1967); trans. Donald Nicholson-Smith, *The Revolution of Everyday Life* (Oakland, California: PM Press, 2012) 25–8.

Sadie Plant
Now, the SI[1]//1992

[...] [Guy Debord's] *The Society of the Spectacle* appeared a decade after the establishment of the Situationist International. The book by no means encompasses the wealth of situationist theory and, read in isolation from the movement's other texts, it is dry and uninspiring, with the only hints of situationist provocation and extravagance appearing in the wealth of italicised enthusiasm and the stolen goods it collects. In line with the movement's tactical subversions of existing texts and materials, much of the book consists of passages plagiarised and subtly rewritten; as a consequence, it is full of Hegelian turns of phrase and vaguely familiar transpositions of the work of Marx and Lukács. But the condensed form in which its arguments are presented makes *The Society of the Spectacle* a rich source for a number of situationist themes, particularly those which define modern capitalist society as a spectacle and identify its internal contradictions.

Vaneigem's book *The Revolution of Everyday Life* was published in the same year as *The Society of the Spectacle* and presented a rather more anecdotal, extravagant and subjective work of propaganda to accompany Debord's theoretical investigations. Vaneigem's rejection of the spectacle was a moral, poetic, erotic, and almost spiritual refusal to co-operate with the demands of commodity exchange. It unleashed witty and compelling tirades against the myths and sacrifices of consumer society, asserting a radical subjectivity which could fire pleasures, spontaneity, and creativity at the all-encompassing equivalence and emptiness of modern life. Above all, it contested the system of social relations which forces us to exist as survivors shackled by needs and forced into labour when all the possibilities of a rich, desiring life are constantly displayed. But although *The Revolution of Everyday Life* expressed the situationists' enduring appeal for life, intensity, passion, and play, it also displayed an impatience with theory and the rather more serious political commitment demanded by Debord. Nobody thought it was very funny when Vaneigem went off on holiday as the great events of 1968 began to unfold, and the tension between having fun in the present and saving it up until after the revolution was an enduring problem which played no small part in the final collapse of the SI.[2]

It was in rather more sober tones, therefore, that Debord presented *The Society of the Spectacle*. More than a decade after its publication, he wrote:

> In 1967 I wanted the Situationist International to have a book of theory. The SI was at this time the extremist group which had done the most to bring back

revolutionary contestation to modern society; and it was easy to see that this group, having imposed its victory on the terrain of critical theory, and having skilfully followed it through on that of practical agitation, was then drawing near the culminating point of its historical action. So it was a question of such a book being present in the troubles that were soon to come, and which would pass it on after them to the vast subversive sequel that they could not fail to open up.[3]

The 'troubles' of 1968 which were indeed 'soon to come' were regarded by the situationists as the mass demonstration of their theory, and if Debord had a single message to convey, it was without doubt the conviction that the 'days of this society are numbered; its reasons and merits have been weighed and found to be lacking; its inhabitants are divided into two parties, one of which wants this society to disappear'.[4] His book contended that although the class and economic structure of capitalist society had suffered no qualitative change since its analysis by Marx, the extension of commodity relations to all aspects of life and culture, accelerated by new systems of technology, information and communication, required the development of a new paradigm within which contemporary society could be understood. The spectacle provided the perfect framework. It captured the contemplative and passive nature of modern life and accounted for the boredom and apathetic dissatisfaction which characterized social experience. It could move beyond the basic categories of orthodox Marxism while at the same time preserving the possibility of a revolutionary critique and providing a perspective from which every aspect of contemporary discourse, culture, social organization and daily existence could be challenged. And although the SI's analysis was not just a response to the increasing role of the mass media, information and advertising, the notion of the spectacle also facilitated a valuable analysis of the ubiquitous messages, signs and images which conspire to confuse appearance with reality and throw into question the possibility of distinguishing true experience, authentic desire and real life from their fabricated, manipulated and represented manifestations. Above all, the notion of the spectacle conveyed the sense in which alienated individuals are condemned to lives spent effectively watching themselves. It suggested that, far from being inevitable attributes of the human condition, the boredom, frustration and powerlessness of contemporary life are the direct consequence of capitalist social relations.

In common with other situationist texts, therefore, *The Society of the Spectacle* painted a picture of a society which believes itself capable of providing everything, satisfying all desire, relieving every burden and fulfilling every dream. But this is also a world which insists that every moment of life must be mediated by the commodity form, a situation which makes it impossible to provide anything for oneself or act without the mediation of commodities. A spectacle can only be watched and enjoyed at a distance, from where it appears glamorous and desirable; participation may be possible, but its form and extent will be predetermined by the context in which it appears. The promises of self-fulfilment and expression, pleasure and independence which adorn every billboard are realizable only through consumption, and the only possible relation to the social world and one's own life is that of the observer, the contemplative and passive spectator. The commodity form places everything in the context of a world organized solely for the perpetuation of the economic system; a tautological world in which the appearance of real life is maintained in order to conceal the reality of its absence. Bombarded by images and commodities which effectively represent their lives to them, people experience reality as second-hand. Everything has been seen and done before; quests for fulfilment are always frustrated, and just as workers find no satisfaction in the products of their labour, so 'no one has the enthusiasm on returning from a venture that they had on setting out on it. My dears', said Debord in one of his films, 'adventure is dead.'[5]

The basis of this characterization of capitalist society was already laid in Marx's early and graphic descriptions of alienation. Performed not in order to satisfy a need but as a means of satisfying other needs, all work undertaken within capitalism is external, alien and 'shunned like the plague' wherever possible. Workers are left debased, exhausted and denied, and the individual only 'feels himself outside his work, and in his work feels outside himself. He feels at home when he is not working, and when he is working he does not feel at home'.[6] Alienated from the products of their labour, their time and their own selves, workers produce and reproduce alienated relations both between themselves and things and between each other. The relations of capitalist production are therefore reproduced in all social relations; circumscribing social reality, alienation comes to be perceived as the necessary reality of daily life. In his later writings too, Marx emphasized the estrangement or alienation intrinsic to capitalist production. The commodity fetishism of *Capital* is a renewed consideration of the phenomenon in which relations between people assume the form of relations between things. In the absence of any real world of unalienated social experience, commodity relations become mysterious and fantastic; labour is turned against the worker and appears as an autonomous power, and because the totality of these relations is presented as a natural order, the worker loses all reason to challenge or understand the experience of alienation.

The situationists argued that these alienated relations of production are now disseminated throughout capitalist society. Leisure, culture, art, information, entertainment, knowledge, the most personal and radical of gestures, and every conceivable aspect of life is reproduced as a commodity: packaged, and sold back to the consumer. Even ways of life are marketed as lifestyles, and careers, opinions, theories and desires are consumed as surely as bread and jam. Constantly creating new markets, the commodity relations of twentieth-century capitalism extend their grasp to the very intimacy of people's everyday lives where nineteenth-century capitalism built its geographical empires. And although Marx had also recognized that commodity relations extend the experience of alienation beyond the workplace, he retained a sense of the worker being at home 'outside his work'. The spectre that has haunted subsequent radical theorists is that this remaining realm of free and unalienated experience is increasingly eroded by the encroachment of capitalist relations. And if alienation really does extend to both work and leisure time, there is a danger that it becomes completely meaningless, since there is nothing with which to compare it and nothing in relation to which it can be defined. The situationists argued that although the ubiquity of alienated relations does indeed make them increasingly difficult to contradict, it is always possible to identify some point of contrast or opposition to them. The desires, imaginings and pleasures of the individual can never be completely eradicated: as a system which operates by transforming objects into commodities and people into their producers and consumers, capitalism cannot but sustain a sense of the reality it distorts. And this suggests that some contradiction between life as it is and life as it could be is preserved regardless of the spectacle's insistence on its own seamless inevitability.

Presenting the spectacle as 'the material reconstruction of the religious illusion',[7] Debord argued that the mediations of church and priest, the separation of body and soul, and the demands of sacrifice and deferred gratification which marked pre-capitalist society are now redeveloped to produce the same experiences of removal, alienation and mystification. Seeking salvation and fulfilment in the spectacle of this world rather than the next, the producers and consumers of the spectacle are equally removed from their own lives and still live in a separated relation to themselves: 'The absolute denial of life, in the shape of a fallacious paradise, is no longer projected onto the heavens, but finds its place instead within material life itself.'[8] The spectacular world presents itself as a natural phenomenon, requiring no organization, denying the existence of any economic foundation, and offering itself as 'an enormous positivity, out of reach and beyond dispute';[9] it is the 'moment at which the commodity completes its colonization of social life. It is not just that the relationship to commodities is now plain to see – commodities are now *all* there is to see; the world we see is the world of the commodity.'[10] And this vision of a united, complete and natural social whole is a representation which compensates for the increasing fragmentation and alienation of daily life and belies the existence of all discontinuity and contradiction. The spectacle is the '*materialization* of ideology';[11] a society in which the particular perspective of the bourgeoisie is given a concrete form. It is a society asleep, in hibernation or a state of suspended animation, for which 'ideology is no longer a historical choice, but simply an assertion of the obvious'.[12]

This absolute realization of commodity relations produces an entirely inverted world, in which everything 'that was directly lived has become mere representation',[13] a 'dull reflection'[14] of itself. Mystified by this removal, it is difficult to understand why the world appears to be so whole, natural and unremarkable, yet is so extraordinarily difficult really to engage and feel at home in. 'The spectator feels at home nowhere, for the spectacle is everywhere',[15] and areas of life which were once untouched by the logic of the commodity form are now possible only within it. Free time is filled with provided forms of leisure and entertainment, and free choice is made from a pre-selected variety of goods, lifestyles, roles and opinions. The content of life is swept aside by the commodity form in which it appears; all other means of judging, evaluating and living in the world are emptied of their real meaning and reduced to the abstract standards of production and consumption. The spectacle is a society which continually declares: 'Everything that appears is good; whatever is good will appear.'[16] A world in which such circularity dominates all social experience is impoverished; only the commodity can exist, and as representations of the whole social world become increasingly tangible, the 'real consumer becomes a consumer of illusions. The commodity is this factually real illusion, and the spectacle is its general manifestation.'[17]

The contradiction which displaces the tautologous unity of capitalist society has long been identified in the tension between the forces and relations of production. In *The Communist Manifesto*, Marx and Engels observed that just as the end of feudal society was necessitated by the development of the forces of production beyond the social relations they supported, so the productive forces unleashed by capitalism project it into a crisis of its own.

> The productive forces at the disposal of society no longer tend to further the development of the conditions of bourgeois property; on the contrary, they have become too powerful for these conditions, by which they are fettered, and so soon as they overcome these fetters, they bring disorder into the whole of bourgeois society … The conditions of bourgeois society are too narrow to comprise the wealth created by them.[18]

The consequent crises of over-production which mark bourgeois society can be temporarily assuaged, primarily by the cultivation of new markets, but their resolution can only be achieved with the abolition of the social and economic relations which lag behind the forces of production. The situationists agreed that the contradiction between the forces and relations of production is the essential antagonism of capitalist society, and were similarly at home with Marxist conceptions of history and class. The spectacle remains a class society, founded on a system of production which separates workers from one another, the products of their labour and the commodities they consume. Regardless of the abundance of spectacular society, the essential poverty of everyday life left the situationists convinced that the proletariat is still reproduced by capitalist social relations as the class capable of realizing and superseding the economic contradictions of capitalism. And the image of unity and seamless self-sufficiency which modern society cultivates is itself a product of the separations, divisions and contradictions which riddle the spectacle. 'The unreal unity the spectacle proclaims masks the class division on which the real unity of the capitalist mode of production is based.'[19] [...]

1   'Now, the SI' is the title of an article in *Internationale Situationniste*, no. 9 (August 1964).
2   [footnote 1 in source] Vaneigem's holiday is a completely unsubstantiated rumour which nevertheless captures the spirit of this debate.
3   [2] Guy Debord, Preface to 4th Italian ed., *The Society of the Spectacle* (London: Chronos, 1979) 8–9.
4   [3] Ibid., 24.
5   [4] Guy Debord, 'Critique of Separation', *Situationist International Anthology*, ed. Ken Knabb (Berkeley: Bureau of Public Secrets, 1981) 37.
6   [5] Karl Marx, 'Economic and Philosophic Manuscripts of 1844', in Karl Marx and Friedrich Engels, *Collected Works*, vol. 3 (London: Lawrence & Wishart, 1975) 274.
7   [6] Guy Debord, *The Society of the Spectacle*, unpublished translation [by Donald Nicholson-Smith] (1990) 20.
8   [7] Ibid.
9   [8] Ibid., 12.
10 [9] Ibid., 42.
11 [10] Ibid., 212.
12 [11] Ibid., 213
13 [12] Ibid., 1.
14 [13] *The Pleasure Tendency, Life and Its Replacement with a Dull Reflection of Itself* (Leeds, 1986).
15 [14] Debord, *The Society of the Spectacle*, op. cit., 30.
16 [15] Ibid., 12
17 [16] Ibid., 47.
18 [17] Karl Marx and Friedrich Engels, 'Manifesto of the Communist Party', in Karl Marx and Friedrich Engels, *Collected Works*, vol. 6 (London: Lawrence & Wishart, 1976) 490.
19 [18] Debord, *The Society of the Spectacle*, op. cit., 72.

Sadie Plant, extract from *The Most Radical Gesture: The Situationist International in a Postmodern Age* (London and New York: Routledge, 1992) 9–14.

I've been quoted a lot as saying, 'I like boring things.' Well, I said it and I meant it. But that doesn't mean I'm not bored by them

Andy Warhol and Pat Hackett, *POPism: The Warhol 60s*, 1980

INDIFFERENCE

John Cage
Silence//1961

[…] Dad is an inventor. In 1912 his submarine had the world's record for staying under water. Running as it did by means of a gasoline engine, it left bubbles on the surface, so it was not employed during World War I. Dad says he does his best work when he is sound asleep. I was explaining at the New School that the way to get ideas is to do something boring. For instance, composing in such a way that the process of composing is boring induces ideas. They fly into one's head like birds. Is that what Dad meant? […]

In Zen they say: If something is boring after two minutes, try it for four. If still boring, try it for eight, sixteen, thirty-two, and so on. Eventually one discovers that it's not boring at all but very interesting.

At the New School once I was substituting for Henry Cowell, teaching a class in Oriental music. I had told him I didn't know anything about the subject. He said, 'That's all right. Just go where the records are. Take one out. Play it and then discuss it with the class.' Well, I took out the first record. It was an LP of a Buddhist service. It began with a short microtonal chant with sliding tones, then soon settled into a single loud reiterated percussive beat. This noise continued relentlessly for about fifteen minutes with no perceptible variation. A lady got up and screamed, and then yelled, 'Take it off. I can't bear it any longer.' I took it off. A man in the class then said angrily, 'Why'd you take it off? I was getting interested.'

John Cage, extract from notes accompanying text originally published as 'Grace and Clarity', *Dance Observer*, vol. 11, no. 9 (November 1944), incorporated in 'Four Statements on Dance', in *Silence: Lectures and Writings* (Middletown, Connecticut: Wesleyan University Press, 1961) 93; followed by extract from 'Experimental Music' (1957), in *Silence*, op. cit., 12.

Moira Roth
The Aesthetic of Indifference//1977

[…] The 1950s were assaulted with literature, popular culture and art describing feelings of indifference, neutrality and passivity in the world of the Cold War; and the Aesthetic of Indifference should be seen in this psychological ambience. A sociological study of this pervasive sense of 'alienation' (which itself became a catch-all term of the period) was undertaken by David Riesman in *The Lonely Crowd* (1950). In film, one of the most famous contemporary portraits of alienation was the James Dean character in *Rebel Without a Cause* (1955), whose impotent defiance of an indifferent world led to his inevitable defeat. The early 1950s also witnessed Beat literature and lifestyle, the curious Beat blend of passion and indifference which was crystallized in Allen Ginsberg's *Howl* (1956) and Jack Kerouac's *On the Road* (1957). In *The Dharma Bums* (1959), Kerouac describes the choice for himself and his generation: 'The only alternative to sleeping out, hopping freights, and doing what I wanted, I saw in a vision would be just to sit with a hundred other patients in front of a nice television set in a madhouse where we could be "supervised".' But in the early 1950s, a growing number of intellectuals consciously espoused indifference as a virtue, as the correct way to deal with an uncertain world.

A language of neutrality developed during the McCarthy period. Marshall McLuhan's *The Mechanical Bride*, published in 1951, […] was an early announcement of this new tone of indifference. *The Mechanical Bride*, a study in advertising manipulations, was written in a cool rather than indignant manner. McLuhan likened his non-judgmental stance to that of the imperilled sailor in Poe's 'The Maelstrom', a figure who saved himself by studying a whirlpool's movements with 'amusement', estimating the velocity of objects as they were drawn downward. McLuhan specifies: 'It is in the same spirit that this book is offered as amusement. Many who are accustomed to the note of moral indignation will mistake this amusement for mere indifference.' In this statement McLuhan defended himself against anticipated criticism that he lacked moral indignation, but more to the point here was his choice of the words 'amusement' and 'mere indifference'. They signalled a new language of neutrality, one cultivated by artists as well as writers.

The key exponents of the Aesthetic of Indifference were Marcel Duchamp, John Cage, Merce Cunningham, Robert Rauschenberg and Jasper Johns. That these artists loosely came together, intellectually and psychologically, in terms of a shared aesthetic during and just after the McCarthy period has received scant attention by art historians and critics. It is time to see their art and artistic stances in the Cold War context in order, first, to understand the art itself, and second, to explain, at least in part, the bizarre disjunction of art and politics that emerged in the 1960s. The radical political movements of the 1960s had virtually no expression in the art of that time, an art that was strangely appealing and acceptable to the very forces – governmental, corporate and middle-class powers – that these radical movements opposed. A major cause of this discrepancy between art and politics was no doubt the enormous impact of the Aesthetic of Indifference on art of the 1960s.

The Aesthetic of Indifference appeared in the early works of Johns and Rauschenberg, and in the Cage/Cunningham music and theatre experiments: all used neutrality as their springboard. These artists made and talked about art characterized by tones of neutrality, passivity, irony and, often, negation. 'Amusement' and 'indifference' became positive values. Parallels and precedents for these ideas were found in Dada and Duchamp. Indeed, Duchamp was a pivotal figure in the aesthetic as well as being, of course, one of its main historical sources. The indifferent aesthetic emerged in the early 1950s, and had three fairly distinct phases: its cool and ironic beginnings in Cage, Rauschenberg and Cunningham (with Duchamp as a major role model); its more poignant expression in the muted anxiety of early Johns; and its weakened final phase in the bland indifference of Pop and minimal art.

By the late 1940s, in the arena of Truman's presidency, one political and moral crisis followed another: the Iron Curtain divided Europe, mainland China was won by the communists in 1949, and a few months later a nuclear device was detonated in the Soviet Union. In the summer of 1950 the Korean war started. These events, and others, caused America to devote more and more of her energy and power to countering this spectre of a communist world take-over. Abroad, the Truman policy, the Marshall Plan, and the policy of containment were attempts to prevent, or at least curtail, communist power. At home, anti-communism dominated politics. In 1947, Truman established a new loyalty programme to weed out 'traitors' and security-risk employees from the federal government. The House Un-American Activities Committee (HUAC) became the stage for endless investigations of loyalty cases, and in 1950 Senator McCarthy, embarking on the first of his charges concerning communist infiltration of the American government, himself became a terrifying force in political life. [...]

As McCarthyism erupted in the world around them, the 'Indifferent' group viewed politics (meaning political bureaucracy and governmental strategies) with distance and irony. If Duchamp himself was later to describe politics as 'a stupid activity which leads to nothing',[1] Cage once envisioned a future in which 'economics and politics as we knew them would disappear and people would be in a position, so to speak, to live anarchistically'.[2] Because of this seemingly indifferent attitude to politics, such artists themselves – and most of their critics – have never acknowledged the influence of the historical context in which this aesthetic was formed, namely the Cold War and McCarthy periods. Such aloofness from political events of the time was part of these artists' general indifference, but today, a quarter of a century later, it is a part of their self-image which should be questioned. I do not see how one could paint the American flag in 1954 and claim, as Johns did, that it was merely inspired by a dream. Perhaps so, but dreams are ultimately connected with reality. Nineteen fifty-four was, in reality, a year of hysterical patriotism. Johns could not have been insensitive to this. […]

Duchamp was the European role model for many of the new notions about the artist: the cool, intelligent artist who disdained manual skills in favour of skilful plays of the mind. But Duchamp was old in 1950 – over sixty – and seemingly not producing much in the way of current art. The actual artistic production of the Aesthetic of Indifference came rather from younger American artists.

In 1950 Cage made a major leap of imagination by entering into his experiments with chance. It was a period of much excitement and exchange between Cage himself, David Tudor and Morton Feldman. But, although the Zen-like chance operations of Cage were exciting to invent, they also exhibited an extreme passivity: a decision not to assert but rather to let happen what may. One of the most famous of these early passive chance pieces by Cage was his *4'33"*. First performed in 1952, Cage's 'empty' composition lasted four minutes and thirty-three seconds, its only sounds being incidental noises from a restless audience and the outside environment. A similar theme of emptiness and passivity resided in Rauschenberg's white paintings of a year or so earlier. The large all-white canvases contained no image except the fleeting shadows of passers-by. The paintings had perplexed the public who saw them for the first time in 1953, a year after Cage's *4'33"* perplexed *its* first audience. In 1953, Cage wrote a description of these all-white paintings. His haiku-like response constitutes a poetic manifesto of the Aesthetic of Indifference:

> To whom
> No subject
> No image
> No taste
> No object
> No beauty
> No message
> No talent
> No technique (no why)

No idea
No intention
No art
No feeling ...³

The American public at large had been presented, in that year of the silent, empty white paintings, with the violent sounds and gestures of Joe McCarthy's performance in his new role as chairman of the Government Operations Committee, following the victory of Eisenhower and the emergence of a Republican majority in the Senate. In the spring of 1953, McCarthy's henchmen Roy M. Cohn and G. David Schine made a lightning censorship tour of the American overseas information programme in Europe. Their search for 'subversive' communist literature led to a monstrous 'cleaning up' of libraries and, literally, to book burning. In the political ambience of hysterical anti-communism and right-wing action, the Cage poem reads like an unconscious tragic acknowledgment of total paralysis. The Aesthetic of Indifference had literally gone 'blank'. There are no messages, no feelings and no ideas. Only emptiness. [...]

1 [footnote 4 in source] Pierre Cabanne, *Dialogues with Marcel Duchamp*, trans. Ron Padgett (New York: Viking, 1971) 103.
2 [5] Richard Kostelanetz, 'Conversation with John Cage', in Kostelanetz, ed., *John Cage* (New York: Praeger, 1970) 8.
3 [13] Reprinted in Richard Kostelanetz, ed., *John Cage*, op. cit., 111; a statement originally distributed in 1953 by the Stable Gallery, which had put on the first show of the Rauschenberg *White Paintings* that year.

Moira Roth, extracts from 'The Aesthetic of Indifference', *Artforum* (November 1977); reprinted in *Difference / Indifference* (Amsterdam: G+B Arts International, 1998) 34, 35–7, 40–41.

Jonathan D. Katz
Identification//1998

[…] In exploring the relationship between Cold War discursive modalities and these new aesthetic and erotic identities, Moira Roth's essay points toward the possibility of a social history of the mappings of gay identity in postwar American art – the first such analysis ever published.

Yet her ascription of indifference to a group of gay artists has long troubled me, for the term implies the presence of a choice; her implication that they did not become involved assumes that they could have. But the fact is that queer artists and straight artists were not playing on a level field in Cold War America. On the contrary, this was arguably the single most actively homophobic decade in American history, and queers who hoped to survive it had to engage in a constant negotiation with the dangers of self-disclosure. Silence ensured survival. Grouping a number of these gay artists together under the rubric of indifference and then chastising them for remaining silent during some of the most acrimonious debates on homosexuality in American history thus seems a bit unfair.

Although compelled, these gay artists' choice of silence and indifference was moreover not exactly a mode of the closet, for the closet uncompromisingly demands that one ape the larger cultural requirements as seamlessly as possible. Truly closeted artists would have simply painted abstract expressionist canvases. Instead, Cage stood before the assembled abstract expressionist multitude in 1948 and gave his 'Lecture on Nothing', with its famous tag line, 'I have nothing to say and I'm saying it.'[1] A few years later, Rauschenberg would complete his empty *White Paintings* and Cage his silence piece, *4'33"*. And yet a few years later, Johns would create a painting called *Disappearance II* that featured two layers of canvas, one atop the other, the top one folded in on itself so as to obscure its inner surface. In all these works silence and absence is thematized, made palpable as a silencing. The argument I want to make here is that this is not silence at all, but rather the *performance* of silence, and that – we shall find – is a very different thing. To call this silencing indifference is to mistake cause and effect. Duchamp had found a way to critique the natural without marking himself off as its enemy. He offered a recipe for destabilizing the operations of power without recourse to any articulated form of direct opposition. This, too, would prove enormously useful to a subsequent generation of closeted artists. Duchamp was never *against* anything; he was, as Roth correctly asserts, merely indifferent to that which he did not like. In a context of extreme constraint, such as that suffered by gay artists of the Cold War era, this ability to enact an opposition without articulating or embodying it would prove highly useful.

Opposition without oppositionality served to camouflage the dissident, and surely Duchamp was the most polite, respectable radical around. In Duchamp's case, this politesse was a useful performative strategy; for the gay artists who came later, it would become much, much more. In a context of institutionalized homophobia – among other constraints –opposition without oppositionality spelled the difference between success and censure, liberty and interdiction. Gay artists couldn't be against the naturalized masculine expressivity of abstract expressionism, but they could be, and were, indifferent to it. As Cage said in his 'Lecture on Nothing', 'I have nothing to say and I'm saying it.'

Moreover, because of this lack of oppositionality, the Duchampian model was able to secure a form of resistance to established power which did not enact or embody otherness. In the Cold War cultural context, otherness was useful to avoid, especially for gay men, who were moreover generally aligned with that ultimate other, the Communist.[2] And since the nomination of 'otherness' has long proved useful to the solidification of domination and control – becoming the outside that allows the inside to look past all differences and cohere as a united front – in denying an other, dominant culture was robbed of one of its chief supports. Hegemony generally required an other in order to define itself in antithesis. Thus, within this highly policed Cold War society, straightforward resistance to power, especially for gay men, could result, paradoxically, in its reinforcement. It was better, then, to approach power with the stealthy indirection of a Duchamp.

Not surprisingly, this is precisely what gay artists did during the Cold War. In unexpressive expressionism, silent music and white paintings, Johns, Cage and Rauschenberg, respectively, made a statement of non-statement. In their hands nothingness, emptiness and silence grew articulate. Though music was supposed to have arranged sound, painting organized colour, and expressionism the manifestation of emotions, their work had none of these tropes. But just as Duchamp interrogated the conditions of meaning in art through an act of negation – substituting a purchased mass-produced commodity for the autographic intensity of the authentic creative act – so too did these gay artists negate, and accordingly interrogate, other normative conditions of art meaning.

Here the act of negation constitutes an active, political praxis. And the negations of this Cold War generation of queer artists were both purposeful and successful, ultimately seeding and nourishing a resistance to the masculinized, hence naturalized, 'meaning-making' of the Cold War avant-garde. Through a seemingly indifferent aesthetic practice, these closeted artists nonetheless succeeded in destructuring hegemonic art world assumptions.

In short, I am arguing that what Roth refers to as 'an aesthetic of indifference' can be more accurately termed 'a politics of negation', wherein negation functions as an active resistance to hegemonic constructions of meaning as natural or inherent in the work. For negation to achieve this level of political engagement, it requires two preconditions: first, a context of extreme constraint such that direct opposition is both dangerous and ineffectual; and second, a practice so rigorously hegemonic that the negation of it would in and of itself signify. Surely, if ever these conditions occurred in the US, it was during the Cold War era. In navigating the distance between saying and meaning, these acts of negation opened up the process of signification for an audience-centred examination of the conditions of aesthetic statement. […]

Queer artists found in negation a mode useful precisely for its ability to obscure its investments; indeed that was one of its central purposes. Its potential invisibility is therefore not a flaw but a strength, and such camouflage would prove highly useful in the policed context of Cold War culture. But equally, as literary theorist Ross Chambers argues, the act of negation brings a work so close to its target that it may seem hardly different from it at all. As Chambers sums it up, 'negation shares with grammatical negation an inescapable feature … negation necessarily "mentions" therefore acknowledges the power of what it negates (whereas an affirmation does not have to have to acknowledge that which it is negating).'[3]

Silent music or empty painting – as in the work of Cage or Rauschenberg, respectively – depend for their signification on traditional music and painting. This dependence, which may from one perspective seem like a detriment, from another perspective yields great instrumental benefits, for it achieves two related and highly useful goals. First, negation avoids the recolonizing force of the oppositional – that which permits the opponent to solidify and suture through recourse to the excluded other. Second, negation operates as a closeted relation, mediating between the negating and the negated in such a way as to exclude all who are not already at the very least sympathetic to its case.

There is a remarkable symmetry between this analysis of the politics of negation and Derrida's notion of indecidability. Derrida has argued that the only exit from the binaries that structure and enable systems of knowing is through the use of what he called 'indecidables'. He named them indecidables because they operate like ball bearings in a binary system, overturning and negating first in this direction, then in that, so as to keep the binary itself from being re-established. What makes something an indecidable is that it cannot be fitted into the totalizing oppositional economy of binarism. Indecidables do not constitute or construct a third term in a traditional Hegelian dialectic, for that would only produce yet another binary logos. Instead they subject the binarism itself to scrutiny. This irritating resistance of indecidables to the polarizing either/or of our habitual epistemology is what makes them so effective in deconstruction.

I want therefore to substitute Derrida's term 'indecidable' for Roth's 'indifferent' as a way of restoring the particular political utility to this Cold War practice of negation. Fred Orton has elegantly defined indecidability as a strategic way 'of using the only available language while not subscribing to its premises, a mode of operating according to the vocabulary of the very thing …' delimited.[4] The trope of negation is thus coterminous with the Derridian concept of indecidability; both depend on, and then negate, that which they oppose as the sole means of marking out their difference. Cage's silence, whether before the rowdy abstract expressionists at the Club or a formal concert hall audience, was just such an indecidable, dependent upon that which it sought to oppose – respectively, abstract expressionist aesthetic discourse and 'music', among many other targets – in order to describe difference. In this context silence is a negation because an audience has gathered to hear something; of course in other audience contexts that would not necessarily be the case.

As with Cage's embrace of silence in his 1948 'Lecture on Nothing' at the Club, Rauschenberg, too, in his 1951 *White Paintings* chose silence as a means of refusal. When these paintings were finally exhibited in 1953, they were interpreted by critics as nihilistic, as a joke, as a Dada gesture, as, in Cage's words, 'airports for light and shadow'.[5] What wasn't noticed at the time was that these paintings are the absolute negation of abstract expressionism in terms of mood, surface, colour; a silencing of abstract expressionism, if you will. The paintings are a sort of pure anti-abstract expressionism, and though of abstract expressionist scale, so without autographic or gestural content of any kind that Rauschenberg decreed they were to be painted by others, using a roller and housepaint.

The *White Paintings* thus ironically negated the broad outlines of the habitual abstract expressionist aesthetic universe. In this sense, the fact that these paintings were not discussed at the time as oppositional is evidence of their successful incorporation of a politics of oppositionality, for oppositionality here lies less in their legibility as acts of resistance than in their indecidable status. And they are indecidable because as absolute negations, there is nothing here, nothing *to* decide. […]

1   [footnote 12 in source] John Cage, *Silence: Lectures and Writings* (Middletown, Connecticut: Wesleyan University Press, 1973) 109.
2   [34] John D'Emilio, 'The Homosexual Menace: The Politics of Sexuality in Cold War America', in *Passion and Power: Sexuality in History*, ed. Kathy Peiss and Christina Simmons (Philadelphia: Temple University Press, 1989) 226–40.
3   [36] Ross Chambers, *Room for Manoeuvre: Reading Oppositional Narrative* (Chicago: University of Chicago Press, 1991).
4   [37] Fred Orton's article first suggested to me the applicability of these Derridean concepts to art

history. I am heavily indebted to his pioneering work. See his 'On Being Bent "Blue" (Second State): An Introduction to Jacques Derrida/A Footnote on Jasper Johns', *Oxford Art Journal*, vol. 12, no. 1 (1989) 35–46.

5   [38] John Cage, 'On Robert Rauschenberg, Artist, and His Work', *Metro* (May 1961); reprinted in *Silence*, op. cit., 98.

Jonathan D. Katz, extracts from 'Identification', in Moira Roth, ed., *Difference/Indifference* (Amsterdam: G+B Arts International, 1998) 53, 62–5.

Dick Higgins
Boredom and Danger//1968

Boredom was, until recently, one of the qualities an artist tried most to avoid. Yet today it appears that artists are deliberately trying to make their work boring. Is this true, or is it only an illusion? In either case, what is the explanation?

There was a time, not so very long ago, when music was considered a form of entertainment, perhaps on a higher level than some other forms, but still part of the same world as theatre vaudeville, circuses, etc. Similarly, apart from religious art and purely functional art, the fine arts were basically used for decorative purposes. But with the rise of the idea that the work of art was intended first and foremost as an experience, that its function could be spiritual, psychological and educational, the situation began to change. Kandinsky's view of art as a means of deepening one's spiritual life is a landmark along this way. The musical parallel to this conception is found in Arnold Schoenberg's writings, in the letters and in *Style and Idea*.

But it is still a very long way from musical expressionism, which merely denies that entertainment values are at all to the point, to the situation in which boredom and other, related feelings might actually play a part. In music the key personality in this development, as in many others, is Erik Satie. Satie composed a piece shortly before World War I, *Vieux Sequins et Vieilles Cuirasses*, a characteristically programmatic piece in which he spoofs the military and the glories of nationalism. At the end of the piece there appears an eight-beat passage evocative of old marches and patriotic songs, but which is to be repeated 380 times. In performance the satirical intent of this repetition comes through very clearly, but at the same time other very interesting results begin to appear. The music first becomes so familiar that it seems extremely offensive and objectionable. But after that the mind slowly becomes incapable of taking further offence, and a very strange, euphoric acceptance and enjoyment begin to set in. Satie appears to have been fascinated by this effect, because he also wrote *Vexations* […] an utterly serious 32-bar piece (although the bar lines are not written in) intended to be played very softly and very slowly 840 times. Today it is usually done by a team of pianists, and lasts over a period of roughly 25 hours. Is it boring? Only at first. After a while the euphoria I have mentioned begins to intensify. By the time the piece is over, the silence is absolutely numbing, so much of an environment has the piece become. […]

If it can be said that Satie's interest in boredom originated as a kind of gesture – there is a certain bravura about asking a pianist to play the same eight beats 380 times – and developed into a fascinating, aesthetic statement, then I think it can be said with equal fairness that Cage was the first to try to emphasize in his work and his teaching a dialectic between boredom and intensity. I recall a class with him at the New School for Social Research in the summer of 1958, where George Brecht had brought in a piece which simply asked each performer to do two different things, each once. When each participant had done two, the piece was over. Cage suggested that we perform this piece in darkness, so as to be unable to tell, visually, whether the piece had ended. This was done. The result was fascinating, both for its own sake and for the extraordinary intensity that appeared in waves, as we wondered whether the piece was over or not, what the next thing to happen would be, etc. Afterwards we were asked to guess how long we had been in the dark. The guesses ranged from four minutes to 25. The actual duration was nine minutes. The boredom played a comparable role, in relation to intensity, to that which silence plays with sound, where each one heightens the other and frames it.

The point which we have been coming to, then, is that in the context of work which attempts to involve the spectator, boredom often serves a useful function: as an opposite to excitement and as a means of bringing emphasis to what it interrupts, causing us to view both elements freshly. It is a necessary station on the way to other experiences, as in the case of the Satie.

The arts in which boredom has been a structural factor have been predominantly the performing arts (as emphasized in Cage's class), and the kind of performances in which boredom has been most structurally implicit and useful are the events (miniature Happenings) associated with the Fluxus movement. Fluxus was an attempt to provide a coordinating rostrum for a large body of Happenings and events activities which were not oriented towards the visual arts, and were therefore unable to effect continuity of information through the art galleries, as the visual Happenings did. Just to indicate the variety of backgrounds of the participants, among the original Fluxus members were

George Brecht, the maker of small art objects and early minimal art; Jackson Mac Low, the poet; La Monte Young, the composer; myself, a composer and poet; and ten or twenty others of similarly disparate original concerns. […]

The Fluxus performance arose from a feeling that the best of the performing arts should not be entertaining nor should they inherently even be educational. It was felt they should serve as stimuli which made one's life and work and experience more meaningful and flexible. The use, in Fluxus format works, of boredom became not so much a structural factor as an implicit factor, as, for example, when Jackson Mac Low proposed a project, a film which, for financial reasons, was not executed till recently (but which was published). The film was to be made of a tree on which the camera would be trained for any length of time. This film would clearly have been more environmental than entertaining, cinematic or educational. One would relate to it in direct proportion to the ability to look with concentration at it. Boring? Of course; if one were to ignore the more intense activity involved, which we might call 'super boring', and which took one beyond the initial level of simple boredom. This has very much to do with the Satie idea.

In the same vein, La Monte Young composed a musical piece which consisted of a *B* and *F* sharp, to be played simultaneously on as many instruments as available with as little variation as possible. But the performed result established a drone over which, while it was intended to have the most neutral, blank character possible and was therefore made of plain, open fifths, one would begin to imagine all kinds of goings-on. In fact, most of La Monte Young's most recent performances have consisted of the playing of just such fantastic patterns over a similar drone.

In a parallel spirit, I tried to achieve a similar effect in a series of pieces by using 'blank stuctures', in which I simply established a rule matrix for the performance, and gave neither explicit clues to my intentions nor any working materials, apart from the matrix, to the performers. What they or the audience contributed became both subject matter and perceptible form. At a Fluxus performance in Copenhagen in 1962 the extremes of this kind of work were tested – with the excitement inseparable, again, from the boredom. During my second *Contribution*, each performer chooses something in the environment of the performance to cue him to perform an action, which he has also determined. The poet Emmett Williams and the composer Eric Andersen each chose to do his action when he became the last person on the stage. The resulting hours of waiting to see which would break became very exciting. Each stood motionless. The audience became bored, impatient and upset. But the word began to circulate, through those who knew the piece, as to what had happened. And then the audience quieted down and became fascinated. Very few left. The end of the performance came by accident – one of the performers, offered a drink by someone, misunderstood and thought he was being ordered off stage. It was a very fortunate misunderstanding, since Williams and Andersen are sufficiently tough-minded to be there still today, six years later, if necessary. […]

Dick Higgins, extract from 'Boredom and Danger', *Something Else Press Newsletter*, vol. 1, no. 9 (December 1968) (New York: Something Else Press, 1968), originally drafted in 1966; reprinted in *A Dialectic of Centuries*, 2nd ed. (New York and Barton, Vermont: Printed Editions, 1978) 42–6.

Ina Blom
Boredom and Oblivion//1998

In 1966 Dick Higgins published his influential 'Intermedia' essay, stating that the new and interesting forms of art did not limit their field of operation to a question of artistic media, but tended to operate between or outside particular media or categories.[1] A comparison between this essay and the actual artistic developments it described might lead to more precise definitions. As a term, 'intermedia' was designed to cover those instances where the artist did not simply combine different artistic media, but worked against the grain of any categorial organizations by means of strategies of displacement. In contrast to the term 'multimedia', 'intermedia' did not denote a formal identification but rather a strategic intent or a performative.[2] Then the medial aspect of the work could be described in terms of *transmedia*: that is, as an agent of change or transcoding. Intermedia's many attempts to formulate 'betweens' or 'outsides' did not express a dream about the idyllic state of the unmediated. It simply dealt with the principle of mediation as a passage from one state to another.

Around the same time, however, Higgins' lesser-known essay on boredom and danger somehow seems to strike closer to the core of the particular intermedial strategies that developed in the late 1950s and early 60s. Higgins sets out as if he desperately needs to make sense of this puzzling concept, but it is immediately apparent that for him boredom is a positive term, a point of departure for a new orientation. The apparent lack of stimuli in boring art involves the surroundings in ways not apparent when stimuli appear as exciting along certain lines of expectation. When Higgins tries to explain the effect of boring art such as, for instance, Erik Satie's *Vexations*, in which an 'utterly serious 32-bar piece' is played very slowly 840 times (a performance takes twenty-five hours), he repeatedly returns to the way in which such works will fade into their environment, become an integral part of their surroundings.[3] Boredom destroys the boundaries that keep the surge of intensities within the fenced-off space of the work. Now the intensities move along different lines, as in a Cage class experience referred to by Higgins, where the students were instructed to do two different things each, in total darkness, so that one could not visually determine the beginning and the end of the piece.[4] Higgins describes the way in which the intensities in this piece 'appeared in waves' as expectation of structure mingled with the experience of non-structure; how the sense of time was warped as work and non-work could not be distinguished as separate areas of perception.

In a set of notes dealing with the experience the spectator would have with his play *St Joan of Beaurevoir*, Higgins comments on a different aspect of boredom. Anticipating audience reactions, he describes different levels of involvement developing through the piece, such as boredom, irritation, understanding and new boredom. 'Then', he writes, 'the witness will ideally disappear into the piece. He will stop seeing himself and start seeing events as events. The general stasis of the piece will be soothing. Quantities will become relative and not numerical.'[5] Boredom, in other words, has the capacity to cause disappearance on two different levels which must be experienced as reciprocal: the work will disappear into the surroundings, and the spectator will disappear into the work.

This situation describes the kind of symmetrical relationship where the two sides are different by being the reverse of one another, as in a mirror. The work sees 'itself' in the surroundings, as the surroundings sees 'itself' in the work. But in this throwing back and forth, the identity of each is cancelled – one no longer knows which side of the mirror one is on. Usually identity is established with a simple self-reflexivity: I know that I am. When Higgins describes the experience of the piece in the darkened room, he describes a situation where this simple reflexivity proliferates into a series of repetitive questions concerning the boundaries between work and perceiving subject. The intensities of the piece move along the lines of questions such as 'whether the piece was finished or not, what the next thing to happen would be, etc.'[6] And this repetition has the capacity to undo identity. It works to highlight the simulacral quality of a mirroring in which the two sides of the mirror are confused so that 'nothing' or 'everything' is finally mirrored. Boredom – or the level beyond the initial experience of boredom which Higgins calls 'super boring' – essentially has to do with indistinction, disappearance and oblivion.

Oblivion on the level of the work, oblivion on the level of the spectator who engages with the reality of the work. In 1959 Higgins worked with a series of works called 'Contributions' and which developed from this principle. One piece calls for the production of a sound 'that is neither opposed to nor directly derived from' the environment in which it will be produced.[7] The piece is in fact an instructive riddle. How can one determine that which is neither opposed to nor derived from a context? Obviously, there is no way to avoid either of these parameters as long as sound is reflected in terms of predetermined relationships and as long as one sees the context as a given, closed whole. The only way to arrive at the freedom of this neither/nor situation seems to be to accept a fundamental independence of sounds and an equally fundamental dispersion of context. Then anything will do, and this anything will simply contribute to the oblivion of the situation. […]

1   [6] Dick Higgins, 'Intermedia', *The Something Else Newsletter* (February 1966).
2   [7] Ina Blom, 'The Intermedia Dynamic: An Aspect of Fluxus', Dissertation, University of Oslo, 1993.
3   [8] Dick Higgins, 'Boredom and Danger', *Something Else Newsletter* (December 1968). The essay was originally written in the summer of 1966.
4   [9] Ibid. The piece was originally by George Brecht; John Cage, however, suggested that it should be done in darkness.
5   [10] Dick Higgins, notes to *St Joan of Beaurevoir*, 'What Part Does a Witness to St Joan of Beaurevoir Play?'; Silverman Collection, Detroit and New York.
6   [11] Higgins, 'Boredom and Danger', op. cit.
7   [12] Dick Higgins, *Contribution 1* (November 1959).

Ina Blom, extract from 'Boredom and Oblivion', in *The Fluxus Reader*, ed. Ken Friedman (London: Academy Editions, 1998) 65–6.

Andy Warhol
In Conversation with Joseph Gelmis//1969

Joseph Gelmis What was the reaction of the college audiences to your films last year?

Andy Warhol We showed them so much they didn't know whether they liked them or not.

Gelmis Is that the reaction of most people?

Warhol When people go to a show today they're never involved any more. A movie like *Sleep* gets them involved again. They get involved with themselves and they create their own entertainment.

Gelmis Your audience is forced to do the work themselves?

Warhol It becomes fun.

Gelmis Do you mean people who don't like your films or are bored by them just aren't working hard enough?

Warhol I don't know. But it's a lot of fun.

Gelmis Most of your films have little or no editing. You keep the camera in one spot and keep shooting until the reels run out. Your characters enter and leave the frame. But there's no cutting, just reels spliced together. Why?

Warhol The reason we did that was because whatever anybody did was always good. So you can't say one was better than the other. You get more involved and time goes by quicker if you stay with one scene.

Gelmis Have you changed your opinions about the need for editing?

Warhol Well, now we really believe in entertainment, and that's a different scene.

Gelmis You've said 'I like boring things.' How can entertainment be boring?

Warhol When you just sit and look out of a window, that's enjoyable.

Gelmis Why? Because you can't figure out what's going to happen, what's going to be passing in front of you?

Warhol It takes up time.

Gelmis Are you serious?

Warhol Yeah. Really. You see people looking out of their windows all the time. I do.

Gelmis Mostly it's people who are stuck where they have to be, like an old person or a housewife waiting for the kid to get out of school or the husband to come home from work. And they're usually bored.

Warhol No. I don't think so. If you're not looking out of a window, you're sitting in a shop looking at the street.

Gelmis Your films are just a way of taking up time?

Warhol Yeah.

Andy Warhol and Joseph Gelmis, extract from Joseph Gelmis, 'Andy Warhol' (Spring 1969), first published in Gelmis, *The Film Director as Superstar* (Garden City, New York: Doubleday, 1970); reprinted in Kenneth Goldsmith, ed., *I'll Be Your Mirror: The Selected Andy Warhol Interviews 1962–1987* (New York: Carroll & Graf, 2004) 168–9.

Jonas Mekas
Notes after Reseeing the Movies of Andy Warhol//1970

[…] To do this once is forgivable. It is a kind of dadaesque joke mocking art – and hell, I'm all for it. People and artists do tend to take themselves too seriously at times. If one has enough money for selling Brillo boxes at $200 apiece to waste on six hours of raw stock and developing (such as in the movie *Sleep*), to create a mammoth joke – well, man, go ahead.

But to do it again and again, and then ask people to sit through it, is pushing things

a bit too far. A joke's a joke, but I for one would be embarrassed to play the same boring joke on people more than once.
– Peter Goldman.[1]

During the early years of the decade, the early period of Warhol's film work, whenever I went to a university, lecturing, I used to take one of Andy's films, usually *Eat*. And always the same thing used to happen. The film starts rolling, the audience sits quietly, for a minute or two. The catcalls and crack remarks begin. In the fourth or fifth minute, however, they begin to realize that I have no intention of stopping the film, and the reports from the back lines reach the front lines, that the reel is *big* (45 minutes). The most unsettling, however, is the fact that no amount of noise or cracks seems to do any harm to the film! Its nonchalant, obstinate and don't-give-a-damn imperturbability on the screen seems to reject or absorb anything you can throw at it. It almost grows stronger with every whistle. So the students begin to leave the auditorium. After ten minutes or so the impatient ones leave or give up, others resign, and the rest of the show proceeds quietly. Later, from the discussions, it becomes clear that there is always a period – to some five minutes, to others fifteen, to some still longer – a period of *jumping the reality gap*, or what we could also call the period of aesthetic weightlessness; a period of adjusting to the aesthetic weightlessness, to the different gravitational pull. From there on you are floating through your mind, from there on the movie – *Sleep*, *Eat*, *Haircut*, and exactly the same applies to the later sound movies, say *The Imitation of Christ* – from there on everything becomes very rich. You are watching now from a new angle, every detail reveals a new meaning, the proportions and perspectives change – you begin to notice not only the hundred-mile movements but also one-inch movements; not only a crashing blow on the head is an action, a touch of a butterfly wing is also an action. A whole new world opens because of this shifted angle of vision, of seeing, a world in which there is as much action, suspense, tension, adventure, and entertainment as on the former plane – and more! […]

1   [footnote 21 in source] Peter Goldman, *Village Voice* (27 August 1964).

Jonas Mekas, extract from 'Notes after Reseeing the Movies of Andy Warhol', in *Andy Warhol*, ed. John Coplans (Greenwich, Connecticut: New York Graphic Society, 1970) 144.

Tan Lin
Warhol's Aura and the Language of Writing//2001

[...] Most of Warhol's films are about people not changing because not changing was what most people do most of the time. Change is atypical. Not changing is also known as boredom and Warhol liked 'boring things', attenuated time frames, desultory and unpredictable mechanical 'systems' of production, variable repetition, occasional violence, open schedules, haphazard talk and blasé mediation. A film about the Empire State building, a film about a man sleeping, a film about a man getting fellated – these were ways Warhol flirted with things that were not yet 'happening'. That is why Warhol claimed to have never grown up: 'I'm missing some chemicals and that's why I have this tendency to be more of a – mama's boy. A – sissy ... I'm immature, but maybe something could happen to my chemicals and I could get mature.' That is also why Warhol liked things that are exactly the same: '... most people love watching the same basic thing, as long as the details are different. But I'm just the opposite: If I'm going to sit and watch the same thing I saw the night before, I don't want it to be essentially the same – I want it to be *exactly* the same. Because the more you look at the same exact thing, the more the meaning goes away, and the better and emptier you feel.' Not surprisingly, Warhol disavowed orchestrating the destruction (change) of particular individuals like Edie Sedgwick. No one makes an artwork and no one changes somebody else: 'When people are ready to, they change. They never do it before then, and sometimes they die before they get around to it. You can't make them change if they don't want to, just like when they do want to, you can't stop them.'

The eye produces serial images, automatically, and without thought. The mouth produces serial words, automatically, and without thought. Eye and mouth are both surrogate modes of 'being oneself'. The most interesting mode of being oneself used to be 'having a memory'. Not surprisingly, Warhol's two favourite surrogates were his tape-recorder and his camera, which functioned as his ears and eyes respectively. Both lacked memory. Similarly, the screen tests were about waiting for someone to walk in and sit for a few minutes and manifest, as a kind of deaf-mute image, that thing known as 'screen presence'. For this reason, beauty that occurs there occurs in the background and still strikes its viewers dumb. Warhol, in Monte Carlo, at the Hotel Mirabeau remarks: 'Damian looked beautiful in a navy-blue Dior.' In Rome: 'Just then, Ursula Andress appeared at the top of the stairs. She looked beautiful.' In *Blowjob*, the hustler finally comes after 41 minutes. Somewhere in the middle of an eight-hour *Empire*, the floodlights go on and the Empire State Building begins to shine or give off something filmic, much like the face of Marilyn or Jackie.

The films (like his novel *A*) are experiments in slowing down viewing (or reading) time or creating a lag between clock time and the rate at which we register perceptual changes. One of the things that slow-motion does is make change harder to see. Oddly, boredom, which most people associate with things not changing, creates for Warhol a heightened state of anticipation, a place where beauty might erupt. In this sense, Warhol's films and novels mimic the endless staying the same that is existence and the endless continual change that is also and simultaneously existence. One might say that beauty for Warhol was that point where boredom and change overlap. A typical Warhol film was shot at sound speed or 24 frames per second, but played back at silent speed, or 16 frames per second, thus literally slowing down the rate at which an image changes and prolonging the rate at which things stay the same. The slower speed enabled Warhol to capture what he called 'nothing': '... we ran it at a slower speed to make up for the film I didn't shoot.' The slowed-down film heightens the fact that something that we can't quite perceive or register is going on in the background, something unnoticed like wallpaper or something accidentally recorded, like off-screen voices.

All of these repeated elements or serial patterns are forms of 'nothing' that make up our day-to-day perceptions, the things we almost register consciously. For this reason, it takes much longer to transcribe or read *A* then it did to actually say it. The best language is the language that just takes place somewhere in the background, language we hear but don't remember, language that merely fills up the time slowly and completely without us fully processing or consciously thinking about it. It is often hard to tell who is speaking to whom; arguments are left unfinished; body language is lost; only one half of telephone conversations are recorded; when people speak simultaneously, multiple voices are often transcribed out of order. Transcribing a life in this manner renders it almost impossibly opaque and difficult to apprehend, much less remember. Fame is the best kind of background noise; it obscures who we are not. The opposite of being successful is being nothing. Fifteen minutes is a short time for someone who wants to be famous. Novelistic time, like art time, is artificially constructed to feign speed, suspense and resolution. Warhol preferred boredom, empty spaces, killing time, and no memory. 'My mind is like a tape recorder with one button – Erase. If I wake up too early to check in with anyone, I kill time by watching TV and washing my underwear. Maybe the reason my memory is so bad is that I always do at least two things at once.'

Tan Lin, extract from 'Warhol's Aura and the Language of Writing', *Cabinet*, no. 4 (Fall 2001). (www.cabinetmagazine.org) [Quotations are from *POPism: The Warhol 60s* and *The Philosophy of Andy Warhol*]

SINCE THERE WAS NOTHING ELSE TO DO, I WORKED. WORKED MECHANICALLY AND AT TIMES DESPAIRINGLY ON MOVEMENT. IT WAS NECESSARY TO FIND A DIFFERENT WAY TO MOVE

Yvonne Rainer, On *Parts of Some Sextets*, 1965

SILENCE

Yvonne Rainer
On Parts of Some Sextets//1965

The Work

[…] We next spent six weeks in Dusseldorf [in September and October 1964]. Bob [Robert Morris] prepared sculpture for a show. I went every day to a tiny sixth-floor walk-up ballet studio in the Altstadt; I could see the Rhine beyond the old rooftops. One day there was a fire in the next block. Much smoke and scurrying around. I felt like a cuckoo in a Swiss clock observing an intricate mechanized toy go thru its paces. All those little firemen and townsfolk seemed wound up. And in the distance that flat river and green-washed Rhine meadow. The whole scene was decidedly depressing.

    Since there was nothing else to do, I worked. Worked mechanically and at times despairingly on movement. It was necessary to find a different way to move. I felt I could no longer call on the energy and hard-attack impulses that had characterized my work previously, nor did I want to explore any further the 'imitations-from-life' kind of eccentric movement that someone once described as 'goofy glamour'. So I started at another place – wiggled my elbows, shifted from one foot to the other, looked at the ceiling, shifted eye focus within a tiny radius, watched a flattened, raised hand moving and stopping, moving and stopping. Slowly the things I made began to go together, along with sudden sharp, hard changes in dynamics. But basically I wanted it to remain undynamic movement, no rhythm, no emphasis, no tension, no relaxation. You just *do* it, with the coordination of a pro and the non-definition of an amateur. It's an ideal, still to be worked on.

    I was also doing a lot of thinking about my group piece. […] How I decided upon the system that I ultimately used is now not too clear to me, especially since in retrospect it seems there were many solutions that might have more successfully achieved what I had in mind. However, it was clear that there must not be a flowing or developmental type of progression in the action, but rather whatever changes were to take place must be as abrupt and jagged as possible, perhaps occurring at regular brief intervals. So I resorted to two devices that I have used consistently since my earliest dances: repetition and interruption. In the context of this new piece, both factors were to produce a 'chunky' continuity, repetition making the eye jump back and forth in time and possibly establishing more strongly the differences in the movement material – especially the 'dancey' stuff – that some of the movement episodes were simply small fragments used randomly and some were elaborate sequences made from consecutive phrases.

Interruption would also function to disrupt the continuity and prevent prolonged involvement with any one image. So it began to take shape in my head: dance movement of various kinds; activities with mattresses; static activities (sitting, standing, lying); continuous simultaneous actions changing abruptly at perhaps thirty-second intervals, sometimes the whole field changing at the same time, sometimes only a portion of it, but every thirty seconds something changing. Thirty seconds began to seem like the right interval-length. I did not realize until much later that a given duration can *seem* long or short according to what is put into it. So my scheme, when applied to the diversity of materials that finally filled it out, did not really produce the insistent regularity I had thought it might. However, by the time I made this basic discovery I had begun to like the irregularities of the piece.

Returned to New York beginning of Nov. 1964. Had already decided on the soundtrack for the piece. Spent the next five weeks in the NY Public Library perusing the index of and copying excerpts from the *Diary of William Bentley, D.D.*, a late eighteenth-century Episcopal minister who lived in Salem, Mass. and kept careful stock of the local goings-on during his forty-year tenure. Continued to work on movement material. Began to assemble the chart that would dictate the final arrangement of materials and people.

The chart, reading down, lists 31 choices of material; reading across, numbers consecutively thirty-second intervals 1 thru 84. The piece is as long as two sheets of 22 x 17 inch graph paper allow with one-half inch of ruled space equivalent to thirty seconds. The chart is divided into squares, each indicating the juncture of a given piece of material with a given interval in time. The physical space of the dance – where the material would take place – was to be decided by necessity and whim as rehearsals progressed.

The 31 possibilities as briefly described on the chart are: 1. Duet: Corridor Solo; 2. Duet: Bob's entrance thru Y's squeals; 3. Duet: Leaning away thru 1st embraces; 4. Duet: Diagonal run to end; 5. Bird run; 6. Running thru; 7. Racing walk; 8. Solo beginning with shifting of weight; 9. Standing figure; 10. Bent-over walk; 11. Quartet; 12. Rope duet (with rope); 13. Rope movements 1 thru 4; 14. Rope movements 5 thru 8; 15. Rope movements 9 thru 13; 16. One vertical mattress moving back and forth on single layer; 17. 'Swedish werewolf' (always off-stage); 18. Human flies on mattress pile; 19. Formation no. 1 (fling); 20. Formation no. 2 (with 'bug squash'); 21. Move pile to other side; 22. Peel one at a time; 23. Crawl thru below top mattress; 24. Standing figure on top of pile; 25. House lights; 26. One person running another into pile; 27. Bob's diagonal; 28. Sitting figure; 29. Sleeping figure; 30. Vague movement; 31. Formation no. 3 (pile-up).

In December began asking people to perform in the piece. The cast materialized as Lucinda Childs, Judith Dunn, Sally Gross, Deborah Hay, Tony Holder, Robert

Morris, Steve Paxton, Me, Robert Rauschenberg, Joseph Schlichter. [...]

Began teaching the dance material. (The non-trained people, Morris, and Rauschenberg, learned everything except 'Quartet'.) Had been putting off the actual filling in of the chart, but now with the mattresses bought and rehearsals proper ready to start, there could be no more delay. So one night I took the plunge and with a pencil made random marks all over the chart paper. Mostly in isolated squares, but sometimes in two, three or even four consecutive ones.

Then the work began: in column no. 1 (the first thirty seconds) marks fell in the square indicating Duet: Corridor Solo, Bird run, Bent-over walk, Quartet, Peel one at a time, House Lights, Sitting Figure. The remaining decisions to make were who – and how many – were to do these and where they were to do them. Column by column I filled in initials of the cast. The decisions were based both on expediency (e.g. 'do the rope movements wherever you happen to be' or 'J. can't continue doing that because she has to do Corridor Solo here', etc.) and my feeling about the constantly shifting churned-up quality I was after. So when one activity went on for more than two columns (one minute), I usually added to or reduced the number of people doing it or even replaced them half way thru.

The final problem was that of cues. Eventually we would take word cues from the taped reading of the diary, but I hadn't yet made the tape because I thought it would be too difficult to learn movement sequences and cues at the same time. So I made a work tape with my voice saying 'change' every thirty seconds. Now I feel that using the double learning process from the very beginning would have meant a considerable saving in time and work. As things stood, after we had learned the dance with the work tape, we had to plod thru it innumerable times for the extra familiarizing process involving the cues in the reading.

The dance took eight weeks to learn. For the first four weeks we rehearsed four times a week; after that two or three times a week. It proved to be dry, plodding work, partly due to the length and repetitiousness. Also, since there was no 'organic' or kinaesthetic continuity, some of us found it extraordinarily difficult to learn and ended up memorizing it by rote, like multiplication tables or dates in history. [...]

Postscript

All I am inclined to indicate here are various feelings about *Parts of Some Sextets* and its effort in a certain direction – an area of concern as yet not fully clarified for me in relation to dance, but existing as a very large NO to many facts in the theatre today. (This is not to say that I personally do not enjoy many forms of theatre. It is only to define more stringently the rules and boundaries of my own artistic game of the moment.)

NO to spectacle no to virtuosity no to transformations and magic and make-believe no to the glamour and transcendency of the star image no to the heroic no to the anti-heroic no to trash imagery no to involvement of performer or spectator no to style no to camp no to seduction of spectator by the wiles of the performer no to eccentricity no to moving or being moved.

The challenge might be defined as how to move in the spaces between theatrical bloat with its burden of dramatic psychological 'meaning' – and – the imagery and atmospheric effects of the non-dramatic, non-verbal theatre (i.e. dancing and some 'happenings') – and – theatre of spectator participation and/ or assault. I like to think that *Parts of Some Sextets* worked somewhere in these spaces, at the risk of losing the audience before it was half over (but that is yet another matter of concern, not to be investigated here). Its repetition of actions, its length, its relentless recitation, its inconsequential ebb and flow all combined to produce an effect of nothing happening. The dance 'went nowhere', did not develop, progressed as though on a treadmill or like a 10-ton truck stuck on a hill: it shifts gears, groans, sweats, farts, but doesn't move an inch.

Perhaps next time my truck will make some headway; perhaps it will inch forward – imperceptibly – or fall backward – headlong.

Yvonne Rainer, extract from 'Some Retrospective Notes on a Dance for 10 People and 12 Mattresses Called 'Parts of Some Sextets', Performed at the Wadsworth Atheneum, Hartford, Connecticut, and Judson Memorial Church, New York, in March, 1965', *The Tulane Drama Review*, vol. 10, no. 2 (Winter 1965) 168–78; reprinted in *Work 1961–73* (Halifax, Nova Scotia: The Press of the Nova Scotia College of Art and Design, 1974) 46–51.

Robert Morris
Three Folds in the Fabric and Four Autobiographical Asides as Allegories (or Interruptions)//1989

[…] I first met the elderly Barnett Newman at a party at Frank Stella's on 73rd Street in 1965, if memory serves. When I introduced myself, he looked at me through his monocle and said, 'Yes, I know your work.' I was very surprised but learned later that he was intensely interested in the newer work that was just being shown then and made a point to see as much of it as possible. 'Yes', he continued in his gravelly voice, 'you're that guy who makes those low grey things, all those plinths and boxes and slabs. It's all so low and hugs the ground. But don't you know the difficult thing is to get it up?'

At thirty I had my alienation, my Skilsaw and my plywood. I was out to rip out the metaphors, especially those that had to do with 'up', as well as every other whiff of transcendence. When I sliced into the plywood with my Skilsaw, I could hear, beneath the ear-damaging whine, a stark and refreshing 'no' reverberate off the four walls: no to transcendence and spiritual values, heroic scale, anguished decisions, historicizing narrative, valuable artefact, intelligent structure, interesting visual experience. [...]

Robert Morris, extract from 'Three Folds in the Fabric and Four Autobiographical Asides as Allegories (or Interruptions)', *Art in America* (November 1989) 142–51; reprinted in Morris, *Continuous Project Altered Daily* (Cambridge, Massachusetts: The MIT Press, 1993) 263, 265.

Barbara Rose
ABC Art//1965

[...] It seems clear that the group of young artists I am speaking of were reacting to more than merely formal chaos when they opted not to fulfil Ad Reinhardt's prescription for 'divine madness' in 'third generation Abstract Expressionists'. In another light, one might as easily construe the new, reserved impersonality and self-effacing anonymity as a reaction against the self-indulgence of an unbridled subjectivity, just as one might see it in terms of a formal reaction to the excesses of painterliness. One has the sense that the question of whether or not an emotional state can be communicated (particularly in an abstract work) or worse still, to what degree it can be simulated or staged, must have struck some serious-minded young artists as disturbing. That the spontaneous splashes and drips could be manufactured was demonstrated by Robert Rauschenberg in his identical action paintings, *Factum I* and *Factum II*. In fact, it was almost as if, toward the *Götterdämmerung* of the late fifties, the trumpets blared with such an apocalyptic and Wagnerian intensity that each moment was a crisis and each 'act' a climax. Obviously, such a crisis climate could hardly be sustained; just to be able to hear at all again, the volume had to be turned down, and the pitch, if not the instrument, changed.

Choreographer Merce Cunningham, whose work has been of the utmost importance to young choreographers, may have been the first to put this reaction into words (in an article in *trans/formation*, no. 1, 1952): 'Now I can't see that crisis any longer means a climax, unless we are willing to grant that every breath of wind has a climax (which I am), but then that obliterates climax, being a surfeit of such. And since our lives, both by nature and by the newspapers, are so full of crisis that one is no longer aware of it, then it is clear that life goes on regardless, and further that each thing can be and is separate from each and every other, *viz*: the continuity of the newspaper headlines. Climax is for those who are swept by New Year's Eve.' In a dance called *Crises*, Cunningham eliminated any fixed focus or climax in much the way the young artists I am discussing here have banished them from their works as well. Thus Cunningham's activity, too, must be considered as having helped to shape the new sensibility of the post-abstract expressionist generation. [...]

Mainly this shift toward a new sensibility came, as I've suggested, in the Fifties, a time of convulsive transition not only for the art world, but for society at large as well. In these years, for some reasons I've touched on, many young artists found action painting unconvincing. Instead they turned to the static emptiness of Barnett Newman's eloquent chromatic abstractions or to the sharp visual punning of Jasper Johns' object-like flags and targets.

Obviously, the new sensibility that preferred Newman and Johns to Willem de Kooning or his epigoni was going to produce art that was different, not only in form but in content as well, from the art that it spurned, because it rejected not only the premises, but the emotional content of abstract expressionism. I think we cannot treat the revolt of these young artists as we would that of artists of the age of the second generation, that is, artists now roughly forty. For the art of that generation, the assumption that form and content are identical, the fundamental assumption of formalist criticism, seems adequate to describe the work. But in the work of the younger people, one has the sense that form and content do not coincide, that, in fact, a bland, neutral-looking form is the vehicle for a hostile, aggressive content. Even in instances such as the work of Walter Darby Bannard or Larry Zox, where perhaps a purist reading might appear justifiable, there remains something that jars and sets the teeth just slightly on edge. Why, for example, are the pastel tints so unpleasant? Why is surface tension stretched to the breaking point? Why do we feel, in the end, vaguely deprived or frustrated? That such matters crop up, and that they are ultimately unanswerable, is part of the elusiveness and ambiguity that seem to be prime qualities of the new art. Of the sculptors one might ask similar questions: Why is it so big, so blunt, so graceless, so inert? And why are the films and dances and music so boring, so repetitious, so gratuitously long or short? In the art of these young people, form and content no longer mesh, with the result that the customer gets more or less than he bargained for.

The problem of the subversive content of these works is complicated, though it has to be approached, even if only to define why it is peculiar or corrosive.

Often, because they appear to belong to the category of ordinary objects rather than art objects, these works look altogether devoid of art content. This, as it has been pointed out in criticism of the so-called contentless novels of Alain Robbe-Grillet, is quite impossible for a work of art to achieve. The simple denial of content can itself constitute the content of such a work. That these young artists attempt to suppress or withdraw content from their works is undeniable. That they wish to make art that is as bland, neutral and as redundant as possible also seems clear. The content, then, if we are to take the work at face value, should be nothing more than the total of the series of assertions that it is this or that shape and takes up so much space and is painted such a colour and made of such a material. Statements from the artists involved are frequently couched in these equally factual, matter-of-fact descriptive terms; the work is described but not interpreted and statements with regard to content or meaning or intention are prominent only by their omission.

For the spectator, this is often all very bewildering. In the face of so much nothing, he is still experiencing something, and usually a rather unhappy something at that. I have often thought one had a sense of loss looking at these big, blank, empty things, so anxious to cloak their art identity that they were masquerading as objects. Perhaps, what one senses is that, as opposed to the florid baroque fullness of the angst-ridden older generation, the hollow, barrenness of the void has a certain poignant, if strangled, expressiveness. [...]

A rose is a rose is a rose:
Repetition as rhythmic structuring

… the kind of invention that is necessary to make a general scheme is limited in everybody's experience, every time one of the hundreds of times a newspaper man makes fun of my writing and of my repetition he always has the same theme, that is, if you like, repetition, that is if you like the repeating that is the same thing, but once started expressing this thing, expressing any thing there can be no repetition because the essence of that expression is insistence, and if you insist you must each time use emphasis and if you use emphasis it is not possible while anybody is alive that they should use exactly the same emphasis. (Gertrude Stein, 'Portaits and Repetition' in *Lectures in America*, 1935)

Form ceases to be an ordering in time like ABA and reduces to a single, brief image, an instantaneous whole both fixed and moving. Satie's form can be extended only by reiteration or 'endurance'. Satie frequently scrutinizes a very simple musical object; a short unchanging ostinato accompaniment plus a fragmentary melody. Out of this sameness comes subtle variety. (Roger Shattuck, *The Banquet Years*, 1955)

In painting the repetition of a single motif (such as Larry Poons's dots or Gene Davis's stripes) over a surface usually means an involvement with Jackson Pollock's all-over paintings. In sculpture, the repetition of standard units may derive partly from practical considerations. But in the case of Judd's, Morris's, Andre's and Flavin's pieces it seems to have more to do with setting up a measured, rhythmic beat in the work. Judd's latest sculptures, for example, are wall reliefs made of a transverse metal rod from which are suspended, at even intervals, identical bar or box units. For some artists – for example, the West Coast painter Billy Al Bengston who puts sergeants' stripes in all his paintings – a repeated motif may take on the character of a personal insignia. Morris's four identical mirrored boxes, which were so elusive that they appeared literally transparent, and his recent L-shape plywood pieces were demonstrations of both variability and interchangeability in the use of standard units. To find variety in repetition where only the nuance alters seems more and more to interest artists, perhaps in reaction to the increasing uniformity of the environment and repetitiveness of a circumscribed experience. Andy Warhol's Brillo boxes, silk-screen paintings of the same image repeated countless times and films in which people or things hardly move are illustrations of the kind of life situations many ordinary people will face or face already. In their insistence on repetition both Satie and Gertrude Stein have influenced the young dancers who perform at the Judson Memorial Church Dance Theater in New York. Yvonne Rainer, the most gifted choreographer of the group (which formed as a result of a course in dance composition taught by the composer, Robert Dunn, at Merce Cunningham's New York dance studio) has said that repetition was her first idea of form:

> I remember thinking that dance was at a disadvantage in relation to sculpture in that the spectator could spend as much time as he required to examine a sculpture, walk around it, and so forth – but a dance movement – because it happened in time – vanished as soon as it was executed. So in a solo called *The Bells* [performed at the Living Theatre in 1961] I repeated the same seven movements for eight minutes. It was not exact repetition, as the sequence of the movements kept changing. They also underwent changes through being repeated in different parts of the space and faced in different directions – in a sense allowing the spectator to 'walk around it'.

For these dancers, and for composers like La Monte Young (who conceives of time as an endless continuum in which the performance of his *Dream Music* is a single, continuous experience interrupted by intervals during which it is not being performed) durations of time much longer than those we are accustomed to are acceptable. Thus, for example, an ordinary movement like walking across a stage may be performed in slow motion, and concerts of the *Dream Music* have lasted several days, just as Andy Warhol's first film, *Sleep*, was an eight-hour-long movie of a man sleeping. Again, Satie is at least a partial source. It is not surprising that the only performance of his piano piece, *Vexations*, in which the same fragment is ritualistically repeated 840 times, took place over two years ago in New York. The performance lasted 18 hours, 40 minutes and required the participation in shifts of a dozen or so pianists, of whom John Cage was one. Shattuck's statement that 'Satie seems to combine experiment and inertia' seems applicable to a certain amount of avant garde activity of the moment.

Repetition as taedium vitae

What tedium. And I call that playing. (Samuel Beckett, *Malone Dies*)

This vast section of the world is inhabited by only one man: a negro. He is getting bored laughing himself to death. (Erik Satie, *Venomous Obstacles*)

In Zen they say: if something is boring after two minutes, try it for four. If still boring, try it for eight, sixteen, thirty-two, and so on. Eventually one discovers that it's not boring but very interesting. (John Cage, *Silence*)

The public venerates boredom. For boredom is mysterious and profound.
The Listener is defenceless against boredom. Boredom subdues him. (Erik Satie)

It seems probable that the human capacity for being bored, rather than man's social or natural needs, lies at the root of man's cultural advance. (Ralph Linton, *Study of Man*)

If, on seeing some of the new paintings, sculptures, dances or films, you are bored, probably you were intended to be. Boring the public is one way of testing its commitment. The new artists seem to be extremely chary; approval, they know, is easy to come by in this seller's market for culture, but commitment is nearly impossible to elicit. So they make their art as difficult, remote, aloof and indigestible as possible. One way to achieve this is to make art boring. Some artists, often the most gifted, finally end by finding art a bore. It is no coincidence that the last painting Duchamp made, in 1918, was called *Tu m'*. The title is short for *tu m'ennuie* – you bore me.

There is one theory which holds that wars start when people are bored. In our particular historical situation, without the threat of famine or plague, it is not surprising that boredom should be a common experience or that artists should find it a subject for study. [...]

That all this new art is so low-key, and so often concerned with little more than nuances of differentiation and executed in the *pianissimo* we associate with, for example, Morton Feldman's music, makes it rather out of step with the screeching, blaring, spangled carnival of American life. But, if pop art is the reflection of our environment, perhaps the art I have been describing is its antidote, even if it is a hard one to swallow. In its oversized, awkward, uncompromising, sometimes brutal directness, and in its refusal to participate, either as entertainment or as whimsical, ingratiating commodity (being simply too big or too graceless or too empty or too boring to appeal) this new art is surely hard to assimilate with ease. And it is almost as hard to talk about as it is to have around, because, of the art that is being made now, it is clearly the most ambivalent and the most elusive. For the moment one has made a statement, or more hopeless still, attempted a generality, the precise opposite then appears to be true, sometimes simultaneously with the original thought one had. As Roger Shattuck says of Satie's music, 'the simplest pieces, some of the humouristic works and children's pieces built out of a handful of notes and rhythms are the most enigmatic for this very reason: they have no beginning middle and end. They exist simultaneously.' So with the multiple levels of an art not so simple as it looks.

Barbara Rose, extracts from 'ABC Art', *Art in America*, vol. 53, no. 5 (October/November 1965) 61–2, 65–6, 69.

Susan Sontag
The Aesthetics of Silence//1967

IV

How literally does silence figure in art?

Silence exists as a *decision* – in the exemplary suicide of the artist (Kleist, Lautréamont), who thereby testifies that he has gone 'too far'; and in the already cited model renunciations by the artist of his vocation.

Silence also exists as a *punishment* – self-punishment, in the exemplary madness of artists (Hölderlin, Artaud) who demonstrate that sanity itself may be the price of trespassing the accepted frontiers of consciousness; and, of course, in penalties (ranging from censorship and physical destruction of artworks to fines, exile, prison for the artist) meted out by 'society' for the artist's spiritual nonconformity or subversion of the group sensibility.

Silence doesn't exist in a literal sense, however, as the *experience* of an audience. It would mean that the spectator was aware of no stimulus or that he was unable to make a response. But this can't happen; nor can it even be induced programmatically. The non-awareness of any stimulus, the inability to make a response, can result only from a defective presence on the part of the spectator, or a misunderstanding of his own reactions (misled by restrictive ideas about what would be a 'relevant' response). As long as audiences, by definition, consist of sentient beings in a 'situation', it is impossible for them to have no response at all.

Nor can silence, in its literal state, exist as the *property* of an artwork – even of works like Duchamp's readymades or Cage's *4'33"*, in which the artist has ostentatiously done no more to satisfy any established criteria of art than set the object in a gallery or situate the performance on a concert stage. There is no neutral surface, no neutral discourse, no neutral theme, no neutral form. Something is neutral only with respect to something else – like an intention or an expectation. As a property of the work of art itself, silence can exist only in a cooked or nonliteral sense. (Put otherwise: if a work exists at all, its silence is only one element in it.) Instead of raw or achieved silence, one finds various moves in the direction of an ever receding horizon of silence – moves which, by definition, can never be fully consummated. One result is a type of art that many people characterize pejoratively as dumb, depressed, acquiescent, cold. But these privative qualities exist in a context of the artist's objective intention, which is always discernible. Cultivating the metaphoric silence suggested by conventionally lifeless subjects (as in much of Pop art) and constructing 'minimal' forms that seem to lack emotional resonance are in themselves vigorous, often tonic choices.

And, finally, even without imputing objective intentions to the artwork, there remains the inescapable truth about perception: the positivity of all experience at every moment of it. As Cage has insisted, 'There is no such thing as silence. Something is always happening that makes a sound.' (Cage has described how, even in a soundless chamber, he still heard two things: his heartbeat and the coursing of the blood in his head.) Similarly, there is no such thing as empty space. As long as a human eye is looking, there is always something to see. To look at something which is 'empty' is still to be looking, still to be seeing something – if only the ghosts of one's own expectations. In order to perceive fullness, one must retain an acute sense of the emptiness which marks it off; conversely, in order to perceive emptiness, one must apprehend other zones of the world as full. (In *Through the Looking Glass*, Alice comes upon a shop 'that seemed to be full of all manner of curious things – but the oddest part of it all was that whenever she looked hard at any shelf, to make out exactly what it had on it, that particular shelf was always quite empty, though the others round it were crowded full as they could hold.')

'Silence' never ceases to imply its opposite and to depend on its presence: just as there can't be 'up' without 'down' or 'left' without 'right', so one must acknowledge a surrounding environment of sound or language in order to recognize silence. Not only does silence exist in a world full of speech and other sounds, but any given silence has its identity as a stretch of time being perforated by sound. (Thus, much of the beauty of Harpo Marx's muteness derives from his being surrounded by manic talkers.)

A genuine emptiness, a pure silence are not feasible – either conceptually or in fact. If only because the artwork exists in a world furnished with many other things, the artist who creates silence or emptiness must produce something dialectical: a full void, an enriching emptiness, a resonating or eloquent silence. Silence remains, inescapably, a form of speech (in many instances, of complaint or indictment) and an element in a dialogue. […]

X

Silence is a metaphor for a cleansed, non-interfering vision, appropriate to artworks that are unresponsive before being seen, unviolable in their essential integrity by human scrutiny. The spectator would approach art as he does a landscape. A landscape doesn't demand from the spectator his 'understanding', his imputations of significance, his anxieties and sympathies; it demands, rather, his absence, it asks that he not add anything to *it*. Contemplation, strictly speaking, entails self-forgetfulness on the part of the spectator: an object worthy of contemplation is one which, in effect, annihilates the perceiving subject.

Toward such an ideal plenitude to which the audience can add nothing, analogous to the aesthetic relation to nature, a great deal of contemporary art aspires – through various strategies of blandness, of reduction, of de-individuation, of alogicality. In principle, the audience may not even add its thought. All objects, rightly perceived, are already full. This is what Cage must mean when, after explaining that there is no such thing as silence because something is always happening that makes a sound, he adds, 'No one can have an idea once he starts really listening.'

Plenitude – experiencing all the space as filled, so that ideas cannot enter – means impenetrability. A person who becomes silent becomes opaque for the other; somebody's silence opens up an array of possibilities for interpreting that silence, for imputing speech to it.

The way in which this opaqueness induces spiritual vertigo is the theme of Bergman's *Persona*. The actress's deliberate silence has two aspects: considered as a decision apparently relating to herself, the refusal to speak is apparently the form she has given to the wish for ethical purity; but it is also, as behaviour, a means of power, a species of sadism, a virtually inviolable position of strength from which she manipulates and confounds her nurse-companion, who is charged with the burden of talking.

But the opaqueness of silence can be conceived more positively, as free from anxiety. For Keats, the silence of the Grecian urn is a locus of spiritual nourishment: 'unheard' melodies endure, whereas those that pipe to 'the sensual ear' decay. Silence is equated with arresting time ('slow time'). One can stare endlessly at the Grecian urn. Eternity, in the argument of Keats' poem, is the only interesting stimulus to thought and also the sole occasion for coming to the end of mental activity, which means interminable, unanswered questions ('Thou, silent form, dost tease us out of thought / As doth eternity'), in order to arrive at a final equation of ideas ('Beauty is truth, truth beauty') which is both absolutely vacuous and completely full. Keats' poem quite logically ends in a statement that will seem, if the reader hasn't followed his argument, like empty wisdom, a banality. As time, or history, is the medium of definite, determinate thought, the silence of eternity prepares for a thought beyond thought, which must appear from the perspective of traditional thinking and the familiar uses of the mind as no thought at all – though it may rather be the emblem of new, 'difficult' thinking. [...]

XIII

[...] [I]n an overpopulated world being connected by global electronic communication and jet travel at a pace too rapid and violent for an organically sound person to assimilate without shock, people are also suffering from a revulsion at any further proliferation of speech and images. Such different factors as the unlimited 'technological reproduction' and near universal diffusion of printed language and speech as well as images (from 'news' to 'art objects'), and the degeneration of public language within the realms of politics and advertising and entertainment, have produced, especially among the better-educated inhabitants of modern mass society, a devaluation of language. (I should argue, contrary to McLuhan, that a devaluation of the power and credibility of images has taken place no less profound than, and essentially similar to, that afflicting language.) And, as the prestige of language falls, that of silence rises. [...]

Explicitly in revolt against what is deemed the desiccated, categorized life of the ordinary mind, the artist issues his own call for a revision of language. A good deal of contemporary art is moved by this quest for a consciousness purified of contaminated language and, in some versions, of the distortions produced by conceiving the world exclusively in conventional verbal (in their debased sense, 'rational' or 'logical') terms. Art itself becomes a kind of counterviolence, seeking to loosen the grip upon consciousness of the habits of lifeless, static verbalization, presenting models of 'sensual speech'.

If anything, the volume of discontent has been turned up since the arts inherited the problem of language from religious discourse. It's not just that words, ultimately, are inadequate to the highest aims of consciousness; or even that they get in the way. Art expresses a double discontent. We lack words, and we have too many of them. It raises two complaints about language. Words are too crude. And words are also too busy – inviting a hyperactivity of consciousness that is not only dysfunctional, in terms of human capacities of feeling and acting, but actively deadens the mind and blunts the senses.

Language is demoted to the status of an event. Something takes place in time, a voice speaking which points to the before and to what comes after an utterance: silence. Silence, then, is both the precondition of speech and the result or aim of properly directed speech. On this model, the artist's activity is the creating or establishing of silence; the efficacious artwork leaves silence in its wake. Silence, administered by the artist, is part of a program of perceptual and cultural therapy, often on the model of shock therapy rather than of persuasion. Even if the artist's medium is words, he can share in this task: language can be employed to check language, to express muteness. Mallarmé thought it was the job of poetry, using words, to clean up our word-clogged reality – by creating silences around things. Art must mount a full-scale attack on language itself, by means of language and its surrogates, on behalf of the standard of silence. […]

XV

In his Fourth Duino Elegy, Rilke gives a metaphoric statement of the problem of language and recommends a procedure for approaching as near the horizon of silence as he considers feasible. A prerequisite of 'emptying out' is to be able to perceive what one is 'full of', what words and mechanical gestures one is stuffed with, like a doll; only then, in polar confrontation with the doll, does the 'angel' appear, a figure representing an equally inhuman though 'higher' possibility, that of an entirely unmediated, translinguistic apprehension. Neither doll nor angel, human beings remain situated within the kingdom of language. But for nature, then things, then other people, then the textures of ordinary life to be experienced from a stance other than the crippled one of mere spectatorship, language must regain its chastity. As Rilke describes it in the Ninth Elegy, the redemption of language (which is to say, the redemption of the world through its interiorization in consciousness) is a long, infinitely arduous task. Human beings are so 'fallen' that they must start with the simplest linguistic act: the naming of things. Perhaps no more than this minimal function can be preserved from the general corruption of discourse. Language may very well have to remain within a permanent state of reduction. Though perhaps, when this spiritual exercise of confining language to naming is perfected, it may be possible to pass on to other, more ambitious uses of language, nothing must be attempted which will allow consciousness to become re-estranged from itself.

For Rilke the overcoming of the alienation of consciousness is conceivable; and not, as in the radical myths of the mystics, through transcending language altogether. It suffices to cut back drastically the scope and use of language. A tremendous spiritual preparation (the contrary of 'alienation') is required for this deceptively simple act of naming. It is nothing less than the scouring and harmonious sharpening of the senses (the very opposite of such violent projects, with roughly the same end and informed by the same hostility to verbal-rational culture, as 'systematically deranging the senses').

Rilke's remedy lies halfway between exploiting the numbness of language as a gross, fully installed cultural institution and yielding to the suicidal vertigo of pure silence. But this middle ground of reducing language to naming can be claimed in quite another way than his. Contrast the benign nominalism proposed by Rilke (and proposed and practised by Francis Ponge) with the brutal nominalism adopted by many other artists. The more familiar recourse of modern art to the aesthetics of the inventory is not made – as in Rilke – with an eye to 'humanizing' things, but rather to confirming their inhumanity, their impersonality, their indifference to and separateness from human concerns. (Examples of the 'inhumane' preoccupation with naming: Roussel's *Impressions of Africa*; the silk-screen paintings and early films of Andy Warhol; the early novels of Robbe-Grillet, which attempt to confine the function of language to bare physical description and location.)

Rilke and Ponge assume that there are priorities: rich as opposed to vacuous objects, events with a certain allure. (This is the incentive for trying to peel back language, allowing the 'things' themselves to speak.) More decisively, they assume that if there are states of false (language-clogged) consciousness, there are also authentic states of consciousness – which it's the function of art to promote. The alternative view denies the traditional hierarchies of interest and meaning, in which some things have more 'significance' than others. The distinction between true and false experience, true and false consciousness is also denied: in principle, one should desire to pay attention to everything. It's this view, most elegantly formulated by Cage though its practice is found everywhere, that leads to the art of the inventory, the catalogue, surfaces; also 'chance'. The function of art isn't to sanction any specific experience, except the state of being open to the multiplicity of experience – which ends in practice by a decided stress on things usually considered trivial or unimportant.

The attachment of contemporary art to the 'minimal' narrative principle of the catalogue or inventory seems almost to parody the capitalist world-view, in which the environment is atomized into 'items' (a category embracing things and persons, works of art and natural organisms), and in which every item is a commodity – that is, a discrete, portable object. A general levelling of value is encouraged in the art of inventory, which is itself only one of the possible approaches to an ideally uninflected discourse. Traditionally, the effects of an artwork have been unevenly distributed, to induce in the audience a certain sequence of experience: first arousing, then manipulating, and eventually fulfilling emotional expectations. What is proposed now is a discourse without emphases in this traditional sense. (Again, the principle of the stare as opposed to the look.)

Such art could also be described as establishing great 'distance' (between spectator and art object, between the spectator and his emotions). But, psychologically, distance often is linked with the most intense state of feeling, in which the coolness or impersonality with which something is treated measures the insatiable interest that thing has for us. The distance that a great deal of 'anti-humanist' art proposes is actually equivalent to obsession – an aspect of the involvement in 'things' of which the 'humanist' nominalism of Rilke has no intimation. [...]

XX

Contemporary artists advocate silence in two styles: loud and soft.

The loud style is a function of the unstable antithesis of 'plenum' and 'void'. The sensuous, ecstatic, translinguistic apprehension of the plenum is notoriously fragile: in a terrible, almost instantaneous plunge it can collapse into the void of negative silence. With all its awareness of risk-taking (the hazards of spiritual nausea, even of madness), this advocacy of silence tends to be frenetic and overgeneralizing. It is also frequently apocalyptic and must endure the indignity of all apocalyptic thinking: namely, to prophesy the end, to see the day come, to outlive it, and then to set a new date for the incineration of consciousness and the definitive pollution of language and exhaustion of the possibilities of art-discourse.

The other way of talking about silence is more cautious. Basically, it presents itself as an extension of a main feature of traditional classicism: the concern with modes of propriety, with standards of seemliness. Silence is only 'reticence' stepped up to the nth degree. Of course, in the translation of this concern from the matrix of traditional classical art, the tone has changed – from didactic seriousness to ironic openmindedness. But while the clamorous style of proclaiming the rhetoric of silence may seem more passionate, its more subdued advocates (like Cage, Johns) are saying something equally drastic. They are reacting to the same idea of art's absolute aspirations (by programmatic disavowals of art); they share the same disdain for the 'meanings' established by bourgeois-rationalist culture, indeed for culture itself in the familiar sense. What is voiced by the Futurists, some of the Dada artists and William Burroughs as a harsh despair and perverse vision of apocalypse is no less serious for being proclaimed in a polite voice and as a sequence of playful affirmations. Indeed, it could be argued that silence is likely to remain a viable notion for modern art and consciousness only if deployed with a considerable, near systematic irony. […]

Susan Sontag, extracts from 'The Aesthetics of Silence', *Aspen*, no. 5 + 6, item 3, unpaginated; reprinted in *Styles of Radical Will* (New York: Farrar, Straus & Giroux, 1969) 9–11, 16–17, 21–6, 32–3.

Nicolas Bourriaud
The Legacy of Indifference//1987

It is indeed in the early 1960s, which are marked by the joint arrival of Minimalism and Pop art, that mechanization acquires the unchecked strength of an ideology in the contemporary imagination. Yet it was with the Marquis de Sade that, for the first time, the human body was subjected to a set of operations close to that of the assembly line. In his work, the body was no longer anything but an assemblage of parts manipulable at will. And there is a bit of the panicked terror that the 'Divine Marquis' inspires in us in our fascination with the 'systemic' that is developed in these years. Andy Warhol and his repetitive imagery, the declarations of Sol LeWitt ('the idea becomes the machine that makes the art'), the glacial appearance of a Lichtenstein or a Rosenquist – all point to a 'becoming-machine' that responds to the 'becoming-animal' of a Goya. In *Saturn*, André Malraux wrote: 'Behind Goya, for the first time, there is no human system.' With Warhol or LeWitt, we find a set of systems that only concern the human because it is excluded from them, and that drive us to feel, faced with a can of soup or a geometric figure, the same irrational fear that the ancients felt before their idols. Both are beyond our control, and reflect an order without origin or known destination.

If Pop art and Minimalism are linked, apart from the fact they were both born of a rejection of Abstract Expressionism, it's that they pit a world of phenomena against the world of manifested being. Enthusiasts of simple, regular forms (points, chevrons, circles) and smooth surfaces, having recourse to industrial lacquers and mechanical means of reproduction, they both refuse touch and obvious gesture; they refuse any internal disorder to highlight the preponderance of orders that are external to us. There is always expression, even if it is a predetermined conceptual order, and no longer action, that underlies being. […]

Robert Rauschenberg, when in 1957 he exhibited *Factum I* and *Factum II*, showed two absolutely indistinguishable splashes of paint: he thus defined Abstract Expressionism as a rhetoric, likening automatism to an industrial product, the mask of a grimace. Eleven years later, Sigmar Polke proceeds identically in *Moderne Kunst*, saying aloud that seismic recordings of sincerity-in-action have no value whatsoever.

Rauschenberg erasing de Kooning, parodying Action Painting; […] and today the facsimiles of Sherrie Levine or John Armleder's installations – all come under an aesthetic of *disenchantment* that has its roots (or its forerunners) in two great ancestors. First of all Duchamp, the first to advocate the use of mechanical techniques, to exercise a 'precision painting' and to practice 'the beauty of indifference'. He was mentor of a whole generation of artists in the United States, first through the intermediary of John Cage, then directly. Duchamp's cynicism was, however, only apparent, and his phlegm, nourished by Zen, camouflaged the fantastic demonstration that he addressed to his time. His resounding success: the bewildered mimicry of his zealots, who failed to perceive that they were following an absent leader; and that of critics who fell into the traps of meaning set by the *Large Glass*. Duchamp's disenchantment was merely a new way to enter the game, to invert the roles of all the chess pieces, just to see what would happen. Cage, Johns and Rauschenberg submitted to their fascination with this scepticism, without realizing that it was stoked to a white heat. Unlike many others, they however understood that the aim of the 'readymades' was not the equivalence of all values and the abolition of all rules, but the exaltation of individual choice made by a sovereign ego. We are thus closer to Nietzschean ethics than to a nihilistic anything goes. […]

The second source of disenchantment is Manet – the Manet who was proclaimed the founding father of modern art (not counting the Spanish?), to whom we owe, in the words of Bataille, 'the birth of this kind of painting devoid of any signification other than the art of painting itself'. He adds, regarding *Olympia*: 'the meaning of the picture is not in the text behind it but in the obliteration of that text … Her real nudity (not merely that of her body) is the silence that emanates from her, like that from a sunken ship.' […]

Nicolas Bourriaud, extracts from 'L'Héritage de l'indifférence', *Artstudio*, no. 6 ('Art minimal') (Autumn 1987) 30–31, 33. Translation by Tom McDonough, 2016.

Jonathan Flatley
Allegories of Boredom//2004

A work needs only to be interesting.
– Donald Judd[1]

[Pop art] is liking things.
– Andy Warhol[2]

Allegory consists in the withdrawal of [the] self-sufficiency of meaning from a given representation.
– Fredric Jameson[3]

Despite their significant differences, Andy Warhol and Donald Judd held similar ideas about the kind of aesthetic experience they hoped to create with their work. They each sought to solicit from their audience and produce for themselves an apparently mundane form of emotional attachment, which Judd called 'interest' and Warhol 'liking'. In doing so, they happily ignored loftier (and more widely recognized and respected) artistic goals such as the creation of transcendent beauty or sublimity; the representation of truth or reality; or the expression of one's genius, complex inner feelings or unique interpretation of the world. Moreover, they each seemed to feel that the only art that could create an emotionally resonant aesthetic experience was one that was maximally emptied of subjective or expressive intent. As Alex Potts wrote (speaking of Judd, but just as accurately describing Warhol's work), 'a situation has been reached where it is felt that any intensified bodily or libidinal charge will be blocked if these qualities are seen to be objectified in the work.'[4] In other words, for Judd and Warhol the only affecting art was one that appeared to be utterly affectless.

When Warhol and Judd first started showing their art in galleries in the early 1960s, the 'purging of authorial feeling and demonstrable intention', as James Meyer put it, 'was poorly received by viewers steeped in the aesthetics of abstract expressionism, who insisted that a work of art was by definition the handmade product of a subjective self.'[5] The distinctions that would later seem so significant and obvious – Judd's emphasis on non-referentiality and construction versus Warhol's mimetic appropriation, Judd's apparent distance from consumer culture and Warhol's proximity to it, Judd's butch intellectuality and Warhol's fey naïveté – were less visible than what Judd and Warhol shared: the turn toward a cool, non-composed, affectless art to which 'meaning' is difficult to attribute. I am interested in focusing on this moment of commonality between Judd and Warhol in order to consider the nature of the historical situation to which they were both responding. My aim is to examine what is at stake in their differences by determining the logics and limits of the field of contestation that they shared.

In my effort to understand what the artworks of Warhol and Judd are saying about the world in which these artists lived, my central question will be: what is the emotional context, the historical mood, in which the aesthetic experience offered to viewers in the work of Warhol and Judd is attractive? My presumption here is that the affective nature of aesthetic experience is always at least partly compensatory. In other words, the experience of art has an emotional force because it offers us something in the space of 'art' that we do not get elsewhere. Art, in this view, always contains a utopian element. In giving us something that is otherwise missing, each aesthetic experience provides a picture of the world from which it has sprung. However, it does so in reverse, like a photographic negative. Within this view of what is missing from the world lies an implicit theory of it – a theory of the aggregate of shifting, competing and contradictory forces that shape everyday life. The task of the critic, then, is to reconstruct this aggregate and determine its logic – which we might also call 'history' – in order to make sense of the attractions of the specific experience that the artwork offers. This reconstruction must start from the aesthetic experience that the art promotes because it is precisely here, on the level of affect, I will contend, that we can most clearly see the residue of historicity. Subjective affect is the shuttle on which history gets into art and how it comes back. I should add that history, in the sense that I am using it here, is not 'there' in any immediately observable way. Rather, history is only conceivable as an absent cause, the problem or contradiction to which an aesthetic practice tries to offer a solution.

In proposing a different idea about what art is and does, Judd's 'interesting' and Warhol's 'liking' each also suggests a new understanding of the problem to which art is responding. By seeking to produce emotion without representing it, they neatly reversed the model that had held for Abstract Expressionism and, more broadly, for modernism. There, the paintings were understood to be representing an emotional truth that had been repressed by the 'manufactured bonhomie of the white-collar workplace and the willed optimism of the culture promoted by advertising',[6] but the critical voice that championed them was one that engaged with the paintings through a Kantian 'disinterest'. In other words, art should represent emotion but not solicit it. Indeed, it was this space of disinterestedness that gave the beholder the necessary distance to have insights about the emotions that were otherwise too immediate in their domination of everyday life. In this understanding, the disinterested moment of aesthetic experience and judgement is attractive precisely in as much as it is 'shadowed by the wildest interest'. In fact, we might say 'the dignity of artworks', as Theodor Adorno argued, 'depends on the intensity of the interest from which they are wrested.'[7]

What then to do with an art that reverses this model and seeks the beholder's interest while representing no emotion? If (as Adorno suggests) art always contains an element of what it repulses, then we might hypothesize that Juddian interest and Warholian liking are attractive precisely in as much as the world from which they spring is characterized by an anaesthetizing boredom. Like Charles Baudelaire – who faced an audience seized by ennui, that 'monstre délicat', who would 'willingly make rubble of the earth and swallow up creation in a yawn'[8] – so, too, Judd and Warhol seem to be responding to a world in which it is difficult to be interested in anything at all, in which, as Warhol said, 'it would be so much easier not to care … it's too hard to care'.[9] Judd and Warhol replace the dialectic between interest and disinterest with one between interest and boredom.

There was a lot of anxiety about boredom in the 1950s and early 60s. In books such as C. Wright Mills's *White Collar: The American Middle Classes* (1951), David Riesman's *The Lonely Crowd: A Study of Changing American Character* (1950) and William H. Whyte's *The Organization Man* (1956), the increasing power of large impersonal institutions – such as corporations, government bureaucracies, universities, the military establishment and mass media – in structuring work and leisure alike was adduced as a source of a disabling sense of dissociation, especially among the new, white, middle classes. White-collar workers certainly had it no worse than their wives, Betty Friedan argued in *The Feminine Mystique* (1963), since the 'endless, monotonous, unrewarding' nature of a housewife's work, combined with her social isolation and lack of avenues for individual expression, turns her into 'an anonymous biological robot in a docile mass'.[10]

Men and women both shared the experience of a mass culture that treated them as passive recipients of 'mechanically vivified experiences', giving them their parts to play in the 'scheme for pre-scheduled, mass emotions'.[11] In promising to distract us from our boredom (enforcing the idea that boredom is something horrible and to be avoided) while never surprising us, entertainment perpetuates the boredom that is supposedly being relieved. Moreover, in supporting the simple idea that one need escape 'work' or 'life', 'leisure' activities also naturalize the bindingness and inescapability of the nature of work and the economic system on which it depends. The society in which we live becomes that-from-which-we-must-be-distracted. In comparison to entertainment, politics becomes 'dull and threadbare'. Thus, despite a widespread sense of alienation, Mills writes, 'there were no plain targets of revolt; and the cold metropolitan manner had so entered the soul of overpowered men that they were made completely private and blasé, down deep and for good.'[12]

In his social history of melancholy, Wolf Lepenies argues that boredom typically appears as a collective phenomenon in classes that for one reason or another feel a lack of political agency, which means that boredom contains within it a readiness and desire for social transformation.[13] Thus Baudelaire could write of converting a disillusioned ennui into 'spleen', an active interest in and anger about the losses one suffered and a sense of urgency about the need to address them right now. The success of the civil rights movement in interesting and mobilizing large numbers of people, black and white, and the subsequent explosion in the 1960s of social movements and countercultures testifies to the desire and readiness for transformation that lay nascent within the boredom that writers like Friedan and Mills decried.

In creating affectless works, Warhol and Judd were also presuming that there were affects in their audiences just waiting to find a space in which they could appear. If, as Siegfried Kracauer wrote, the problem is that 'even if one perhaps isn't interested in it, the world itself is much too interested for one to find the peace and quiet necessary to be as thoroughly bored with the world as it ultimately deserves',[14] then Judd's and Warhol's task was to create work that did not promise to distract, nor claim to represent repressed feelings (like Abstract Expressionism), but instead create a space in which one's affective experience of everyday life could come into being. By mimicking the lack of affect that one might feel toward the everyday world of things and images (as against the overcharged emotionality that characterizes the mode of address of that world), Judd's and Warhol's works allow boredom, which is the basic structure of feeling of late capital, to come into existence as such. And then something interesting happens: a different boredom emerges, one that is 'an apogee of mental relaxation' rather than withdrawal. This is the boredom that Walter Benjamin called 'the dream bird that hatches the egg of experience'.[15] In Benjamin's view, boredom characterizes an emotional openness that is the condition of possibility for being affected and transformed, for being interested and surprised by one's desires, attractions and imaginations. […]

Unearthly

If … one has … the sort of patience specific to legitimate boredom, then one experiences a kind of bliss that is almost unearthly. A landscape appears in which colourful peacocks strut about, and images of people suffused with soul come into view. And look – your own soul is likewise swelling, and in ecstasy you name what you have always lacked: the great passion. Were this passion – which shimmers like a comet – to descend, were it to envelop you, the others and the world – oh, then boredom would come to an end, and everything that exists would be …
– Siegfried Kracauer[16]

I have been arguing for affectlessness as an aesthetic strategy that facilitates emotional involvement in as much as it de-identifies the object of perception in a way that makes these objects available for transferences of affect from various quarters of everyday life. The relaxed, bored state that Judd's and Warhol's work may be seen to create is thus a kind of transitional state, the mood in which affects can emerge from viewers who may otherwise keep them throttled inside. The promise of the work of both, as in the Kracauer quote, is that a patient experience of boredom will allow unexpected and unpredictable passions to emerge.

I have also been suggesting that the strategy of affectlessness only makes sense in a specific historical context, one in which people are experiencing difficulty being emotionally involved in the world around them because they have withdrawn from a world that makes too many aggressive emotional demands on them. It was difficult to care in part because there was too much to care about: the ever-increasing violence of warfare, which by the 1950s had reached the point where the annihilation of the human race itself had become a possibility; the automatic, repetitive and sensorially demanding quality of work and consumption alike; the scale and size of city space and the masses of people encountered there; and the number of other lives and deaths and sufferings that one comes into contact with via the 'news'. In such environments the finer antennae of our mimetic faculties are dulled; we lose our ability to notice similarities and enact them. In as much as affects appear according to a mimetic logic, this loss, this blunting of our ability to perceive similarities, means that our own emotional lives become obscure to us; our agency in relation to them decreases.

Both Judd and Warhol seek to give us more agency in relation to our emotional lives by making our affects available to us in the carefully framed environment of their work, an environment that resembles our everyday life enough to allow our affects to be transferred from there, but which is 'unearthly' enough to defamiliarize them at the same time. Judd's specific objects allow us to consider how our shared reification causes us to resemble each other; Warhol's serial silkscreens remind us of the melancholic imitations in which we all regularly engage. Thus Judd and Warhol share an opposition to universal fungibility and the illusion of the 'genuine' that it produces as a distracting side effect.

In conclusion, it is worth emphasizing that Judd's and Warhol's insistence on similarity and non-identity as keys to emotional involvement are not promotions of homogeneity. The perception of likeness is a mode of metaphorical thinking (the right use of which, as Aristotle noted, requires 'an eye for resemblances') and, like metaphor, the strategies that Judd and Warhol employ do not erase the differences between things that resemble each other, but instead reassert their specificity. In part, this is because things that resemble each other require no intervening abstraction to be in relation – they cannot be made to *equal* each other. That both Judd and Warhol knew they were likely themselves to be subject to the application of universal standards of value – whether it is provided by the art market or by critics – only made the assertion of resemblance more attractive. Thus it is in an effort to promote a metaphorical 'transaction of contexts' that I here juxtapose Judd and Warhol in my own attempt to mimic and perpetuate the production of similarities that I have argued are central to their aesthetic projects.

1   Donald Judd, 'Specific Objects' (1965), in Judd, *Complete Writings 1959–1975* (Halifax, Nova Scotia: The Press of the Nova Scotia College of Art and Design, 1975) 184.
2   Andy Warhol, 'What is Pop Art?', interview by G.R. Swenson, *ARTnews*, vol. 62, no. 7 (November 1963) 26.
3   Fredric Jameson, *Brecht and Method* (London and New York: Verso, 1998) 122.
4   Alex Potts, *The Sculptural Imagination: Figurative, Modernist, Minimalist* (New Haven and London: Yale University Press, 2000) 305
5   James Meyer, *Minimalism: Art and Polemics in the Sixties* (New Haven and London: Yale University Press, 2001) 3. […]
6   [footnote 8 in source] Jackson Lears, *Fables of Abundance: A Cultural History of Advertising in America* (New York: Basic Books, 1994) 363.
7   [9] Theodor W. Adorno, *Aesthetic Theory* (1970); trans. Robert Hullot-Kentor (Minneapolis: University of Minnesota Press, 1997) 11.
8   [10] Charles Baudelaire, 'To the Reader', in *The Flowers of Evil* (1857); trans. Stanley Kunitz (New York: New Directions, 1989) 2.
9   [11] Warhol, in 'Nothing to Lose: An Interview with Andy Warhol' by Gretchen Berg, *Cahiers du Cinéma*, no. 10 (1967); reprinted in *Andy Warhol: Film Factory*, ed. Michael O'Pray (London: British Film Institute, 1989) 61.
10 [13] Betty Friedan, *The Feminine Mystique* (New York: Dell Publishing, 1963) 307–8.
11 [14] C. Wright Mills, *White Collar: The American Middle Classes* (New York: Oxford University Press, 1956) 329, 333.
12 [16] Ibid., 329.
13 [17] Wolf Lepenies, *Melancholy and Society*, trans. Jeremy Gaines and Doris Jones (Cambridge, Massachusetts: Harvard University Press, 1992); see esp. 50–60 passim.
14 [18] Siegfried Kracauer, 'Boredom', in *The Mass Ornament: Weimar Essays*, trans. Thomas Y. Levin (Cambridge, Massachusetts: Harvard University Press, 1995) 332.
15 [19] Walter Benjamin, 'The Storyteller' (1936), in *Illuminations*, trans. Harry Zohn (New York: Schocken Books, 1969) 91.
16 [117] Kracauer, 'Boredom', op. cit., 334.

Jonathan Flatley, extracts from 'Allegories of Boredom', in *A Minimal Future?: Art as Object, 1958–1968*, ed. Jane Hyun (Los Angeles: The Museum of Contemporary Art/Cambridge, Massachusetts: The MIT Press, 2004) 51–3, 74–5.

John Miller
No More Boring Art//2001

[...] Once, when I talked about John Baldessari's Super 8 films with Gregor Stemmrich's class at the Hochschule der Künste in Berlin, several students were quick to point out that I never mentioned how funny these films are. They were right to bring this up; humour is important in Baldessari's work. It has a particular quality. It is more a reality check than entertainment. (Reality, of course, necessarily includes artifice.) Its scepticism makes it an oddly sober humour. Even so, it is mildly subversive as well. It sets such low – 'reasonably low' – hurdles for itself, that winning the race becomes insidiously somehow beside the point. In one video, when the artist half-heartedly promises to make 'no more boring art', is the problem making art or being boring? Rather than defy the rule, Baldessari pretends to be contrite. He writes the command over and over and, by atoning, transgresses the standing demand to transgress. He keeps writing that next time he'll do better. But we can never trust him; each new promise breaks the rule once more.

From artist to art-making as a hobby
Although it's invisible (yet the product of a point of view), humour is as much a representation to be reckoned with as any of the formal elements in these Super 8s. With deceptive modesty, it dismisses, out of hand, an Abstract Expressionist legacy of bar brawls, angst and heroic posturing. Instead it admits that, from now on, American artists will be college-educated, middle-class professionals, middle class in an era of unprecedented affluence, middle class in a nation that boasts of being the most powerful in history. The new prosperity means freedom from doubt and privation. Thus, the bohemian loses his last vestiges of credibility and Artaud's artist 'suicided by society' comes to seem laughable. Middle-class status is 'laughable' too – because it's blasé and self-reflexive. But that's not exactly the stuff of whimsy. In the case of these films, the humorous excess (not 'structurally' necessary) is an index of social legitimation and prestige – like Thorstein Veblen's conspicuous consumption. Even under pressure, however, the ethos of artistic marginalization dies hard. For example, after Allan Kaprow proclaimed the artist to be 'a man of the world', he still dreamed of 'merging' art and life. For Baldessari, that was missing the point. Art was already part of life. To see that, he didn't have to look any farther than the colleges and art schools where he worked on a regular basis. School was, after all, the overarching metaphor in *I Will Not Make Any More Boring Art* (1971); the artist simply mocked his inscription into its regime.

For artists of Baldessari's generation, professionalism was wedded to education, but divorced from technical training. After Duchamp's edict that tools that require skill are no good, this suggests a shift in class orientation toward the more managerial style of conceptual art. If technique was a stigma, wit was a virtue. Popularly, however, artistry still meant technique – which, in turn, meant realism. Better art meant better technique. In contrast, the Abstract Expressionists decided not only that art couldn't be taught, but also that their kind of painting could not be reduced to skill, let alone technique. Even so, the existential confrontation between painter and canvas remained paramount. Ironically, because it mediated between skill and 'unknowable' artistry, Abstract Expressionism emerged as the penultimate style in American art schools and remained so for decades. Against this, the suppression of technique and mystique informs Baldessari's decision to work in Super 8. The format was flagrantly amateur, the medium of birthday parties and family vacations. In place of the existentialist came the hobbyist.

While technical prowess might now compromise one's artistic standing, the new protocols of professionalism became 1) a calculated indifference to the old ones, 2) a turn to less melodramatic subject matter and 3) a more detached, ironic treatment of that subject matter. Together, these represented a paradigm shift – for which Andy Warhol had been the catalyst. For Baldessari, the new sensibility meant a more nuanced, yet more matter-of-fact, look into the minutiae of everyday life. Camera in hand, he set out to capture less, not more: postcards, flip books, a Christmas card, buttons, a thermometer or an egg timer. It was a small world, after all. And the growing affordability of air travel made it seem even smaller. It exposed Middle America to the stultifying paradox of tourism, in which the tourist unwittingly transported his ideological props wherever he went. In an expansive spirit, the California Institute of the Arts, where Baldessari taught for so many years, launched its 'post-studio' art programme. Instead of withering away, however, leaving its occupant to consort with the world at large, Baldessari's studio shrank to the size of a desktop.

The Super 8 films
In his Super 8s, Baldessari seeks out small, flat surfaces and vestigial signs of mark making. Often, an anonymous hand manipulates the objects that fall on screen. Thus, Baldessari's lens brings some of the old concerns of Action Painting into fresh focus. The films, in their own way, are educational – which is to say slightly didactic, like filmstrips. The points they make are simple, so these films are concise, typically less than three minutes. In *New York City Art History* (1971) the camera takes close-ups of coloured cards and art history illustrations paraded through the streets of Soho. Views of pedestrians and traffic flood in between cards and around their edges. This juxtaposition seemingly reflects the art-historical process itself. Artworks as icons lose their ability to alter the way viewers see – that instead is the

capacity of less codified art. In *New York Green Postcard #2* (1971) and *City Postcard Painting* an incessant brush blots out the picturesque views featured in a series of postcards. Here, New York School painting would seem to be the discursive subject. The panoramic views suggest a monumental scale (much like Oldenburg's proposed monuments), but one nonetheless circumscribed by the postcards on which they are printed. The drama of self-confrontation through paint becomes a souvenir, too. Even so, the painting in question is as good as any other. Gertrude Stein once said she loved all kinds of painting, just so long as it was paint on a surface. Similarly, Baldessari says – in line with John Cage – that anywhere you point the camera is a composition. The postcards are the painted equivalents of his photographic approach. *Black Out* (1971) is more reductive; a felt-tip frenetically scribbles over a piece of white paper until it turns black. *Water to Wine to Water* (1972–73) reduces a Biblical miracle to the status of a magic trick or science fair experiment – but manages to dupe the camera all the same. This, like many of Baldessari's other Super 8 films, is a loop originally shot in 16 mm. With no beginning or end to the transformation, the liquid won't stop changing, turning the miracle itself into a slight annoyance. The artist as shaman or alchemist proves to be a tedious fraud. In *Time/Temperature* (1972–73) a small hourglass and thermometer measure properties that are otherwise invisible. Like the camera, these are indexical instruments, but where the camera would ordinarily be taken for granted, these devices seem self-evident.

The film industry is another concern in Baldessari's Super 8s. Of course it is implied by the choice of medium, but some works reflect it thematically. *Dance* (1971), for example, records a flip book in action. This is nothing less than a demonstration of how film works. It implies, among other things, that the cinematic apparatus is less a matter of technology than it is a desire to structure seeing a certain way. In the various versions of *Taking a Slate* (1974), Baldessari presents the kind of footage that ordinarily lands on the cutting-room floor. Sometimes we see a sequence just as it was shot. Other times, we see that same strip of film moving back and forth on a viewer. This means Baldessari sometimes had to film his own film. Moreover, there is no slate. An actor simply mimics one with his hands. Both versions of *Ted's Christmas Card* feature tight close-ups of an old-fashioned, winter landscape printed on foil paper. The card keeps tilting so that it reflects a hallucinatory light straight back at the camera. The camera is in so close that we only see fragments of the scene. Tinsel Town beckons in *The Hollywood Film* (1972–73) where the same thing happens again, only this time with two buttons with starlets' portraits on one side and mirrors on the other. When not confined to a universe of shallow facades, the viewer is accordingly 'blinded by the light' of a reverse projection.

As a group, Baldessari's Super 8s negotiate what was once a confrontation between paintbrush and camera. Now, however, digital technology has become a kind of common denominator not only for painting and cinema, but also for drawing, photography and video as well; together they form an unbroken continuum of image making. This, of course, corresponds to an ideological complex – through which an optical unconscious might be glimpsed.

Film as a medium
Sergei Eisenstein believed that the cinema embodied the most acute aspects of American capitalism. He, of course, was thinking in terms of representation, but the political economy of cinema is sharper still. According to Jonathan Crary, Edison's primary genius was to use this medium to forge an economic link between hardware and software; what cinema ultimately offered was a new system of quantification and distribution based on the reciprocity of photography and money as homologous forms of social power:

> They are equally totalizing systems for binding and unifying all subjects within a single global network of valuation and desire. As Marx said of money, photography is also a great leveller, a democratizer, a 'mere symbol', a fiction 'sanctioned by the so-called universal concept of mankind. Both are magical forms that establish a new set of abstract relations between individuals and things and impose those relations as real.[1]

As Eisenstein argued, this is most true in the United States. Of all the industrialized nations, it has the greatest gap between rich and poor, but most Americans believe that they are, more or less, without class – that they are, in short, middle class. Photography's levelling effect remains naturalistic within the confines of the medium; when Baldessari retroactively applies it to painting, it seems manipulative. Traditionalists might see it as 'cruel', 'unfair' or 'cynical'. Here, humour takes on a more compensatory Freudian role as the vehicle for otherwise unacceptable revelations. Perversely, Baldessari's films exclude montage just where it would normally be expected. Instead, they reflect the principle Eisenstein called *typage*, which, in conventional film appears as typecasting or shooting on location. More broadly, it is a principle of minimum interference through which reality finds its analogy in film. The presumed veracity of the photo, according to Michael Taussig, is like sympathetic magic in so far as the belief system rests on contact between photons emitted by the subject and the photographic plate. Andy Warhol's films *Empire*, *Sleep*, *Eat* and *Blowjob* all seemingly guarantee that this contact remains continuous: no cuts, no camera movement and a relatively stationary subject. These movies demand a surplus 'persistence of vision' that will transcend rational knowledge of film's intrinsically fragmentary structure. This is the mythos of 'real time'. Filming the Empire State Building this way seemingly reconstitutes its mythic, existential status. Within the gallery system of the 1990s, Warhol's auratic use of the camera paves the way for the reintegration of film and video as updated forms of painting. When Baldessari brings a similar approach to bear on a mixed collection of ephemera, the viewer must accept it, too, as mythic – or else call into question cinema's documentary authority.

Photographic works

As opposed to his film approach, Baldessari typically constructs his photo works around the principle of montage. Here, unlike Eisenstein's classic version, Baldessari's photo montage is apparently non-signifying. For raw material, he typically uses an intervalvometer to shoot stills from film or television. What the exact shot will be is arbitrary. Thus, the shots are not 'composed' in the usual sense. Rather, actors – or the camera – are caught in transition. By combining these pictures with unrelated shots from other movies, Baldessari wrenches them out of their intended narrative. Thus montage foregrounds latent meanings within a given still. (In this regard, the photograph itself is literally metonymic, because the 35 mm negative derives directly from film stock.) The misuse of these photos frees them from their regular denotative function. They return to a more fundamental materiality, i.e. what Eisenstein called 'the factual immutability of the shot'. However, because the camera always produces surplus information, the shot can't be reduced to a univocal meaning; that is the role of the caption. What is immutable, then, is not necessarily invariable – at least on the level of the way it's read. This return to photo-materiality releases a liberatory glee. In short, the artist uses still photos to unpack film grammar, a system so thoroughly ingrained that it ordinarily goes unnoticed. Baldessari's reflexivity thus addresses film and TV as mass culture's dominant signifying practices, as sites where subjectivity is most powerfully formed and transformed. The focus on subtext not only undermines the overdetermination of conventional narrative imagery, it also indicates how film and television cultivate a deeper form of apperception in mass culture.

Between glamour and boredom

Boredom in Warhol's work derives primarily from apperception, namely the generalized experience of shock in mass culture. Not surprisingly, Warhol is also a key figure in the transvaluation of Action Painting aesthetics. Put bluntly, he substituted piss for paint. More discursively, by claiming he wanted to be a machine, he exchanged authenticity for a romantic inversion of it. This accounts for the fatal glamour that runs through Warhol's films. The fundamental tragedy, of course, is the camera's destruction of the authentic: 'The Superstars are fading.' This is exactly what confounded Jackson Pollock when Hans Namuth tried to film him painting. Namuth had asked Pollock to paint over a sheet of glass, so that he could record the action from underneath, at the point of impact. For this Pollock had to pretend to paint a picture on the glass. What pretend meant, more exactly, was to paint something he did not plan to show, to paint on glass instead of canvas. Although this posed a personal crisis for Pollock, earlier on he had, in fact, considered painting on glass as a way to integrate painting and architecture. So, it could only be the camera, the inserted technical apparatus, which was the falsifying element, that for which he performed and that which turned his gestures into theatre, or a spectacle. From the more objective standpoint of film form, it is difficult to say whether Namuth's approach was naturalistic or anti-naturalistic. Baldessari's camera specializes in de-glamorizing. Since whatever tiny events that unfold do so in real time, this is a recipe for boredom: boredom with a trace of humour, a classic surrealist formula. The effect, however, is far from surreal, yet, if the viewer is willing to make the requisite mental adjustments, i.e. to disregard the quotidian facticity of the filmed objects, these too might become sublime. That's exactly the problem the camera always poses: making the requisite mental adjustment. In this sense, Pollock was not simply exploited by the camera; he exploited it, too. *Life* magazine and *Vogue* (including a fashion feature shot by Cecil Beaton) ran big spreads of his work. These, together with his good looks and personal charisma, helped catapult him into national celebrity. As early as 1946, Mark Rothko remarked, 'Pollock is a self-contained and sustained advertising concern.'[2] In fact, none of that is true, even at the level of polemic. He was not self contained, but promoted by a media system. His role was more that of product than promoter. By putting himself behind the camera, however, Baldessari turns the tables. Only as a joke could he ever exclaim, 'I am Nature!' Nor would Ed Harris ever film his life story. When *Saturday Night Live* featured a regular skit called 'Bad Conceptual Art' in the late 1970s, perhaps Baldessari's work might have made it on. Yet, if praise is damning, parody might be the sincerest form of flattery. Otherwise, boredom keeps the producers at bay. Baldessari, for his part, promises to entertain next time, then fails to make good on the promise.

1   [footnote 4 in source] Jonathan Crary, 'Modernity and the Problem of the Observer', in *Techniques of the Observer: On Vision and Modernity in the Nineteenth Century* (Cambridge, Massachusetts: The MIT Press, 1999) 13.

2   [5] T. J. Clark, 'Jackson Pollock's Abstraction', in Serge Guilbaut, ed., *Reconstructing Modernism* (Cambridge, Massachusetts: The MIT Press, 1990) 176.

John Miller, 'No More Boring Art', in *Kunst/Kino: Jahresring 48* (Cologne: Oktagon Verlag, 2001) 69–78.

Life in a 'society' made by and for creatures who, when they are not grim and depressing are <u>utter bores</u>, can only be, when not grim and depressing, an <u>utter bore</u>

Valerie Solanas, S.C.U.M. Manifesto, 1967

NOTHING HAPPENS

Betty Friedan
The Feminine Mystique//1963

[...] The ultimate, in housewife happiness, is finally achieved by the Texas housewife, described in 'How America Lives' (*Ladies' Home Journal*, October 1960), who 'sits on a pale aqua satin sofa gazing out of her picture window at the street. Even at this hour of the morning (it is barely nine o'clock), she is wearing rouge, powder and lipstick, and her cotton dress is immaculately fresh.' She says proudly, 'By 8.30 a.m., when my youngest goes to school, my whole house is clean and neat and I am dressed for the day. I am free to play bridge, attend club meetings, or stay home and read, listen to Beethoven, and just plain loaf.'

'Sometimes, she washes and dries her hair before sitting down at a bridge table at 1.30. Mornings she is having bridge at her house are the busiest, for then she must get out the tables, cards, tallies, prepare fresh coffee and organize lunch … During the winter months, she may play as often as four days a week from 9.30 to 3 p.m. … Janice is careful to be at home before her sons return from school at 4 p.m.'

She is not frustrated, this new housewife. An honour student at high school, married at eighteen, remarried and pregnant at twenty, she has the house she spent seven years dreaming and planning in detail. She is proud of her efficiency as a housewife, getting it all done by 8.30. She does the major housecleaning on Saturday, when her husband fishes and her sons are busy with the Boy Scouts. ('There's nothing else to do. No bridge games. It's a long day for me.')

'"I love my home", she says … The pale grey paint in her L-shaped living and dining room is five years old, but still in perfect condition … The pale peach and yellow and aqua damask upholstery looks spotless after eight years' wear. "Sometimes, I feel I'm too passive, too content", remarks Janice, fondly, regarding the wristband of large family diamonds she wears even when the watch itself is being repaired … Her favourite possession is her four-poster spool bed with a pink taffeta canopy. "I feel just like Queen Elizabeth sleeping in that bed", she says happily. (Her husband sleeps in another room, since he snores.)'

'"I'm so grateful for my blessings", she says. "Wonderful husband, handsome sons with dispositions to match, big comfortable house … I'm thankful for my good health and faith in God and such material possessions as two cars, two TVs and two fireplaces."'

Staring uneasily at this image, I wonder if a few problems are not somehow better than this smiling empty passivity. If they are happy, these young women who live the feminine mystique, then is this the end of the road? Or are the seeds of something worse than frustration inherent in this image? Is there a growing divergence between this image of woman and human reality?

Consider, as a symptom, the increasing emphasis on glamour in the women's magazines: the housewife wearing eye make-up as she vacuums the floor – 'The Honour of Being a Woman'. Why does 'Occupation: housewife' require such insistent glamorizing year after year? The strained glamour is in itself a question mark: the lady doth protest too much.

The image of woman in another era required increasing prudishness to keep denying sex. This new image seems to require increasing emphasis on *things*: two cars, two TVs, two fireplaces. Whole pages of women's magazines are filled with gargantuan vegetables: beets, cucumbers, green peppers, potatoes, described like a love affair. The very size of their print is raised until it looks like a first-grade primer. The new *McCall's* frankly assumes women are brainless, fluffy kittens; the *Ladies' Home Journal*, feverishly competing, procures rock-and-roller Pat Boone as a counsellor to teenagers; *Redbook* and the others enlarge their own type size. Does the size of the print mean that the new young women, whom all the magazines are courting, have only first-grade minds? Or does it try to hide the triviality of the content? Within the confines of what is now accepted as woman's world, an editor may no longer be able to think of anything big to do except blow up a baked potato, or describe a kitchen as if it were the Hall of Mirrors; he is, after all, forbidden by the mystique to deal with a big idea. But does it not occur to any of the men who run the women's magazines that their troubles may stem from the smallness of the image with which they are truncating women's minds?

They are all in trouble today, the mass-circulation magazines, vying fiercely with each other and television to deliver more and more millions of women who will buy the things their advertisers sell. Does this frantic race force the men who make the images to see women only as thing-buyers? Does it force them to compete finally in emptying women's minds of human thought? The fact is, the troubles of the image-makers seem to be increasing in direct proportion to the increasing mindlessness of their image. During the years in which that image has narrowed woman's world down to the home, cut her role back to housewife, five of the mass-circulation magazines geared to women have ceased publication; others are on the brink.

The growing boredom of women with the empty, narrow image of the women's magazines may be the most hopeful sign of the image's divorce from reality. But there are more violent symptoms on the part of women who are committed to that image. In 1960, the editors of a magazine specifically geared to the happy young housewife – or rather to the new young couples (the wives are not considered separate from their husbands and children) – ran an article asking, 'Why Young Mothers Feel Trapped' (*Redbook*, September 1960). As a promotion stunt, they invited young mothers with such a problem to write in the details, for $500. The editors were shocked to receive 24,000 replies. Can an image of woman be cut down to the point where it becomes itself a trap?

At one of the major women's magazines, a woman editor, sensing that American housewives might be desperately in need of something to enlarge their world, tried for months to convince her male colleagues to introduce a few ideas outside the home into the magazine. 'We decided against it', the man who makes the final decisions said. 'Women are so completely divorced from the world of ideas in their lives now, they couldn't take it.' Perhaps it is irrelevant to ask, who divorced them? Perhaps these Frankensteins no longer have the power to stop the feminine monster they have created.

I helped create this image. I have watched American women for fifteen years try to conform to it. But I can no longer deny my own knowledge of its terrible implications. It is not a harmless image. There may be no psychological terms for the harm it is doing. But what happens when women grow up in an image that makes them deny the reality of the changing world?

The material details of daily life, the daily burdens of cooking and cleaning, of taking care of the physical needs of husband and children – these did indeed define a woman's world a century ago when Americans were pioneers, and the American frontier lay in conquering the land. But the women who went west with the wagon trains also shared the pioneering purpose. Now the American frontiers are of the mind, and of the spirit. Love and children and home are good, but they are not the whole world, even if most of the words now written for women pretend they are. Why should women accept this picture of a half-life, instead of a share in the whole of human destiny? [...]

Betty Friedan, extract from *The Feminine Mystique* (1963); 10th ed. (New York: W.W. Norton, Inc., 1974) 63–7.

Simone de Beauvoir
Les Belles Images//1966

[…] He searched among his gramophone records. No hi-fi system: only a great many lovingly-chosen discs. 'I'm going to play you something very fine, a new recording of *L'Incoronazione di Poppea*.'

Laurence tried to concentrate. A woman was saying farewell to her country and her friends. It was beautiful. She looked at her father: oh to be able to sink into oneself like that. He alone possessed what she thought she had found in Jean-Charles and Lucien; upon his face there was a reflection of the infinite. To be delightful company for oneself: to be a hearth that sends out warmth. I indulge in the luxury of remorse: I blame myself for my neglect: but it is I who need him. She looked at her father; she wondered where his secret lay and whether she would ever be able to discover it. She did not listen. For a long while now music had no longer said anything to her. Monteverdi's pathos, the tragic utterances of Beethoven, referred to pains of a kind that she had never felt – huge, vehement, mastered pains. She had experienced a piercing anguish now and then, a certain wretchedness of mind, forlornness, perturbation, emptiness, boredom – above all boredom. No one celebrates boredom in music.

'Yes, it's perfectly splendid', she said fervently. (Say what you think, said Mlle Houchet. Even with her father it was impossible. You say what people expect you to say.) […]

Simone de Beauvoir, extract from *Les belles images* (Paris: Gallimard, 1966); trans. Patrick O'Brian, Les Belles Images (London: Collins, 1968) 30–31.

Mierle Laderman Ukeles
MANIFESTO! MAINTENANCE ART – Proposal for an Exhibition 'CARE'//1969

I. IDEAS:

    A. The Death Instinct and the Life Instinct:

The Death Instinct: separation, individuality, Avant-Garde par excellence; to follow one's own path to death – do your own thing, dynamic change.

The Life Instinct: unification, the eternal return, the perpetuation and MAINTENANCE of the species, survival systems and operations, equilibrium.

B. Two basic systems: Development and Maintenance. The sourball of every revolution: after the revolution, who's going to pick up the garbage on Monday morning?
Development: pure individual creation; the new; change; progress, advance, excitement, flight or fleeing.
Maintenance: keep the dust off the pure individual creation; preserve the new; sustain the change; protect progress; defend and prolong the advance; renew the excitement; repeat the flight.

> show your work – show it again
> keep the contemporaryartmuseum groovy
> keep the home fires burning

Development systems are partial feedback systems with major room for change.
Maintenance systems are direct feedback systems with little room for alteration.

C. Maintenance is a drag; it takes all the fucking time (lit.)
The mind boggles and chafes at the boredom. The culture confers lousy status on maintenance jobs = minimum wages, housewives = no pay.

clean your desk, wash the dishes, clean the floor, wash your clothes, wash your toes, change the baby's diaper, finish the report, correct the typos, mend the fence, keep the customer happy, throw out the stinking garbage, watch out don't put things in your nose, what shall I wear, I have no sox, pay your bills, don't litter, save string, wash your hair, change the sheets, go to the store, I'm out of perfume, say it again – he doesn't understand, seal it again – it leaks, go to work, this art is dusty, clear the table, call him again, flush the toilet, stay young.

D. Art:

Everything I say is Art is Art. Everything I do is Art is Art.
'We have no Art, we try to do everything well.' (Balinese saying).

Avant-garde art, which claims utter development, is infected by strains of maintenance ideas, maintenance activities, and maintenance materials.
– Process art especially claims pure development and change, yet employs almost purely maintenance processes.

E. The exhibition of Maintenance Art, 'CARE', would zero in on pure maintenance, exhibit it as contemporary art, and yield, by utter opposition, clarity of issues.

II. THE MAINTENANCE ART EXHIBITION: Three parts: personal, general, and Earth Maintenance.

   A. Personal Part:

> I am an artist. I am a woman. I am a wife. I am a mother (random order).
> I do a hell of a lot of washing, cleaning, cooking, renewing, supporting, preserving, etc. Also, (up to now separately) I 'do' Art.

Now, I will simply do these maintenance everyday things, and flush them up to consciousness, exhibit them, as Art. I will live in the museum as I customarily do at home with my husband and my baby (right, or if you don't want me around at night I would come in every day) for the duration of the exhibition, and do all these things as public Art activities: I will sweep and wax the floors, dust everything, wash the walls (i.e. 'floor paintings, dust works, soap-sculpture, wall-paintings'), cook, invite people to eat, clean up, put away, change light bulbs. I might save and make agglomerations and dispositions of all functional refuse. The exhibition area might look 'empty' of art, but it will be maintained in full public view.

My working will be the work

   B. General part:

Everyone does a hell of a lot of noodiling maintenance work.

The general part of the exhibition would consist of interviews of two kinds.

1. Previous interviews of, say, 50 different classes and kinds of occupations that run a gamut from 'maintenance man', maid, sanitation man, mailman, union man, construction worker, librarian, grocerystore man, nurse, doctor, teacher, museum director, salesman, baseball player, child, criminal, bank president, mayor, movie star, artist, etc., about what they think maintenance is; how they feel about spending whatever parts of their lives on maintenance activities; what is the relationship between maintenance and freedom; what is the relationship between maintenance and life's dreams.

   These interviews will be typed and exhibited.

2. Interview Room – for spectators at the Exhibition:
   A room of desks and chairs where professional (?) interviewers will interview the spectators at the exhibition along same questions as typed interviews (in 1. above). The responses should be personal.

   These interviews are taped and replayed throughout the exhibition area.

C. Earth Maintenance

Everyday, a container of the following kinds of refuse will be delivered to the Museum: 1) the contents of one sanitation truck; 2) a container of polluted air; 3) a container of polluted Hudson River; 4) a container of ravaged land. Once at the exhibition, each container will be serviced: purified, depoluted, rehabilitated, recycled, and conserved by various technical (and / or pseudo-technical) procedures either by myself or scientists.

These servicing procedures are repeated for the duration of the exhibition.

Mierle Laderman Ukeles, typeset transcript from the original typewritten manuscript: *MANIFESTO! / MAINTENANCE ART – Proposal for an Exhibition / 'CARE'* (Philadelphia, 1969); courtesy of the artist and Ronald Feldman Gallery, 2016.

Faith Wilding
Waiting//1971

Waiting …   waiting …   waiting …
Waiting for someone to come in
Waiting for someone to hold me
Waiting for someone to feed me
Waiting for someone to change my diaper   Waiting …

Waiting to scrawl, to walk, waiting to talk
Waiting to be cuddled
Waiting for someone to take me outside
Waiting for someone to play with me
Waiting for someone to take me outside
Waiting for someone to read to me, dress me, tie my shoes
Waiting for Mommy to brush my hair
Waiting for her to curl my hair
Waiting to wear my frilly dress
Waiting to be a pretty girl
Waiting to grow up   Waiting …

Waiting for my breasts to develop
Waiting to wear a bra
Waiting to menstruate
Waiting to read forbidden books
Waiting to stop being clumsy
Waiting to have a good figure
Waiting for my first date
Waiting to have a boyfriend
Waiting to go to a party, to be asked to dance, to dance close
Waiting to be beautiful
Waiting for the secret
Waiting for life to begin   Waiting …

Waiting to be somebody
Waiting to wear make-up
Waiting for my pimples to go away
Waiting to wear lipstick, to wear high heels and stockings

Waiting to get dressed up, to shave my legs
Waiting to be pretty   Waiting …

Waiting for him to notice me, to call me
Waiting for him to ask me out
Waiting for him to pay attention to me
Waiting for him to fall in love with me
Waiting for him to kiss me, touch me, touch my breasts
Waiting for him to pass my house
Waiting for him to tell me I'm beautiful
Waiting for him to ask me to go steady
Waiting to neck, to make out, waiting to go all the way
Waiting to smoke, to drink, to stay out late
Waiting to be a woman   Waiting …

Waiting for my great love
Waiting for the perfect man
Waiting for Mr Right   Waiting …

Waiting to get married
Waiting for my wedding day
Waiting for my wedding night
Waiting for sex
Waiting for him to make the first move
Waiting for him to excite me
Waiting for him to give me pleasure
Waiting for him to give me an orgasm   Waiting …
Waiting for him to come home, to fill my time   Waiting …

Waiting for my baby to come
Waiting for my belly to swell
Waiting for my breasts to fill with milk
Waiting to feel my baby move
Waiting for my legs to stop swelling
Waiting for the first contractions
Waiting for the contractions to end
Waiting for the head to emerge
Waiting for the first scream, the afterbirth
Waiting to hold my baby
Waiting for my baby to suck my milk

Waiting for my baby to stop crying
Waiting for my baby to sleep through the night
Waiting for my breasts to dry up
Waiting to get my figure back, for the stretch marks to go away
Waiting for some time to myself
Waiting to be beautiful again
Waiting for my child to go to school
Waiting for life to begin again   Waiting …

Waiting for my children to come home from school
Waiting for them to grow up, to leave home
Waiting to be myself
Waiting for excitement
Waiting for him to tell me something interesting, to ask me how I feel
Waiting for him to stop being crabby, reach for my hand, kiss me good morning
Waiting for fulfilment
Waiting for the children to marry
Waiting for something to happen   Waiting …
Waiting to lose weight
Waiting for the first grey hair
Waiting for menopause
Waiting to grow wise
Waiting …
Waiting for my body to break down, to get ugly
Waiting for my flesh to sag
Waiting for my breasts to shrivel up
Waiting for a visit from my children, for letters
Waiting for my friends to die
Waiting for my husband to die   Waiting …
Waiting to get sick
Waiting for things to get better
Waiting for winter to end
Waiting for the mirror to tell me that I'm old
Waiting for a good bowel movement
Waiting for the pain to go away
Waiting for the struggle to end
Waiting for release
Waiting for morning
Waiting for the end of the day
Waiting for sleep   Waiting …

Faith Wilding, 'Waiting' (1971), 15-minute poem/monologue, performed by the artist at Womanhouse, Los Angeles, the feminist installation and performance space organized by Judy Chicago and Miriam Schapiro (30 January – 28 February 1972); published in *Ms magazine* (December 1973). (http://faithwilding.refugia.net/waiting.html)

Ivone Margulies
On *Jeanne Dielman*//1996

[…] For the first two hours, all in Chantal Akerman's *Jeanne Dielman, 23, Quai Du Commerce, 1080 Bruxelles* (1975) is startling order. This rigour supports a comparison of the film's structure to a game of 'What is wrong with this picture?' The rhyming of formal and structural tone with the pro-filmic event in Jeanne Dielman is akin to the strategic engagement of the spectator's expectations in structural film. As minimal art, structural film reduces the number of elements involved in its scrutiny. Structural film offers a paradigm (formal repetition, seriality, etc.) through which the viewer can reconstruct its governing system, and in a way predict its 'narrative'; it thus invites one to read the development of the film as a 'natural' sequence of events, as an organic match between pro-filmic and cinematic orders. The interplay between recognizing the utter arbitrariness of this sequencing and noticing that which might break its expected pattern is a basic component of the structural film's vocabulary and intention.

Akerman sets a formal and a behavioural paradigm only the better to expose its underside. The narrative is predicated on the difference between the first two days and the third day of Jeanne's routine. In its didactic exposure of the fragility of order, this discrepancy implies a moral tale: a fork falls, dishes remain sudsy, the brush flies as Jeanne shines the shoes, and she arrives either too early or too late to each of her routine stations. Objects seem animistically fraught, with a will of their own, and time, Jeanne's motor, starts being felt (by her and by us) as the reverse and constitutive side of boredom: as impatience and anguish.

It is on the third day that, because of an initial derangement of Jeanne's chronology (she wakes before her alarm clock rings), we see her sit apathetically at the kitchen table, then suddenly go to the back balcony, pick up a broom, leave it, and return to the chair. She stands up again, taking some coffee from the thermos bottle. She pours in some milk, and … the coffee tastes bad. She tastes the milk, brings out the sugar, carefully choosing perfect cubes which she joins symmetrically in a tiny rectangle before putting them in her drink – and the coffee still tastes bad. Then she starts making more coffee from scratch. Her apathy is given a purpose – to wait for the coffee to seep slowly through the Melita filter. Thierry de Duve has described this figuration of time – the water seeping through a domestic apparatus shaped rather like an hourglass – as a representation of one of the temporalities administered by Jeanne and by Akerman. Providing a metaphoric level for all the film's scenes in real time, the Melita coffee scene constitutes an image of 'time as entropy, as irreversibility'.[1]

The extra activity does not rebalance Jeanne's chronology. She sits in an old mustard-coloured armchair, taking its shape and faded tone, only breathing. It is on the third day of the film's narrative that we watch Jeanne sit for long periods of time, doing nothing, then abruptly standing, or doing something unnecessary (like cleaning the bibelots) or unusual (like trying to play with the neighbour's baby, who normally sits alone as Jeanne has her snack). If, at a certain point in the film, we begin to suspect a change in the pace of what we've been watching for two and a half hours, this has to do with the introduction of signs of anxiety, shots where the action is in 'disaster mode'. In *Jeanne Dielman*, the disruptions in the scene are relatively small; they could be analogues for the images that classic analytic editing would privilege, through cut-aways and close-ups, as suggestions of something about to happen.

Nevertheless, in showing all of Jeanne's vicissitudes – small disasters such as a falling fork, the loss of her usual coffee time, a baby howling – in an unchanged medium long shot, Akerman fixes these signs in the present time of their dramatic and material repercussions. Such mishaps are not to be read as forebodings, then, although they eventually function this way. To the extent that they are dramatic, it is through their actual noise and visual disturbance. The unease is felt through the disruption of the pace of the earlier scenes, with their untroubled movement (for the spectator) and domestic order (for Jeanne). The fact that *Jeanne Dielman* involves the spectator's attention in what in the hierarchy of spectacle is a minor hermeneutic chain leads more to the viewing of what is happening than to the prospect of what will happen. Although we have learned to decode Jeanne's routine, and thus know what to expect in the order of events, Akerman's episodic narrative structure holds surprises having nothing to do with the notion of a turn of events. One adjusts very slowly to the fact that the irruption of differences holds the promise of some dramatic change. In *Jeanne Dielman*, the suspension of expectation generates another kind of suspense: the film experiments with the possibility of an attention to silence, blankness and minor events, but not as either a sign of some form of asceticism (a moralistic standpoint against traditional narrative, for example) or the absolute precondition for or even announcement of drama (like the stillness that reinforces the suspense of a thriller). *Jeanne Dielman* constitutes a radical experiment with being undramatic and, paradoxically, with drama's absolute necessity. [...]

1   [footnote 28 in source] Thierry de Duve, 'Les trois horloges', in Chantal Akerman, *Cahier 1*, ed. Jaqueline Aubenas (Brussels: Atelier des Arts, 1982) 89. [...]

Ivone Margulies, extract from *Nothing Happens: Chantal Akerman's Hyperrealist Everyday* (Durham, North Carolina: Duke University Press, 1996) 78–80.

Jennifer Doyle
I Must Be Boring Someone//2006

And then there's always the soup. Now, the soup of the meal is, uh, very very important because soup is very very easy to digest and it doesn't really fill you up that much, unless you're sick. Now, there's all different kinds of soups. Different kinds of soups. Soup – it's just so much fun, and, like, so easy to make. Say you wanna make a vegetable soup. All you do is take a big pot and fill it up with some water or some broth and start chopping potatoes and onions and carrots and peas and lettuce and celery and cucumbers and everything, uh, and noodles and meat and fish and lobsters and shrimp and just mix it all together in a big garbage soup [here, she lowers the other strap of her dress] and, really, it tastes so delicious and you season it with salt and pepper and garlic salt, you drop a couple of fried eggs in it, make sure they don't get runny, and, uhm, and then if the leaves get curly you take an iron and ya iron the leaves out. And, uh, I mean, soup is just so divine, my dear. It really is. And then the second, the uh third course of course would be the salad, which I've already discussed. Now for the fifth course, I would like to make you some roast beef.
[– Ingrid Superstar, in Andy Warhol's film *Bike Boy*, 1967–68]

At which point Ingrid Superstar asks Bike Boy (but without really engaging him), 'Do you like roast beef?' She cocks her head to the side, leaving room for a reply without, however, appearing to expect one. After a beat, she continues: 'Well I don't care if you like roast beef, because *I* like roast beef and that's all that matters: What *I* like, not what you like. So, uh. Roast beef. Well you just stick the roast in the oven for a couple hours ...' As her soliloquy picks up a rhythm, she relaxes into her position as *not* Bike Boy's object of interest. In fact, it becomes increasingly obvious as the camera stays on them that he does not even seem to be bored by her – he seems, rather, to participate in a different economy of interest altogether (that of the trade hustler, leaning against a bar, waiting for someone else). It is not clear that he is even listening to her.

So Superstar kills time, emptying out her speech until the viewer can hardly stand it because the dynamics of interest in the scene have become so perverse. […] [She] is simply filling up the time and space of the scene. Her passive resistance to the demand that she interest Bike Boy becomes fascinating as a performance of the desire to be boring, of, even, the production of boredom as a critical mode. Toward this effect, she interrupts her strange culinary excursus and sighs wistfully, 'I must be boring someone', as if this were her hope.

As she says this, she outlines the difficulty of her position on the screen. What she lacks (to quote the feminist critic Naomi Schor, writing about Emma Bovary) 'is not a lover, but a receiver'.[1] She is talking to herself – and, worse, she is talking to herself not because she is alone but because her on-screen partner is not listening to her. Carla Kaplan writes that 'no form of talk is as self-effacing, humiliating or damaging to social standing as is talking to ourselves.'[2] The disempowered subject 'longs' for talk, longs for a listener who might engage her talk and turn it into conversation. Superstar, however, seems very comfortable in her chatter – we might, in fact, compare her performance with that of *le bavard*, the title character of a 1946 experimental novel that charts the aimless, non-stop chatter of its narrator. Eleanor Kaufman, in an essay on chatter and philosophical friendship, suggests that this experimental transcription of meaningless talk renders speech into a play of forms – in which form stands 'slightly apart from content', to 'far surpass … anything that the content might disclose'.[3] Toward this end, Maurice Blanchot writes of *le bavard* that 'chatter is the shame of language. To chatter is not to speak. The stuff of speech destroys silence while at the same time impeding speech. When one chatters, nothing true is said, even if nothing false is said, because one is not truly speaking.'[4] It is speech, Kaufman writes (drawing on Blanchot's words), and not chatter, that 'risks shutting language down', in so far as it is in chatter that we play with language – with happy accidents and strange conjunctions.[5] She wonders, then, if 'saying exactly nothing is really saying nothing … in laying bare the nothingness of a text, in making that nothingness excessive, perhaps something extraordinary is being iterated.'[6] Superstar offers us a cinematic version of *le bavard*'s excessive nothingness. She seems to luxuriate in the meaningless of her talk and in her own boredom, displacing any discomfort with her situation onto the audience and leaving us to wonder at the point of it all. Her performance – which conjoins seduction, nudity and domestic mundanity – furthermore draws to the surface the association of this kind of pointless talk with the housewife.

Her performance in this scene thus parodies the wreckage of heterosexual coupling that Candace Vogler describes in 'Sex and Talk', the kind of breakdown in communication that is the subject of endless talk shows about marriage, and of pop psychology books on the differences between the sexes. In those situations, the man longs for intimacy through sex, and the woman for the same, through talk. Both are after (in Vogler's words) 'depersonalizing forms of intimacy' in which they might be relieved of the burden of producing the contours of the self for the other – but fail to understand the nature of their differences and what ought to be done about it. Drawing from Deborah Tannen's work, Vogler writes that women

> voice fleeting thoughts, impressions, doubts and feelings and mix discussion of minor events in intricate sensory detail with talk of bigger things. This is one of the most common ways exemplary US women engage each other verbally and exemplary US men can't stand it. As one man put it in an interview [with Tannen], 'I do not value my fleeting thoughts, and I do not value the fleeting thoughts of others', having had to engage with a woman's troubles talk for the sake of finding a new partner after his divorce left him 'dizzy from having been bounced around like a yo-yo tied to the string of her self-consciousness.[7]

Superstar acts out for us the humiliation of the woman's position in this domestic drama in so far as it mirrors her place in the world-at-large that ignores her or talks over her as if she were not talking at all. To borrow again from Kaplan's discussion of the ethics and erotics of talk, Superstar's performance satirizes 'the disjunction between the implied promise of dialogue and narrative exchange and the actual social, discursive and material conditions faced by disadvantaged speakers, the conditions in which any dialogic exchange must actually take place'.[8] Her performance is a rather acidic comment on what heterosexuality wants from women (empty speech) […]. Here, the heterosexual woman is literalized as the weak interlocutor – satirized as the woman who won't shut up, exactly because she knows no one is listening to her. And also because, let's not forget, the man she's talking to isn't interested in women – the awkwardness of her presence seems mainly to underscore the film's queerness. The queer frame of their encounter is perhaps the only thing that keeps the scene on the funnier side of the tragic. Her performance is enabled by Bike Boy's, the perfect 'trade' object of homosexual desire; his presence unmoors hers from the seduction narrative and allows our attention to wander. As she says 'I must be boring someone', we bear witness both to her desire for an audience and to her familiarity with talking to an empty house.

Radical Boredoms
Siegfried Kracauer argues for boredom as crucial to the resistance to bourgeois

culture – a willingness to be boring as a kind of luxury that resists capitalist modes of production and the demand to be always productive. He writes, 'People whose duties occasionally make them yawn may be less boring than those who do their business by inclination', and argues against the constant stream of information, images and sound that 'effaces every trace of private existence'.[9] [...] Superstar proves that boredom can 'provide ... a kind of guarantee that one is, so to speak, still in control of one's existence'. Hers is a dialectical reversal of the demand to be interesting, in which the refusal to interest opens up the possibility of something actually happening.

This is the point at which the postmodern readings of Warhol's films – in terms of the death of the author, the erasure of the traces of the author's subjective presence – converge with their potential as feminist texts. Boredom interests Kracauer as a mute negation of the capitalist mandate to production, and Warhol's blank affect, his performance of cosmopolitan boredom, has been taken as definitive of Pop's postmodern turn – its refusal of modernism's weighty self-importance, its negation (emptying out) of the sign.

David Joselit's 'Yippie Pop: Abbie Hoffman, Andy Warhol and Sixties Media Politics' is one of the most interesting essays on this side of Warhol's aesthetic. In his exploration of the harmony between Warhol's aesthetic and Abbie Hoffman's politics, Joselit maps their shared interest in the dissolution of the difference between figure and ground. In particular, Joselit writes, the *Exploding Plastic Inevitable* (multimedia events produced by Warhol around Velvet Underground performances) bred 'a circuit of media feedback ... in which the line between performing oneself and becoming an image was perpetually crossed and re-crossed'.[10] As the audience found itself lit up by the flicker of a strobe light, for example, they seemed to experience themselves as though they were literally on film. His characterization of Warhol's multimedia events is surprisingly evocative of Laura Mulvey's call for the destruction of traditional forms of cinematic pleasure:

> The first blow against the monolithic accumulation of traditional film conventions (already undertaken by radical filmmakers) is to free the look of the camera into its materiality in time and space and the look of the audience into dialectics and passionate detachment. There is no doubt that this destroys the satisfaction, pleasure and privilege of the 'invisible guest', and highlights the way film has depended on voyeuristic active/passive mechanisms. Women, whose image has continually been stolen and used for this end, cannot view the decline of traditional film form with anything much more than sentimental regret.[11]

We can thus read the radicalism of Ingrid Superstar's performance from two angles: the production of boredom as a refusal of traditional forms of cinematic pleasure and as a formal resistance in its confounding of the relationship between figure and ground. As she talks on and on about food, she becomes not only just something to look at (like Bike Boy) but also, in essence, a fixture of the kitchen (anticipating Chantal Akerman).

Mulvey famously denounces narrative cinema's organization of women as objects of interest, as mysteries to be figured out, reined in, re-presented as pure spectacle. As Superstar prattles on about food and inexplicably peels herself out of the top of her dress, she replicates and inverts one of Hollywood cinema's most conservative presentations of the spectacle of feminine sexual difference. Her performance of depersonalized talk (which, in terms of what it says, reveals nothing) calls to mind the musical numbers in suspense films, around which all action would grind to a halt so that the femme fatale might offer herself up as a spectacle. Explaining why suspense films so often arrested the development of plot to offer the spectator apparently pointless musical numbers, Mulvey writes:

> The woman displayed has functioned on two levels: as an erotic object for the characters within the screen's story, and as an erotic object for the spectator within the auditorium, with the shifting tension between the looks on either side of the screen ... the device of the showgirl allows the two looks to be united technically without any apparent break in the diagesis. A woman performs within the narrative; the gaze of the spectator and that of the male characters in the film are neatly combined without breaking narrative similitude. For a moment the sexual impact of the performing woman takes the film into a no man's land outside its own time and space.[12]

The juxtaposition of Superstar's nudity with her pointless speech traces out the ludicrousness of the woman's position on film – that she hold our interest, without, however, becoming narrative's agent.

Ironically, Kracauer argues, 'If one were never to be bored, one would presumably not really be present at all'; one would never encounter one's self 'and would thus be merely one more object of boredom', becoming of a piece with the closed-circuit broadcast that prevents even people waiting in line from finding 'the peace and quiet necessary to be as thoroughly bored with the world as it ultimately deserves'.[13] We might imagine Superstar as suspended within this mandate to always keep the audience interested (and distracted). Superstar's refusal of the imperative to be interesting, her invitation to find her boring (enabled by her own willingness to be bored), allows us to inhabit the scene alongside her – to find her boring, to find him boring, to be bored and to find oneself boring – which, for Kracauer, Adam Phillips, Walter Benjamin (for all the philosophers of boredom), is the first step to taking an interest in the world. The moment Superstar relaxes into her position as not-interesting, we are released from a spell – for at this point, she stops competing with Bike Boy for our attention, and, counter-intuitively, we find ourselves finally able to really see her.

We might place her at one point on a spectrum of feminist takes on boredom (alongside, for example, Akerman), with Valerie Solanas at its extreme. For the heroine of *I, a Man* opens the *S.C.U.M. Manifesto* with a frontal attack on patriarchal normalcy that is […] presented as a response to boredom:

> Life in this society being, at best, an utter bore and no aspect of society being at all relevant to women, there remains to civic-minded, responsible, thrill seeking females only to overthrow the government, eliminate the money system, institute complete automation and destroy the male sex.[14]

These diverse voices are the calls of the twenty-ninth bather, the visible invisible woman who encounters her self only by finding herself in a place she does not belong, on one level surrounded by an audience of people who take no notice of her presence, and confronted on another by the singular spectator who, too bored to follow the plot, discovers that there is more to the story than the story. […]

1 [footnote 38 in source] Naomi Schor, *Reading in Detail: Women, Theory and French Realist Fiction* (New York: Columbia University Press, 1985) 16.
2 [39] Here she summarizes the work of Erving Goffman. See Carla Kaplan, 'Talk to Me: Talk Ethics and Erotics', in *Talk, Talk, Talk: The Cultural Life of Everyday Conversation*, ed. S.I. Salamensky (London and New York: Routledge, 2001) 63.
3 [41] Eleanor Kaufman, 'Chattering Silences', in *The Delirium of Praise: Bataille, Blanchot, Deleuze, Foucault, Klossowski* (Baltimore: The Johns Hopkins University Press, 2001) 21.
4 [42] Maurice Blanchot, 'La Parole vaine', in *L'Amitié* (Paris: Gallimard, 1971) 137; trans. and cited by Kaufman in *The Delirium of Praise*, op. cit., 24.
5 [43] Kaufman, op. cit., 24.
6 [44] Ibid., 22.
7 [45] Candace Vogler, 'Sex and Talk', in *Intimacy*, ed. Lauren Berlant (Chicago: University of Chicago Press, 2000) 359. Here she draws from Deborah Tannen's *You Just Don't Understand: Women and Men in Conversation* (New York: Morrow, 1990) 83, 84.
8 [46] Kaplan, 'Talk to Me', op. cit., 73.
9 [47] Siegfried Kracauer, 'Boredom', in *The Mass Ornament: Weimar Essays*, trans. Thomas Y. Levin (Cambridge, Massachusetts: Harvard University Press, 1995) 331, 333.
10 [48] David Joselit, 'Yippie Pop: Abbie Hoffman, Andy Warhol and Sixties Media Politics', *Grey Room*, no. 8 (Summer 2002) 71, 72.
11 [49] Laura Mulvey, 'Visual Pleasure and Narrative Cinema' (1975), in Mulvey, *Visual and Other*

Pleasures (Bloomington: Indiana University Press, 1989) 26.
12 [50] Laura Mulvey, 'Afterthoughts on "Visual Pleasure and Narrative Cinema" Inspired by King Vidor's *Duel in the Sun* (1946)', in Mulvey, *Visual and Other Pleasures*, op. cit., 29.
13 [51] Kracauer, 'Boredom', op. cit., 334.
14 [52] Valerie Solanas, *S.C.U.M. (Society for Cutting Up Men) Manifesto* (New York, self-published, 1967) 1.

Jennifer Doyle, extract from *Sex Objects: Art and the Dialectics of Desire* (Minneapolis: University of Minnesota Press, 2006) 91–6.

Valerie Solanas
S.C.U.M Manifesto//1967

Life in this society being, at best, an utter bore and no aspect of society being at all relevant to women, there remains to civic-minded, responsible, thrill-seeking females only to overthrow the government, eliminate the money system, institute complete automation, and destroy the male sex.

It is now technically possible to reproduce without the aid of males (or, for that matter, females) and to produce only females. We must begin immediately to do so. Retaining the male has not even the dubious purpose of reproduction. The male is a biological accident: the Y (male) gene is an incomplete X (female) gene, that is, has an incomplete set of chromosomes. In other words, the male is an incomplete female, a walking abortion, aborted at the gene stage. To be male is to be deficient, emotionally limited; maleness is a deficiency disease and males are emotional cripples.

The male is completely egocentric, trapped inside himself, incapable of empathizing or identifying with others, of love, friendship, affection or tenderness. He is a completely isolated unit, incapable of rapport with anyone. His responses are entirely visceral, not cerebral; his intelligence is a mere tool in the service of his drives and needs; he is incapable of mental passion, mental interaction; he can't relate to anything other than his own physical sensations. He is a half-dead, unresponsive lump, incapable of giving or receiving pleasure or happiness; consequently, he is at best an utter bore, an inoffensive blob, since only those capable of absorption in others can be charming. He is trapped in a twilight zone halfway between humans and apes, and is far worse off than the apes because, unlike the apes, he is capable of a large array of negative feelings

– hate, jealousy, contempt, disgust, guilt, shame, doubt – and moreover he *is aware* of what he is and isn't.

Although completely physical, the male is unfit even for stud service. Even assuming mechanical proficiency, which few men have, he is, first of all, incapable of zestfully, lustfully, tearing off a piece, but is instead eaten up with guilt, shame, fear and insecurity, feelings rooted in male nature, which the most enlightened training can only minimize; second, the physical feeling he attains is next to nothing; and, third, he is not empathizing with his partner, but is obsessed with how he's doing, turning in an A performance, doing a good plumbing job. To call a man an animal is to flatter him; he's a machine, a walking dildo. It's often said that men use women. Use them for what? Surely not pleasure.

Eaten up with guilt, shame, fears and insecurities and obtaining, if he's lucky, a barely perceptible physical feeling, the male is, nonetheless, obsessed with screwing; he'll swim a river of snot, wade nostril-deep through a mile of vomit, if he thinks there'll be a friendly pussy awaiting him. He'll screw a woman he despises, any snaggletoothed hag, and, furthermore, pay for the opportunity. Why? Relieving physical tension isn't the answer, as masturbation suffices for that. It's not ego satisfaction; that doesn't explain screwing corpses and babies.

Completely egocentric, unable to relate, empathize or identify, and filled with a vast, pervasive, diffuse sexuality, the male is psychically passive. He hates his passivity, so he projects it onto women, defines the male as active, then sets out to prove that he is ('prove he's a Man'). His main means of attempting to prove it is screwing (Big Man with a Big Dick tearing off a Big Piece). Since he's attempting to prove an error, he must 'prove' it again and again. Screwing, then, is a desperate, compulsive attempt to prove he's not passive, not a woman; but he is passive and does want to be a woman. [...]

Life in a 'society' made by and for creatures who, when they are not grim and depressing are utter bores, can only be, when not grim and depressing, an utter bore. [...]

Valerie Solanas, extracts from *S.C.U.M. (Society for Cutting Up Men) Manifesto* (New York, self-published, 1967) (San Francisco: AK Press, 1996) 1–2, 28.

You know me ...

You see there's nothing behind me

I'm already a has-been

because my future ain't what it was

well I think I know the words that I mean

You know me ...

Buzzcocks, from 'Boredom', *Spiral Scratch*, 1977

NO FUTURE

Peter Fischli
Sigmar Polke – A Contemporary Visionary: In Conversation with Mark Godfrey//2014

Mark Godfrey The idea of time wasting also connects to boredom. What do you make of Sigmar Polke's *Boredom Loop* from 1969, where he stuck awkwardly curved stretches of masking tape on his studio wall and photographed them, with the word *Langeweileschleife* in lettering underneath?

Peter Fischli For me, that's one of the key pieces – if I had to choose four or five works of his, this would be one of them. He redid it in Zurich in the mid 1970s for a show at a place called Ink. He had to fill this empty space, and it was at a moment when he wasn't really keen on doing a lot, so he did another *Boredom Loop*. I remember it as much bigger than the 1969 version. Celebrating boredom was something that I was very interested in. It was in Alighiero Boetti's work too. This mentality is strongly present in our *Equilibres* series. As an artist, if you are always just receptive to the things with which the world entertains you and make your work in response to them, then for me that's not so interesting. The moment when the higher beings are not talking to you, the moment when you are disconnected and go into this deep boredom ... this is really a great experience. And then you go from there ...

Godfrey Yes, it's interesting to think that Polke's *Boredom Loop* came at the end of the 1960s after nearly a decade of painting things around him – foodstuffs, consumables, printed newspaper photographs of holiday destinations and exotic icons, lovers. All these fascinating images. And then you get to boredom. Where do you think it leads him to?

Fischli It's connected in a way to *Höhere Wesen*, to the higher beings, for me. To celebrate boredom was also to be against the whole idea of the 'inspired' artist. As if he were saying: 'We can be bored instead.' It reminds me of the English punk band Buzzcocks in their song 'Boredom': 'I am living in this movie, but it doesn't move me.'[1]

1   The Buzzcocks, 'Boredom', on the album *Spiral Scratch* (1977).

Peter Fischli and Mark Godfrey, extract from 'Interview: A Contemporary Visionary (Part I) Peter Fischli on Sigmar Polke', *Tate Etc.*, no. 32 (Autumn 2014).
(http://www.tate.org.uk/context-comment/articles/contemporary-visionary-part-i)

Jon Savage
England's Dreaming: Anarchy, Sex Pistols, Punk Rock and Beyond//1991

[…] 'The day we wrote "Boredom"', says Pete Shelley, 'Howard was working a night shift at the tie factory, and during the night he'd written these words. I looked at these words and before he went to bed, I wrote the music.' The words were straight out of Ouspensky: 'I've taken this extravagant journey or so it seems to me. I just came from nowhere and I'm going straight back there.' […]

Here also was the everlasting present that had always been pop culture's ideal state and which now found its perfect expression. As Richard Boon wrote later: 'History was burning up. Every second a palpable threat to *being*, a serried, serious hazard to health and *becoming*, a spur to action.' The best records of that time remain those which retain the flavour of this intensity. Time seemed to be accelerating and the only way to freeze the instant was with a snapshot. 'That winter', Boon continues, 'something that had been striving to give birth to itself was beginning to retreat, and there was a feeling that if there was nothing else, there should be a record. The Buzzcocks' phenomenon was desperately unskilled with no industry experience at all, and no resources. It just seemed worth documenting the activity, perhaps as the end result, perhaps the only result.'

In February, the Buzzcocks released their first record, *Spiral Scratch*, on their own label, New Hormones. 'There were no record labels up in Manchester then', says Howard Devoto, 'it's the question of ambition. A lot of people in our situation would have realized, hey, there's something happening here. But we had some other sort of wherewithal, which made us borrow money from Pete's dad, book a recording studio and have records made.'

The picture sleeve of *Spiral Scratch* shows the four youths crowding to get into the picture, as if it were their last. 'There was a feeling amongst the group and myself that the record could illustrate part of the "do it yourself" xerox/cultural polemic that had been generated', says Boon. 'I took the cover picture on the steps of some statue in Manchester Piccadilly with a Polaroid, which was a joke: a very Walter Benjamin, art-in-the-age-of-mechanical-reproduction sort of joke. It was instant replay.' […]

Produced with a hint of ambience by Martin Hannett, the four songs (despite Devoto's reservations about his 'Mickey Mouse, fake cockney' voice) summed up the new aesthetic in phrases that leapt out like the distorted treble of the guitar from a speaker.

'I'm living in this movie, but it doesn't move me', Devoto gabbled in disgust. The Buzzcocks spoke of life as a nagging itch, of 'whining in the dining room', of friends who 'keep me pissing adrenalin'. The keyword 'boredom' had been relocated to England's recession: 'Now I can stand austerity but it gets a little much, when there's all those livid things you never get to touch.'

'I thought Howard's lyrics were very funny', says Boon. 'The period of Buzzcocks with Howard was difficult for people to digest because there was a lot of confusion about the ideas. The humour in Punk has been lost: 'Boredom' was satire, taking the piss out of the whole scene. It was deceptive. Boredom had been a feeling in currency by the time it became a word in currency.'

Yet the Buzzcocks' glee at finding their voice turned facetiousness into liberation: 'Boredom' was broken in half by the siren sound of a perfect, two-note guitar solo. 'I just played the two notes and we all fell about laughing, so we kept it in', says Pete Shelley. 'I'd been in these sub-Heavy Metal bands before, so really Punk evolved from sub-Heavy Metal played badly. That's what it was, fast riffs and singing over the top.'

The implications of *Spiral Scratch* were enormous. There had always been independent record companies, such as Joe Meek's Triumph or Andrew Loog Oldham's Immediate, but they were, in the main, small companies trying to be big, like Island or Virgin. Chiswick and Stiff were releasing Punk-related material, but not as if from within: what was so perfect about the Buzzcocks' EP was that its aesthetics were perfectly combined with the means of production. [...]

Jon Savage, extracts from *England's Dreaming: Anarchy, Sex Pistols, Punk Rock and Beyond* (New York: St. Martin's Press, 1991) 198, 296–7.

Dan Graham
The Producer as Artist//1988

Malcolm McLaren is a typical product of the British art school system. At 42 years of age, he is from the generation caught between the radical movements of the late sixties (Paris '68 and the American counter-culture) as well as Pop and conceptual art's strategies for confronting mass, commercial culture. He is both a Pop artist and hippie entrepreneur. As a rock manager, he automatically follows in the footsteps of American disc jockey Alan Freed, whose manipulation made rock 'n' roll a commercial form of music identified with white, urban, male teenage rebellion. His other predecessor is Brian Epstein, Liverpool record shop owner, intellectual businessman, but in McLaren's words, 'a pathetic (homosexual) closet case'. Both Freed and Epstein (like McLaren) were Jewish. Both had a perverse attraction for adolescent sexuality. Both appeared 'revolutionary' in the way they exploited the media for their own purposes. Both men died tragically, victimized by the media in revenge for their earlier exploitation of it.

In 1974, McLaren went to New York and attempted to manage the New York Dolls: 'I tried to turn them into something that could be a little … dangerous. The Vietnam war was about to end. I said … red was the colour … let's use Mao and … the hammer and sickle … and use all the things that America right now is arrogant about and … make it an event.' Applying this Situationist idea of public spectacle to the group's performances, he designed completely red outfits for the band, who performed against a background of the hammer and sickle. After the Dolls had disbanded, McLaren, who had been influenced by the emerging New York City 'punk rock' scene – the Ramones, Richard Hell and the Voidoids, Patti Smith – decided to apply the 'punk' style to a more English, political context. He created the Sex Pistols out of 'street people', non-musicians who hung about his boutique *Sex* on the King's Road, basing their early songs on the premise that rock is a means of defining a new class, one which Marx hadn't conceived of – youth.

Many of McLaren's ideas derive from Situationism, most obviously the notion that alienation has its roots in the problem of leisure-time and consumption rather than in the contradictions implicit within production. Another Situationist concept, that of the society as spectacle, influenced other key figures of the sixties, notably Abbie Hoffman, whose media-type radicalism was aimed at transforming the passivity of the hippies; Jean-Luc Godard, who used the interview form in Le Gai Savoir to examine the subversiveness of the youth as a class; and Andy Warhol, whose idea that in the future everyone will be famous for fifteen minutes, can be detected in McLaren's creation of anti-stars Johnny Rotten and Sid Vicious.

In the early 1950s, economic changes brought about a new category of consumer, the adolescent, and a new ideology, rock 'n' roll. No longer required after school as an entity within the increasingly automated, productive sphere, teenagers were, in effect, a new class with a huge buying power and little responsibility to the Protestant work-ethic of their elders. Then, as the concept of total leisure turned to boredom, teenagers' understanding of 'freedom' led to revolt, or at least to pseudo-revolt. But adult society must be tolerant; the simple fact is that teenagers and rock music are essential to the economy.

Rock is the first musical form to be totally commercial and consumer-exploitative. It is largely produced by adults for the purpose of exploiting a vast adolescent market whose consciousness it manipulates through radio, film, magazines and television. The industry doesn't care if the message of rock is anarchistic or anti-society as long as it can make money from the music. Yet, at the same time, rock expresses the real ideology of adolescent culture. Although exploited, rock culture redefines the codes of music. Intermediaries from the adult world, such as Alan Freed, play an ambiguous role. On the one hand, he can be seen as a Moses-like, martyred prophet leading the teenagers toward a new musical religion; on the other, he can be viewed as an exploiter and profiteer who manipulated the desires of innocent youths.

Moreover, rock is the first commercial form of music which contains this self-conscious knowledge within its structure. Rock stars, who are both real adolescents and fictions of the entertainment world, become models for a new class which refuses to grow up – the myth of James Dean is exemplary. Taking momentary pleasures of the body to their limits transcends the forces of history and death. Pleasure is oblivion; there are no moral consequences. Death is a technique to achieve fame and eternity.

McLaren obviously saw the consequences of this 'generation gap' as being potentially revolutionary, an inbuilt anarchistic mechanism to disrupt the system. Rock music, he said:

> could change youth into becoming a continuous rebellion … If you're a manager of a rock 'n' roll band … you [can be] a hit-and-run provocateur of new political solutions within youth as a class and within media as such … If you can divorce youth from its seniors … you have a new class [music] which can engineer a solution in which these kids can come together for the purpose of creating as much havoc as possible and changing their lives. […]

Dan Graham, extract from 'The Producer as Artist' (written between 1978 and 1988 and published in various versions), in *Impresario: Malcolm McLaren and the British New Wave*, ed. Paul Taylor (New York: The New Museum of Contemporary Art/Cambridge, Massachusetts: The MIT Press, 1988) 61–3.

Greil Marcus
The Last Sex Pistols Concert … //1989

Now identified with those who had the money and the corporate affiliations to secure the most sophisticated and arcane tools, rock 'n' roll became an old story: a parody of the time had a rock star demanding that his label fund the recording of his next album in outer space, but it didn't come off as a parody. Rock 'n' roll became an ordinary social fact, like a commute or a highway construction project. It became a habit, a structure, an invisible oppression.

A mythical era even as it unfolded, the sixties were based in the belief that since everything was true, everything was possible. Among rock stars, that utopian ideology was by the 1970s reduced to a well-heeled solipsism. On the terms of the barefoot solipsism of extermination camp survival, even a fantasy of resistance – which by its nature almost had to be a fantasy of collectivity, of solidarity – was utopian; insisting on the sensitivity of the individual as the source of all value, rock stars made a utopia out of solipsism. Like movie stars, they had made so much money that they remained untouched by and uninterested in what was happening in the world, and their renderings of a life of ease or of small problems proved attractive to a very large audience. There was no need for change; 'change' began to seem like an old-fashioned, sixties word. The chaos in society at large called for a music of permanence and reassurance; in the pop world, time stood still. For years that seemed like decades, you could turn on the radio with the assurance that you would hear James Taylor's 'Fire and Rain', Led Zeppelin's 'Stairway to Heaven', the Who's 'Behind Blue Eyes', Rod Stewart's 'Maggie May'. It was all right; they were good songs.

Some people began to lose their taste for surprise; others had never known it. 'People pay to see others believe in themselves', Kim Gordon of the New York punk band Sonic Youth wrote in 1983. 'On stage, in the midst of rock 'n' roll, many things happen and anything can happen, whether people come as voyeurs or come to submit to the moment.' Such words would not have been written in the mid 1970s, when people paid to see others believe that others believed in them. As the concerts of the time ended, fans stood up, lit matches, held them high: they were praying.

It was 1974. Malcolm McLaren was briefly in the United States, managing the New York Dolls, then on their last legs. They had wandered into his shop, played him their records; he'd laughed. 'I couldn't believe how anybody could be so bad', he said long after, citing the moment as the inspiration for the Sex Pistols. 'The fact that they were so bad suddenly hit me with such force that I began to realize, "I'm laughing, I'm talking to these guys, I'm looking at them, and I'm laughing with them"; and I was suddenly impressed by the fact that I was no longer concerned with whether you could play well. Whether you were able to even know about rock 'n' roll to the extent that you were able to write songs properly wasn't important any longer … The Dolls really impressed upon me that there was something else. There was something wonderful. I thought how brilliant they were to be this bad.'

No doubt a year later McLaren would be playing Dolls records for the Sex Pistols, just as two decades before Sam Phillips had played old blues records for his new rockabilly singers. A banner McLaren painted up and hoisted over the Dolls' last stages captured the dead time they never escaped: 'WHAT ARE THE POLITICS OF BOREDOM?'

It was, once removed, a situationist slogan. 'Boredom is always counterrevolutionary', the situationists had liked to say. McLaren's question mark was his way of asking how much power might be secreted in the slogans he put such stock in; to find the answer, you had to use the slogans. 'Boredom is always counterrevolutionary' – the line was typical of the situationist style, of its voice, a blindside paradox of dead rhetoric and ordinary language floated just this side of non sequitur, the declarative statement turning into a question as you heard it: what does this mean?

You already know, the situationists had answered: all you lack is the consciousness of what you know. Our project is nothing more than a seductive, subversive restatement of the obvious: 'Our ideas are in everyone's mind.' Our ideas about how the world works, about why it must be changed, are in everyone's mind as sensations almost no one is willing to translate into ideas, so we will do the translating. And that is all we have to do to change the world.

Boredom, to the situationists, was a supremely modern phenomenon, a modern form of control. In feudal times and for the first century of the Industrial Revolution, drudgery and privation produced numbing fatigue and horrible misery, no mystery, just a God-given fact: 'In Adam's fall so sinned we all', and as for those few who knew neither fatigue nor misery, it was easier for a camel to pass through the eye of a needle than for a rich man to enter heaven. As the situationists saw modernity, limited work and relative abundance, city planning and the welfare state produced not happiness but depression and boredom. With God missing, people felt their condition not exactly as a fact, but simply as a fatalism devoid of meaning, which separated every man and woman from every other, which threw all people back upon themselves. I'm not happy – what's wrong with me?

Fatalism is acceptance: 'Que sera, sera' is always counterrevolutionary. But as the situationists understood the modern world, boredom was less a question of work than of leisure. As they set out in the 1950s work seemed to be losing its hold on life; 'automation' and 'cybernetics' were wonderful new words. Leisure time was expanding – and in order to maintain their power, those who ruled, whether capitalist directors in the West or communist bureaucrats in the East, had to ensure that leisure was as boring as the new forms of work. More boring, if leisure was to replace work as the locus of everyday life, a thousand times more. What could be more productive of an atomized, hopeless fatalism than the feeling that one is deadened precisely where one ought to be having fun?

The eight men and women who gathered in the Italian town of Cosio d'Arroscia on 27 July 1957 to found the Situationist International pledged themselves to intervene in a future they believed to be on the verge of banishing both material necessity and individual autonomy. Modern technology had raised the spectre of a world in which 'work' – employment, wage labour, whatever tasks were performed because someone else said they had to be – might soon be no more than a fairy tale out of the Brothers Grimm. In a new world of unlimited leisure each individual might construct a life, just as in the old world a few privileged artists had constructed their representations of what life could be. It was an old dream, the dream of the young Karl Marx – every man his own artist! – but those who owned the present saw the future far more clearly than any of the sodden leftist sects claiming Marx's legacy. Those who ruled were reorganizing social life not merely to maintain their control, but to intensify it; modern technics was a two-edged sword, a means to the domination of the free field of abundance and leisure that revolutionaries had fantasized for five hundred years. Thus boredom. Misery led to resentment, which sooner or later found its rightful target, those who ruled. Boredom was a haze, a confusion, and finally the ultimate mode of control, self-control, alienation perfected: a bad conscience.

In modern society, leisure (What do I want to do today?) was replaced by entertainment (What is there to see today?). The potential fact of all possible freedoms was replaced by a fiction of false freedom: I have enough time and money to see whatever there is to see, whatever there is to see others do. Because this freedom was false, it was unsatifying, it was boring. Because it was boring, it left whoever was unsatisfied to contemplate his or her inability to respond to what, after all, was a hit show. It's a good show, but I feel dead: my God, what's wrong with me? It was leisure culture that produced boredom – produced it, marketed it, took the profits, reinvested them. So the world was going to be changed, announced the first number of *Internationale situationniste* in June 1958, '*because we don't want to be bored* … raging and ill-informed youth, well-off adolescent rebels lacking a point of view but far from lacking a cause – boredom is what they all have in common. The situationists will execute the judgment contemporary leisure is pronouncing against itself.'

The situationists saw boredom as a social pathology; they looked for its negation among sociopaths. In the pages of their journal, lunatic criminals and rioters without manifestos sometimes seem like the only allies the writers are willing to embrace. The situationists meant to define a stance, not an ideology, because they saw all ideologies as alienations, transformations of subjectivity into objectivity, desire into a power that rendered the individual powerless: 'There is no such thing as situationism', they said for years. The world was a structure of alienations and ideologies, of hierarchies and bureaucracies, each of which they saw as a version of the other; thus they celebrated a madman's slashing of a famous painting as a symbolic revolt against a bureaucratically administered alienation in which the ideology of the masterpiece reduced whoever looked at it to nothing. In the same way, they understood the responsible parade monitor who tried to keep people in check during a march against the Vietnam War as a bureaucratic ideologue enforcing a split between desire and comportment – and as much the enemy as General William Westmoreland, or for that matter Ho Chi Minh. Both the painting and the war were hit shows; whether a visit to the museum or a march in the street, both turned the spending of free time into the consumption of repression. The masterpiece convinced you that truth and beauty were someone else's gift from God, the protest in favour of the struggle of the Vietnamese that revolution was a fact of someone else's life. Neither could ever be yours, and so you left each show diminished, with less than you had brought to it. That, the situationists said again and again, was why the show had to be stopped, and could be: just as the tiny humiliations inflicted by the parade monitor were the essence of oppression, a fanatic's exemplary act could prove that liberty was within everyone's grasp.

The situationists announced themselves as revolutionaries, interested only in freedom, and freedom can mean the licence to do anything, with consequences that are indistinguishable from murder, theft, looting, hooliganism, or littering – phenomena that, lacking anything better, the situationists were almost always ready to embrace as harbingers of revolution. But freedom can also mean the chance to discover what it is you truly want to do: to discover, as Edmund Wilson wrote in Paris in 1922, 'for what drama one's setting is the setting'. That too was what the situationists meant by leisure – and it was a lust not simply to discover but to create that drama that drove a twenty-five-year-old Parisian named Guy-Ernest Debord to gather artists and writers from France, Algeria, Italy, Denmark, Belgium, England, Scotland, Holland and West Germany into the Situationist International in 1957. In 1975, with the defunct SI no more than a legend to a few one-time 1960s art students and student radicals, that drama was what McLaren was still seeking. What were the politics of boredom? […]

Who could say that 'Fire and Rain', 'Stairway to Heaven', 'Behind Blue Eyes', and 'Maggie May' were not affirmations of freedom as they were made, and oppressions as they were used? Only those who refused to believe that the affirmation where freedom is grasped is rooted in a negation where freedom is glimpsed – and those people did not include McLaren and the Sex Pistols. Thus they damned rock 'n' roll as a rotting corpse: a monster of moneyed reaction, a mechanism for false consciousness, a system of self-exploitation, a theatre of glamourized oppression, a bore. Rock 'n' roll, Johnny Rotten would say, was only the first of many things the Sex Pistols came to destroy. And yet because the Sex Pistols had no other weapons, because they were fans in spite of themselves, they played rock 'n' roll, stripping it down to essentials of speed, noise, fury and manic glee no one had touched before.

They used rock 'n' roll as a weapon against itself. With all instruments but guitar, bass, drums and voice written off as effete, as elitist accoutrements of a professionalist cult of technique, it was a music best suited to anger and frustration, focusing chaos, dramatizing the last days as everyday life, ramming all emotions into the narrow gap between a blank stare and a sardonic grin. The guitarist laid down a line of fire to cover the singer, the rhythm section put in a pressure drop, and as a response to what was suddenly perceived as the totalitarian freeze of the modern world the music could seem like a version of it. It was also something new under the sun: a new sound.

Greil Marcus, extracts from 'The Last Sex Pistols Concert …', *Lipstick Traces: A Secret History of the Twentieth Century* (Cambridge, Massachusetts: Harvard University Press, 1989) 47–53, 56–7.

Dick Hebdige
Bleached Roots: Punks and White Ethnicity//1979

[…] The punk aesthetic, formulated in the widening gap between artist and audience, can be read as an attempt to expose glam rock's implicit contradictions. For example, the 'working classness', the scruffiness and earthiness of punk ran directly counter to the arrogance, elegance and verbosity of the glam rock superstars. However, this did not prevent the two forms from sharing a certain amount of common ground. Punk claimed to speak for the neglected constituency of white lumpen youth, but it did so typically in the stilted language of glam and glitter rock – 'rendering' working classness metaphorically in chains and hollow cheeks, 'dirty' clothing (stained jackets, tarty see-through blouses) and rough and ready diction. Resorting to parody, the blank generation, 'classified null by society' (Richard Hell, *NME*, 29 October 1977) described itself in bondage through an assortment of darkly comic signifiers – straps and chains, straitjackets and rigid postures. Despite its proletarian accents, punk's rhetoric was steeped in irony.

Punk thus represents a deliberately scrawled addendum to the 'text' of glam rock – an addendum designed to puncture glam rock's extravagantly ornate style. Punk's guttersnipe rhetoric, its obsession with class and relevance were expressly designed to undercut the intellectual posturing of the previous generation of rock musicians. This reaction in its turn directed the new wave towards reggae and the associated styles which the glam rock cult had originally excluded. Reggae attracted those punks who wished to give tangible form to their alienation. It carried the necessary conviction, the political bite, so obviously missing in most contemporary white music.

Dread, in particular, was an enviable commodity. It was the means with which to menace, and the elaborate freemasonry through which it was sustained and communicated on the street – the colours, the locks, the patois – was awesome and forbidding, suggesting as it did an impregnable solidarity, an asceticism born of suffering. The concept of dread provided a key to a whole secret language: an exotic semantic interior which was irrevocably closed against white Christian sympathies (i.e. blacks are just like us) while its very existence confirmed the worst white chauvinist fears (i.e. blacks are nothing like us).

But paradoxically it was here, in the exclusiveness of Black West Indian style, in the virtual impossibility of authentic white identification, that reggae's attraction for the punks was strongest. As we have seen, the clotted language of Rastafarianism was deliberately opaque. It had grown out of patois, and patois itself had been spoken for centuries beneath the Master's comprehension. This was a language capable of piercing the most respectfully inclined white ear, and the themes of Back to Africa and Ethiopianism, celebrated in reggae, made no concessions to the sensibilities of a white audience. Reggae's blackness was proscriptive. It was an alien essence, a foreign body which implicitly threatened mainstream British culture from within and as such it resonated with punk's adopted values – 'anarchy', 'surrender' and 'decline'.

For the punks to find a positive meaning in such a blatant disavowal of Britishness amounted to a symbolic act of treason which complemented, indeed completed, the sacrilegious programme undertaken in punk rock itself (c.f. the Sex Pistols' 'Anarchy in the UK' and 'God Save the Queen', Jordan's rendition of 'Rule Britannia' in Derek Jarman's film *Jubilee*). The punks capitulated to alienation, losing themselves in the unfamiliar contours of an alien form. In this way, the very factors which had dictated the skinheads' withdrawal in the late 60s facilitated the punks' involvement a decade later. Just as the mod and skinhead styles had obliquely reproduced the 'cool' look and feel of the West Indian rude boys and were symbolically placed in the same ideal milieux (the Big City, the violent slum), so the punk aesthetic can be read in part as a white 'translation' of black 'ethnicity'.

This parallel white 'ethnicity' was defined through contradictions. On the one hand it centred, however iconoclastically, on traditional notions of Britishness (the Queen, the Union Jack, etc.). It was 'local'. It emanated from the recognizable locales of Britain's inner cities. It spoke in city accents. And yet, on the other hand, it was predicated upon a denial of place. It issued out of nameless housing estates, anonymous dole queues, slums-in-the-abstract. It was blank, expressionless, rootless. In this the punk subculture can be contrasted against the West Indian styles which had provided the basic models. Whereas urban black youths could place themselves through reggae 'beyond the pale' in an imagined elsewhere (Africa, the West Indies) the punks were tied to present time. They were bound to a Britain which had no foreseeable future.

But this difference could be magically elided. By simple sleight of hand, the coordinates of time and place could be dissolved, transcended, converted into signs. Thus it was that the punks turned towards the world a dead white face which was there and yet not 'there'. Like the myths of Roland Barthes, these 'murdered victims' – emptied and inert – also had an alibi, an elsewhere, literally 'made up' out of vaseline and cosmetics, hair dye and mascara. But paradoxically, in the case of the punks, this 'elsewhere' was also a nowhere – a twilight zone – a zone constituted out of negativity. Like André Breton's Dada, punk might seem to 'open all the doors' but these doors 'gave onto a circular corridor' (Breton, 'Introduction to an Anthology of Surrealist Poetry', 1937).

Once inside this desecrated circle, punk was forever condemned to act out alienation, to mime its imagined condition, to manufacture a whole series of subjective correlatives for the official archetypes of the 'crisis of modern life': the unemployment figures, the Depression, the Westway, Television, etc. Converted into icons (the safety pin, the rip, the mindless lean and hungry look) these paradigms of crisis could live a double life, at once fictional and real. They reflected in a heightened form a perceived condition: a condition of unmitigated exile, voluntarily assumed. But whereas exile had a specific meaning, implied a specific (albeit magical) solution in the context of Rastafarianism and Negro history, when applied metaphorically to *British* white youth it could only delineate a hopeless condition. It could neither promise a future nor explain a past. Trapped in the paradox of 'divine' subordination like Saint Genet, who 'chooses' the Fate which has been bestowed upon him, the punks dissembled, dying to recreate themselves in caricature, to 'dress up' their Destiny in its true colours, to substitute the diet for hunger, to slide the ragamuffin look ('unkempt' but meticulously coutured) between poverty and elegance. Punk, having found an adequate reflection in the shards of broken glass, having spoken through the holes in purposefully torn T-shirts, having brought dishonour on the family name, found itself again at the point from which it had started: as a 'lifer' in 'solitary' despite the fierce tattoos. […]

We can now return to consider the meaning of that uneasy relation between rock and reggae characteristic of punk. We have seen how punk's belligerent insistence on class and relevance was at least partly determined by the ethereal excesses of the glam rock cult, and that the particular form this insistence took (the vagrant aesthetic, a singular music) was also indirectly influenced by the subcultural styles of the black immigrant community. This dialectical movement from white to black and back again is by no means solely confined to the punk subculture. On the contrary [...], the same movement is 'captured' and displayed in the styles of each of the spectacular postwar, working-class youth cultures. More particularly, it runs through rock music (and earlier, jazz) from the mid 50s onwards, dictating each successive shift in rhythm, style and lyrical content. We are now in a position to describe this dialectic.

As the music and the various subcultures it supports or reproduces assume rigid and identifiable patterns, so new subcultures are created which demand or produce corresponding mutations in musical form. These mutations in their turn occur at those moments when forms and themes imported from contemporary black music break up (or 'overdetermine') the existing musical structure and force its elements into new configurations. For instance, the stabilization of rock in the early 1960s (vapid high school bop, romantic ballads, gimmicky instrumentals) encouraged the mods to migrate to soul and ska, and the subsequent reaffirmation of black themes and rhythms by white r & b and soul bands contributed to the resurgence of rock in the mid sixties. Similarly, at the moment when glam rock had exhausted the permutations available within its own distinctive structure of concerns, the punks moved back to earlier, more vigorous forms of rock (i.e. to the 50s and mid 60s when the black influences had been strongest) and forward to contemporary reggae (dub, Bob Marley) in order to find a music which reflected more adequately their sense of frustration and oppression.

However, here as elsewhere in punk, the mutation seems deliberate, constructed. Perhaps, given the differences between them, there can be no easy synthesis of the two languages of rock and reggae. The fundamental lack of fit between these two languages (dress, dance, speech, music, drugs, style, history) exposed in the emergence of black ethnicity in reggae, generates a peculiarly unstable dynamic within the punk subculture. This tension gave punk its curiously petrified quality, its paralysed look, its 'dumbness' which found a silent voice in the smooth moulded surfaces of rubber and plastic, in the bondage and robotics which signify 'punk' to the world. For, at the heart of the punk subculture, forever arrested, lies this frozen dialectic between black and white cultures – a dialectic which beyond a certain point (i.e. ethnicity) is incapable of renewal, trapped, as it is, within its own history, imprisoned within its own irreducible antinomies. [...]

Dick Hebdige, extracts from 'Bleached Roots: Punks and White Ethnicity', *Subculture: The Meaning of Style* (London and New York: Methuen, 1979) 63, 64–6, 69–70 [footnotes not included].

Richard Hell
CBGB as a Physical Space//2006

[…] Its physical space, capacity about 350, has stayed amazingly unchanged. The front two-thirds – entranceway and bar area – of the single long room of the club proper, along with the toilet areas downstairs at the rear, are the same as they always have been. In the venue's first year or two there were a few minor rearrangements made in back, enlarging the stage and dressing-rooms, and installing a first class sound system; but the basic layout and construction, as well as the furniture, lighting and overall atmosphere, have not changed at all since 1974, except that the graffiti has gotten thicker.

The graffiti has gotten thicker, but that happened quickly too. It only took three or four years for the place to acquire the garish veneer within that's become its distinguishing mark: not the place's deathless overall wino-dive griminess, not the long procession of compact neon beer signs dangling like corrupt flags or coats of nauseous arms above the narrow public walkway behind the bar stools, not the blunt, ribbed, white tunnel-roof of canvas overhead outside with its innocuously ugly 'CBGB and OMFUG' logo, all of which stylelessly stylistic elements are virtually unchanged since Hilly Kristal renamed as CBGB what had once been the Palace Bar (adjunct booze hole to the Palace Hotel flophouse next door) … No, it would be a separate consequence of Hilly's stunning and consequential inertia that would ultimately proclaim his physical domain most powerfully – namely, his lack of interest in removing any defacement of the club's interior.

The result of that ultra-passivity regarding decor is the fantastic, ghostly, jewel-smear-for-walls of a palace-for-fun-seeking-children […]. Analytically, all those spectra of marker scrawls, blurred spray-paint swaths and day-glo stickers comprising the interior planes of a shimmering temple of impulse-to-assert, can't truly be seen as 'self-assertion'. It's more like mob behaviour, like what goes on in a mosh pit, or like blank genetic reflexes, than anything to do with anyone's 'self'. It's just about leaving a mark, any mark. The specific words scrawled on the walls are irrelevant. Granted, a viewer almost can't help going in for close-ups and deciphering statements here and there, but the literal messages are unworthy of the overall effect, and interfere with it, like hearing Lindsay Lohan's words on a talk show. (The great '70s street graffiti kids, incidentally, who were of course in a different class altogether, would seem to have concluded the same, quickly evolving tags that were pure style, almost impossible to read.)

Above all, though, the effect of the surfaces of CBGB's dark, crazed insides is eerie, it's haunting. It's like a dead-quiet, chillingly colourful cemetery. Or autopsy:

all of compacted history sliced open. It's not so much that the graffiti evoke the endless procession of individual kids who've attended the club, but that they evoke their absence, their faceless selves buried under the next pretty layer of pointless proclamation. The walls are an onslaught of death and futility as much as they are of life and vitality. The kids believed themselves to be unique individuals; the walls they covered with that claim are the proof that it's a delusion. Or is this what we knew all along, and the walls are sites of revelling in it, revelling in undifferentiation? Because it does seem sweet and innocent and loveable too.

Naturally, the graffiti in CBGB also have a lot in common with the style of music that made the club famous. It's not about an intellectual argument, it's not about opinions, it's about a condition, about being young and hungry; about energy, anger and sex; pure formless assertion. Or not: It's about boredom and frustration. But boredom iterated and reiterated, become drunk, passed out unconscious, and then beginning again. Funnily. It's horrible, but beautifully horrible, like modern ghostly Japanese horror movies with their derelict, peeling, void-riddled spaces; or like the abandoned west side docks of 70s New York where illicit, if somewhat defiantly public, sex was taking place everywhere amongst the filth and scribbled-on rotting wood. It's about abandon and abandonment made visible, and become the environment for where it's made audible as well. It's about ennui and inertia and their perfect realization in violence and sex. It's so pretty it hurts.

Richard Hell, extract from 'CBGB as a Physical Space', *CBGB: Decades of Graffiti* (New York: Mark Batty Publishers, 2006); reprinted in Hell, *Massive Pissed Love* (Berkeley: Soft Skull Press, 2015) 156–7.

Geoff Waite
On the Politics of Boredom (A Communist Pastiche)//1992

WHAT ARE THE POLITICS OF BOREDOM? According to the 'secret history of the twentieth century', as related by Greil Marcus, this was the slogan painted on a banner over the last performances of the proto-punk rock band The New York Dolls (1974), at the instigation of their impresario Malcolm McLaren.[1] […] [I]t is important to recall that the Sex Pistols themselves (who were soon to replace the Dolls as McLaren's major weapon in the politics of boredom and/or, if you prefer, merely his latest commodity at the time) consistently dissociated themselves (more or less seriously) from McLaren's role as their spokesman and from his various agendas. This apparent spat is obviously important (*mutatis mutandis*) since a fundamental, particularly stubborn problem of all politics involves the relationship between leaders and led, and the question whether there ought to be leaders in the first place.

Interviewed in the spring 1992 issue of *Creem* ('America's Only Rock & Roll Magazine'), the following exchange took place with Johnny Rotten/John Lydon:

> *Creem* Is Jamie Reid [who designed all the Sex Pistols' album covers, t-shirts and posters] still around?
>
> *John Lydon* He better not be, for his sake. He's another one of those phonies. All of those people who worked with Malcolm are. Spoiled students, I call them. They always struck me that way and they haven't changed. They don't really care about people. They care about their Decisions, their Ideologies. See, they're from that middle-class English way and when they meet real working-class people they cannot tolerate us. We're not allowed to be intelligent. We're meant to be stupid and easily manipulated, and if we're not then we have to be dispensed with.[2]

Now, this description of himself as 'working class' may seem disingenuous (or at least opportunistic and essentialistic) coming from a former leader of the truly great Sex Pistols and a current leader of much less great but also much more lucrative Public Image Ltd. (PiL), and whose listeners are more middle class than working class. In any case, it is important to raise the stakes beyond what Rotten/Lydon offers here.

Compare and contrast the testimony of Mike Lefevre – the steelworker in Cicero, Illinois, who is the lead-off witness in Studs Terkel's *Working* (1972). In an interview conducted in the early 1970s (before the Sex Pistols shot their glorious wad), Lefevre reflected on the mind- and body-numbing boredom of his job, on the related issue of automation, and on the political implications of both. (Keep in mind, listening to this steelworker, that even computers have metal in them that is still mined by miners who can still strike with powerful effect, that they are still processed by other workers who can also shut down an industry, a nation, etc.) It is difficult to tell whether Lefevre stands on the cusp between pre-capitalist mode of production and Fordism, or on the cusp between Fordism and post-Fordism; in fact, the point is that (back in the early 1970s) he straddles both at once, in the nonsynchronous space that is postmodernity. Lefevre told Terkel: 'It's hard to take pride in a bridge you're never gonna cross, in a door you're never gonna open. You're mass-producing things and you never see the end result of it. I worked for a trucker one time. And I got this tiny satisfaction when I loaded a truck. At least I could see the truck depart loaded. In a steel mill, forget it. You don't see where nothing goes.' About automation, however, Lefevre is more ambivalent. With this ambivalence, he takes a step beyond Rotten/Lydon's squabbles with his former impresario, and he politicizes boredom – not just with fascinating self-contradictions but also directly and disturbingly:

> Automation? Depends on how it's applied. It frightens me it if puts me out on the street. It doesn't frighten me if it shortens my work week. You read that little thing: what are you going to do when this computer replaces you? Blow up computers. [*Laughs.*] Really. Blow up computers. I'll be goddamned if a computer is gonna eat before I do! I want milk for my kids and beer for me. Machines can either liberate man or enslave 'im, because they're pretty neutral. It's man who has the bias to put the thing one place or another.

Then, after reflecting a moment about his own kids' future and a young Leftist coworker intellectual (something of a Trotskyist, it seems, much as Mike has neo-Luddite tendencies), Lefevre continues:

> The twenty-hour week is a possibility today. The intellectuals, they always say there are potential Lord Byrons, Walt Whitmans, Roosevelts, Picassos working in construction or steel mills or factories. But I don't think they believe it. I think what they're afraid of is the potential Hitlers and Stalins that are there too. The people in power fear the leisure man. Not just the United States. Russia's the same. What do you think would happen in this country if, for one year, they experimented and gave everybody a twenty-hour week? How do they know that the guy who digs [George] Wallace today doesn't try to resurrect Hitler tomorrow? Or the guy who is mildly disturbed at pollution doesn't decide to go to General Motors and shit on the guy's desk? You can become a fanatic if you had the time. The whole thing is time. That is, I think, one reason rich kids tend to be fanatic about politics: they have time. Time, that's the important thing.[3]

So it is again that the politics of boredom has to do with the political economy of time, as well as factory and computer space. Cultural politics is undoubtedly involved, too, since the fundamental task of the culture industry in capitalism (the Sex Pistols momentarily blasted off that depressing-repressing-suppressing scale of co-option and commodification on which PiL is closer to the centre) – and in 'existing socialism' as the world has known it – is to make sure that leisure time activities are less interesting, more boring than work, appearances exactly to the contrary.

Beginning at least by the 1950s and fuelled by the Cold War, 'capitalist directors in the West or communist bureaucrats in the East … had to ensure that leisure was as boring as the new forms of work', including not only automation but cybernetics.[4] In other words: a battle not against boredom, but for it. If leisure was experienced as really less boring and more exciting than work, there'd be hell to pay at work – big trouble down the line both in the so-called Workers' Paradise *and* in the dys/utopia known as the Land of the Free, Home of the Brave. Just as 'the triumph of advertising in the culture industry is that consumers feel compelled to buy and use its products even though they see through them.'[5] 'I know [it is not true], but nonetheless …[I believe it and act accordingly]' – this is a main psycho-social mechanism by which real capitalist and so-called socialist cynicism is internalized, embodied, incarnated, and above all incorporated in and by the politics of boredom.[6]

According to Karl Marx in *Capital*, just as to Mike Lefevre in Cicero, in factory work, the *'lightening of the labour, even, becomes a sort of torture*, since the machine does not free the labourer from work, but deprives the work of all interest' (my emphasis).[7] Antonio Gramsci (the leading militant and theorist of the Italian Communist Party in his Fascist prison cell in the 1930s, fighting boredom, depression, and physical distress by struggling to produce something, he said, '*für ewig*', for eternity) still held out hope for a different transformation in Marx's worker-cyborg. Anticipating Roy Batty and his revolutionary cell of 'more human than human' cyborg slaves in *Blade Runner* (who among other things got bored with the thought of dying), Gramsci argued that learning to do a task by rote (Gramsci's examples are athletes and pre-modern mediaeval copyists as well as the Taylorized worker), is not necessarily 'the spiritual death of man'. Gramsci continued:

> The only thing that is completely mechanicized is the physical gesture; the memory of the trade, reduced to simple gestures repeated at an intense rhythm, 'nestles' in the muscular and nervous centres and leaves the brain free and unencumbered for other occupations … American industrialists have understood all too well this dialectic inherent in the new industrial methods … that 'unfortunately' the worker remains a man and even that during his work he thinks more, or at least has greater opportunities for thinking, once he has overcome the crisis of adaptation without being eliminated: and not only does the worker think, but the fact that he gets no immediate satisfaction from his work and realizes that they are trying to reduce him to a trained gorilla, can lead him into a train of thought that is far from conformist.[8]

The culture industry, the Society of the Spectacle, swings directly into this action as well: i.e. the production of maximum boredom in the guise of maximum excitement. But the main point is that if Mike Lefevre is right, what Gramsci's factory worker is (was) thinking about all along is (was) not necessarily a good thing, a communist thing. [...]

Whereas Gramsci sometimes seems to promote or at least legitimate more factory work as a condition or at least possibility for freedom, in volume three of *Capital* Marx suggested (in apparent tension with his other thesis that 'the lightening of the labour, even, becomes a sort of torture') that the condition for freedom was less work. In a famous key passage he wrote:

> Just as the savage must wrestle with Nature to satisfy his wants, to maintain and reproduce life, so must civilized man, and he must do so in all social formations and under all possible modes of production. With his development this realm of physical necessity expands as a result of his wants; but, at the same time, the forces of production which satisfy these wants also increase. Freedom in this field can only consist in socialized man, the associated producers, rationally regulating their interchange with Nature, bringing it under their common control, instead of being ruled by it as by the blind forces of Nature; and achieving this with the least expenditure of energy and under conditions most favourable to, and worthy of, their human nature. But it nonetheless still remains a realm of necessity. Beyond it begins that development of human energy which is an end in itself, the true realm of freedom, which, however, can blossom forth only with this realm of necessity as its basis. The shortening of the working-day is its basic prerequisite.[9]

It was precisely for this reason, however, that the Communist Gramsci deeply (rightly) mistrusted the economistic, social-democratic, reformist aspect of *Capital*, having dubbed the October Revolution 'the revolution against Karl Marx's *Capital*'.[10] But there are two main things to be said from the perspective of the politics of boredom. First, communists need to make hard decisions about whether it is more or rather less work that is revolutionary – and not just any work, but work or the refusal of work under post-Fordist, postmodern conditions. Put differently: When is boredom counter-revolutionary, when revolutionary? But the second and simpler point is: Karl and Toni, meet Johnny, Mike (and Ivan). For that matter, meet Malcolm.

And with this meeting or meetings (for both groups and epochs) we return yet again (but not eternally) to the question: 'What Are the Politics of Boredom?' We ask this question today somewhere *between* Fordism and post-Fordism, modernity and postmodernity, after socialism, and *ever deeper* in the all-digesting belly of the beast of Capital. How can one build real communist alternatives? Where does one look for alternatives to nascent, botched/isolated socialism as well as late, triumphantly swaggering capitalism? In the future but also partly in the past, if history is indeed the contestation of the present (to repeat: this is pretty much the only thing history is good for). Especially interesting in this regard are those sites where the politics of boredom is contested simultaneously in cultural politics and in political economy. Among many other such historical sites, Dada, Surrealism and Situationism may immediately come to mind. (So may 'cultural studies' and their cognates, though precisely as merely 'interdisciplinary' and 'cross-' or 'multicultural' academic pursuits, they to date lack contact with any economic base and hence with effective political struggle.) In a moment I want to consider the possibility (one of many, it is necessary to emphasize, all of which are at best necessary, never sufficient) of a postmodern and communist 'historical bloc', in this case between current 'popular culture', 'street fighters', 'cyberpunks' and readers of *Documents*. But first we need to consider some historical and theoretical precedents.

It is with Dada, surrealism and the Situationist International (SI) that the element of secrecy comes into the slogan 'What are the politics of boredom?' For, according to Marcus, 'It was, once removed, a Situationist slogan.' He continues:

> 'Boredom is always counter-revolutionary', the Situations had liked to say. McLaren's question mark was his way of asking how much power might be secreted in the slogans he put such stock in; to find the answer, you had to use the slogans. 'Boredom is always counter-revolutionary' – the line was typical of the Situationist style, of its voice, a blindside paradox of dead rhetoric and ordinary language floated just this side of non sequitur, the declarative statement turning into a question as you heard it: what does this mean? You already know, the Situationists had answered: all you lack is the consciousness of what you know. Our project is nothing more than a seductive, subversive restatement of the obvious: 'Our ideas are in everyone's mind'.[11]

Leaving its predecessors aside, the first issue of *Internationale situationniste* (June 1958) claimed to inaugurate 'a movement more liberating than the Surrealism of 1924'. The Situationists chose to situate themselves in terms of Surrealism in part because of its attempt to exceed both common reality and art, and in part because of the communist political commitment of some of its members. [...] Writing in 1958:

> For us, Surrealism has been only a beginning of a revolutionary experiment in culture, an experiment that almost immediately ground to a halt practically and theoretically. We have to go further. Why can we no longer be Surrealists? ... If we are not Surrealists it is because we don't want to be bored. Decrepit Surrealism, raging and ill-informed youth, well-off adolescent rebels lacking perspectives but

far from lacking a cause – boredom is what they all have in common. The Situationists will execute the judgement that contemporary leisure is pronouncing against itself.[12]

And (via McLaren, according to Greil Marcus and Jon Savage) the ensuing Situationist politics of boredom came to inform virtually all the lyrics of the Sex Pistols. But the problem of our own contemporary politics of boredom, if not politics per se, is that 'contemporary leisure' has not in fact 'pronounced judgement against itself', has not suicided itself. The SI (like McLaren and Lydon over a decade later) lived in holy (read also *middle-class*?) dread of being bored, or at the very least dreaded being boring. By a similar token, however, when listening to Mike Lefevre talk, a Marx or a Gramsci today, we ought not to be overly surprised that communism has yet to happen, yet to take root in the factory and globally, or that socialism and capitalism turned out to be really one and the same thing – notwithstanding the fact that the one has apparently triumphed, the other definitely failed at least in one major (undemocratic, command-economy) form. But this hardly means that communism is impossible or not worth fighting for. On the contrary.

But what, then, about the politics of boredom in this, our already 'post-contemporary' culture? Is there only one such politics? Are there many? Any? What is boredom? What is politics? As a communist (at a time when communism is, well, discredited to say the least, and for good as well as bad reasons), it seems obvious to me that all such questions have to be asked and answered at once *singularly* and *communally*. How boredom or politics are to be defined ontologically (what boredom is, what politics is) is not for one writer to decide or for this more or less ad hoc collective body – but rather for both. And for neither – to the extent that a singular/collective 'we' is also reaching out toward readers with their own more or less similar points of view, their own plans for further action [...].

'Politics' means not only the attempt to transform present life (as it – the definition and the life – has been at least since Aristotle), but also the more or less successful transformation of life without people's awareness that their lives have been transformed. [...] It is because politics is always also about economics (yes, sure, it is about other things too) that the politics of boredom is also about political economy and just plain capitalist economics. This basic point was once neatly summed up not only by Marx, Lenin and Gramsci but by the Motor City's own Iggy Pop and The Stooges, ventriloquizing the class enemy: 'I'm bored. I'm the Chairman of the Bored.'

Boredom, as Marcus and Savage point out, was indeed a ubiquitous theme and structure of punk music – its 'secret' complicity with the agendas of Situationism and primitive communism – from the Sex Pistols on. Not only Neil

Young and Crazy Horse ('Out of the blue, into the black / The king is gone but not forgotten / This is the story of Johnny Rotten') and Greil Marcus and Jon Savage but also *Rolling Stone*, *Creem*, *Spin* and (alas) *Mondo 2000* and (of course) several major recording companies still perceive and market rock as a series of footnotes to the Pistols, much as the history of Western philosophy is still said to be 'a series of footnotes' to Plato or Aristotle. *Cultural* power, at least, still comes for too many people on earth out of the barrel of a sex pistol. (Though most boredom has likely always been about sex and death, Eros and Thanatos.) Picking a lyric, a footnote almost at random, the chorus of a song by The Clash in 1977 proclaimed: 'I'm so bored with the USA / I'm so bored with the USA / But what can I do?' And the song continued: 'Yankee Detectives are always on the TV / 'Cos killers in America work seven days a week …'[13]

What to do, indeed, about the USA, its cops and soldiers, its producers, its brain police, its criminalization and militarization of society and culture? So asked, in the only way open to them, the people of South Central LA in 1992; and so ask we all, in our different or similar ways. Other lyrics by The Clash in 1977, directly inspired by riots in England ('London's burning / London's burning with boredom now / Dial 99999!'), flash to mind, then fade away:

> Black men gotta lot of problems / But they don't mind throwin' a brick / White people go to school / Where they teach you how to be thick / (Chorus: An' Everybody doin' / Just what they're told to / An' nobody wants / To go to jail / White Riot-White Riot-Riot of me own) / All the power is in the hands / Of people rich enough to buy it / While we walk the streets / Too chicken to even try it / (Repeat Chorus) / Are you taking over – or are you taking orders? / Are you moving backwards – or are you moving forwards?[14]

It ought to surprise nobody that when record company officials (sitting safely on the back benches as chairs began to fly in the Rainbow Theatre in May 1977) heard this version of *Forwards!, Vorwärts!, Avanti Popolo!* they moved quickly to get it on record, patented it, incorporated it. (And to this day The Clash and its subsequent incarnations have resisted better than most.) But the key question of the politics of boredom is: Are the riots, say, in Watts in 1966, at Notting Hill Carnival in 1976 and 1977, in Brixton in 1981, in The City of Quartz in 1992, in Soweto, and in the more or less permanent insurrection that is the South Bronx – are they not also preliminary postmodern communist revolutions not only against Karl Marx's *Capital* (and traditional socialist theory and politics) but also against CAPITAL ITSELF?

The Clash (like McLaren at the time, though at a different level of personal commitment) took the 'traditional' avant-gardist ('Modernist', 'Surrealist'?

'Situationist'? 'Leninist'?) position that a 'historical bloc' was possible and necessary. A *Clash Communiqué* as late as October 1985 reads: 'Wise MEN and street kids together make a GREAT TEAM ... but can the old system be BEAT?? no ... not without YOUR participation ... RADICAL social change begins on the STREET!! ... So if you're looking for some ACTION ... CUT THE CRAP and Get OUT There.'[15] Of course CUT THE CRAP, too, was commodified (the flip side of excessive voluntarism) as the name of a record, a poster, a tour. But the point is that not all aspects of modernist avant-gardism are bad. *Some* sort of 'team' is still required (necessary though insufficient) to push beyond cargo-cult rioting to revolution. It is true that urban rioters and anti-SWAT teams don't have leaders or loyalties in the traditional sense (in addition, the Bloods and the Crips called a truce, etc.), but look where it lands them/us and their/our society. The role as leaders for New Socialized Workers generally are promising but as yet equally ambiguous, equally ... modern. So where, then, might significant 'historical blocs' be found – in this, our politics of post-boredom ?

1 [footnote 15 in source] See Greil Marcus, *Lipstick Traces: A Secret History of the Twentieth Century* (London: Secker & Warburg, 1989) 49.
2 [16] Robert Seidenberg and John Lydon, 'Happiness is a Warm Pistol, or The Public Image of Lydon and Rotten', *Creem*, vol. 1, no. 3 (March 1992) 42. [...]
3 [17] Mike Lefevre, cited in Studs Terkel, *Working People Talk about What They Do All Day and How They Feel about What They Do* (New York: Pantheon Books, 1972) xxxiii–iv.
4 [18] Marcus, *Lipstick Traces*, op. cit., 50.
5 [19] Max Horkheimer and Theodor Adorno, *Dialectic of Enlightenment* (1944); trans. John Cumming (New York: Seabury Press, 1969) 167. [...]
6 [20] See Octave Mannoni, *Clefs pour l'imaginaire ou l'autre scène* (Paris: Seuil, 1969) 163-4; and Slavoj Zizek, *For They Know Not What They Do: Enjoyment as a Political Factor* (London and New York: Verso, 1991) 245-9. [...]
7 [21] Karl Marx, *Capital* (1867-87), trans. Samuel Moore and Edward Aveling (New York: International Publishers, 1967) vol. I, 422-3.
8 [22] *Selections from the Prison Notebooks of Antonio Gramsci*, ed. and trans. Quintin Hoare and Geoffrey Nowell Smith (New York: International Publishers, 1971) 309-10. [...]
9 [26] Marx, *Capital*, op. cit., vol. 3, 820.
10 [27] Antonio Gramsci, *Selections from Political Writings*, ed. Quintin Hoare and John Matthews (New York: International Publishers, 1977) 34.
11 [31] Marcus, *Lipstick Traces*, op. cit., 49-50.
12 [33] Anon., 'The Sound and the Fury' (1958), in *Situationist International Anthology*, ed. and trans. Ken Knabb (Berkeley: Bureau of Public Secrets, 1981) 42.
13 [34] The Clash, 'I'm So Bored with the USA' (1977). Epic/CBS Records, PET 36060.
14 [35] The Clash, 'London's Burning' and 'White Riot' (1977). Epic/CBS Records, PET 36060.

15 [36] *Clash Communiqué* (October 1985). […]

Geoff Waite, extract from 'On the Politics of Boredom: (A Communist Pastiche)', *Documents*, no. 1–2 (Fall/Winter 1992) 98–105.

Everything is equally the other's – the streets, houses, today's tasks and yesterday's, the things surrounding him – all is void-like. Everything means emptiness.

BLOCS OF THE MIND

Alexandr Zinoviev
Homo Sovieticus//1982

The Report
Soviet people are trained to write Reports about everything. It is an indispensable element of the Communist organization of work. Monthly Reports, Quarterly Reports, Yearly Reports, Five-yearly Reports. One old Bolshevik on the books of our institute wrote a Report about his entire life since the revolution. Three thousand pages in very small type. He trundled his epoch-making Report round to the Party office in two battered old shopping bags, and asked the officials to study it and draw lessons from it. The Secretary of the Party bureau entrusted me with this noble mission. In half an hour I wrote my Report on the Report of the old Bolshevik without even looking at it. In the years of Soviet power (so I wrote in my Report) he had consumed so many tons of bread and porridge, drunk so many kegs of vodka, written so many secret denunciations and made so many oral ones, sat for so many years of time at meetings and stood for so many years in queues. 'You are laughing at him', said Secretary. 'No, I'm crying', I said. 'What shall we do?' asked Secretary. 'We'll write to the author on official paper telling him that his manuscript has been transmitted to the Secret Division of the Central Party Archives', I said. 'Why on official paper?' asked Secretary. 'So that the author can frame it and hang it on the wall next to the fifty or so official testimonials that he has received in the course of his inordinately long and stupid life', I said. 'But why to the Secret Division?' asked Secretary. 'So that he won't torment us any more with his reminiscences', I answered. 'But where does this go?' asked Secretary, motioning towards the battered shopping bags that contained the priceless experience of the life of a whole generation. 'To the rubbish dump', I said. 'Go ahead', said Secretary, 'and then write me a short Report about what you've done.'

On another occasion they gave me the task of 'polishing' the Reports of the members of one of our scientific delegations at an international congress. The delegation consisted of 50 people, but there were 60 Reports. Some distinguished scholars, wishing to demonstrate their devotion, had written two Reports each. Each Report was 50 typewritten pages. And what didn't the scholars tell their beloved Organs about! For example, that they could get one Western professor over on to our side by publishing his book in Moscow; that one should invite the director of a secret laboratory to Moscow and fix him up with a reliable girl …

These Reports of the delegation were true and instructive. But we usually write Reports not in order to do a summing-up or extract lessons, but by virtue of certain higher, mystical considerations. For the sake of ordered formality. Therefore we put all we've got into them as a rule, so that it's practically impossible to sift the truth from invention. And indeed there is no need to do this. Nobody reads our Reports anyway. In my Quarterly Report I once wrote that I had discovered ten new elementary particles. I did this with the purely cognitive intention of checking my theory of Reports. The director of the section sent for me. I was on the point of thinking that my theory was mistaken, but I needn't have worried. My Report, Director said, was too short. Would I add a couple of pages? I made a demagogic declaration: the value, I said, of a Report lay not in the number of pages but in what, according to the Report, had been done. 'Read what I have done', I said, 'and compare it with what the others did.' 'Don't try to fool me', said Director calmly. 'Do you think the others have done less than you?' And so I added a couple of pages to the Report in which I communicated the news that I had discovered a method of converting the contents of Moscow's rubbish bins into first-class foodstuffs. 'Well done!' said Director, filing my Report in the bundle of other unread Reports by my colleagues. 'The man who can write a good Report is a good worker.'

But don't imagine that the Report is a superfluous bureaucratic operation. It is a powerful way of integrating people into the Communist system. The important thing is not the contents, just the fact that the Report exists. [...]

The Creative Approach

We Soviet people are also trained to take a creative approach to everything. I remember, in this connection, a very instructive happening. Our spies in the West stole the drawings of a machine tool that was intended for very complex and sophisticated operations. At the same time they picked up the machine tool's component parts. A special group was formed to get the hang of the machine-tool. The high-ups were interested in it because the machine-tool was necessary for tank production. They ordered the group to approach their task in a creative and innovatory spirit and in the most economical manner possible. And they certainly innovated. At the first assembly of the machine tool they found that five of the components were superfluous. The machine tool worked without them. Once more they took it to bits and put it together again. Now there were ten unnecessary parts. And still the machine tool worked. Once more they dismantled and reassembled it. Twenty parts too many. But the machine tool worked. Ho! Ho! How they made fun of the much-vaunted Western technology.

Somebody voiced the proposition that, after five more dismantlings and reassemblies, the machine tool would work without any components at all. What a discovery that would be! The members of the group looked suspiciously at this super-economizer and decided to rest on their laurels. They reported to the management that, as a result of the creative approach, the group had substantially simplified the excessively complicated construction of the machine tool. From then on the machine tool began to perform the most elementary and crude operations. After a month it broke down completely, and for good. But by this time the government had lost interest in it. Western firms had begun to sell us parts of tanks ready-made, and so the machine tool was superfluous.

An even more instructive case occurred in the 'Lenin School' where they train our spies, the leaders of Communist parties and future pro-Soviet government officials for Western countries. One of the pupils who wished to please our government took the demand for a creative approach seriously and began to gibber such nonsense that they wanted to close down the School as a hotbed of Eurocommunism. This Western Communist, although he was a Communist, was also a Westerner, and didn't grasp the real meaning of the 'creative approach'. At a closed meeting of the Central Committee at which the incorrect behaviour of Western Communists was being analysed, the secretary for ideology said that the reason for their mistakes was their inability to approach the concept of the 'creative approach' creatively.

When they had sent me here, the responsible comrades from the Organs ordered me, among other parting words, to adopt a creative approach to my mission. As a Soviet man I understood the real meaning of this farewell: sit quiet and don't make a nuisance of yourself. And as regards creativity, that is needed only for the Report. The worst possible Report is more interesting than the greatest conceivable achievements if it's executed with expertise not in the matter which the Report is about, but in the really important matter, which is the technique of writing a Report. Here my real life is boredom and grey depression in comparison with a whole heap of things I could say about it. You can imagine what would happen in *this* world if we all began to write Reports about our sojourn in the *other* one! […]

Alexandr Zinoviev, extracts from *Homo Sovieticus*, trans. Charles Janson (London: Victor Gollancz, 1985) 14–16, 18–19.

Agne Narusyte
The Aesthetics of Boredom: Lithuanian Photography 1980–1990//2010

[...] Boredom, especially its social circumstances, also became the subject of alternative art in the Soviet Union. Yet the causes of social boredom were very different in this totalitarian country where life was structured around ideological slogans and where the central planning of the economy made competition obsolete and every attempt at free thinking, especially concerning religious issues, was punished. Orrin Klapp, who researched the social aspects of boredom, claimed that this state of mind was characteristic to all societies in the twentieth century, irrespective of their social system or ideology. He supported his statement with an example from the media, which described the Soviet youth of the late 1970s thus: 'Bored, listless, and avoiding state-provided clubrooms, teenagers across the country offend and alarm parents and adults by gathering after school, drinking wine, smoking and preening themselves in Western fashions.'[1] This description shows quite accurately how boredom was identified with an unwillingness to conform to the rules set by the authorities, and even social resistance against the system. However, the sociologist failed to notice that the conditions of boredom were specific behind the 'iron curtain'.

First of all, while Western societies suffered from an overload of information and change that created the impression that life was ephemeral, Soviet society and its social environment could be described as boring in the sense that it simply lacked variety; it was uniform and nothing changed through the decades. A Russian comedy created around that time (1975), *Irony of Fate* (*Ironiya Sudby ili s lyogkim parom!*, directed by Eldar Ryazanov) was an ironic comment on the situation when everything was so standardized that people could easily take somebody else's home for their own. In other words, the environment in the Soviet Union was literally boring. The American writer Saul Bellow recreated the impression by using a monotonous unpunctuated rhythm for his description of Russia as

> the most boring society in history. Dowdiness shabbiness dullness dull goods boring buildings boring discomfort boring supervision a dull press dull education boring bureaucracy forced labour perpetual police presence penal presence, boring party congresses, et cetera. What was permanent was the defeat of interest.[2]

After they had emigrated to the West, the Russian alternative artists Vitaly Komar and Alexander Melamid commented on the situation in a similar way: 'The reader must imagine for him or herself the situation in which they live and work.

Dreary, boring, terrifying Moscow, whose inhabitants are oppressed by a monstrous fear.'[3] The combination of boredom and fear could not remain without consequences. During this period of stagnation, even the Soviet media, which usually avoided any negative description of the socialist system, indicated that monotony was the cause of one of the greatest problems of the society – heavy drinking: 'Some people plead that such are the times; others drink in order to relieve the monotony of life, which turns a human being into some kind of a mechanism.'[4]

The Soviet Union of the 1970s to early 1980s could be described, following Lucien Jerphagnon [on banality], as a world governed by the experience of 'anonymous time': when the environment was presented as if it were a given priori, and the subject could not change it; when everything seemed to be pre-planned and everything happened as if by its own accord, when everything could only be repeated, even experiences, when subjective time had lost value, everything seemed to be banal and boredom was the dominant state of mind. The constant decline of economic and social conditions did not allow for optimism for the future; time seemed to be 'frozen' into an inalterable present where human life passed meaninglessly. Moreover, as Alfonsas Andriuskevicius rightly pointed out, transcendence was purged from life and culture in all possible ways.[5] The need for more varied information, transcendence or meaning could only be realised individually and secretly, and this amounted to an act of spiritual independence and resistance. Meanwhile, the citizens of Western societies always had many opportunities to search for freedom of expression in culture; or seek transcendence in any chosen way. Thus, we may conclude that the Soviet Union could be interpreted as a boring world that did not create conditions to 'discharge', as Otto Fenichel termed it: a Soviet citizen could 'justifiably' blame the society and the state for his or her boredom.

The absurdity of this situation lies in the fact that in this intrinsically 'boring' society boredom was considered to be a deviation from the behavioural model promoted by totalitarian ideology. 'Activity is Our Credo', leading articles declared in the press. In front of their eyes, the readers of magazines were given the positive image of the Soviet man who worked enthusiastically and unhindered by psychological problems. In such a situation it was usual for psychologists to cite an unsuitable lifestyle and a lack of interest in one's social life as the cause of boredom. One of the causes of boredom indicated by official psychology – 'withdrawal into the little world of one's narrow interests' – could also be seen as a conscious dissociation from Soviet society in the form of mental non-cooperation, and as an attempt to acquire different information and spiritual freedom as mentioned before, which did not conform to the interests of ideology and was attributed to the category of dangerous attitudes.

We should note that this situation reminds us of the fatigue that was supposedly overtaking the society of corporate capitalism as described by Jean Baudrillard, who attributed boredom to it as a more general phenomenon. Baudrillard described fatigue (and boredom) as 'passive resistance' because it 'is a concealed form of protest, which turns round against oneself and "grows into" one's own body because, in certain conditions, that is the only thing on which the dispossessed individual can take out his frustration …' Thus social boredom, according to Baudrillard, denotes a passive reconciliation with the present situation when apparent, outward obedience belies secret protest. In 1991 the interpretation of boredom as a form of protest found its way into the Lithuanian press, when the subject of peaceful non-cooperation became an urgent issue after the events of January 13 (when the Soviet army opened fire on a peaceful demonstration and 14 people were killed). We cannot help but notice that the romantic concept of boredom or *spleen* (the dissociation of the romantic personality from the boring society and their inner withdrawal and demonstration of boredom in public), could be interpreted as a form of opposition to the mental violence and unification of the Soviet Union. The individual refuses to participate in a game whose rules are set by ideology, resisting the conformist existence of an alien and aggressive society.

We can recognize boredom in many works produced by the alternative art movement in the Soviet Union: as social protest, as an antidote to the heroic rhetorics imposed on public life and as a comment on the 'boring world'. Among the most renowned examples are the *Albums* (1972–75), early works by Ilya Kabakov, then a member of Collective Actions. These seemingly real but totally fictitious records of anonymous dull lives that the artist invented are almost empty, marked only by insignificant details that are completely at odds with the image of the society presented by Soviet propaganda. Or, for instance, the painter Oskar Rabin who conveyed social apathy by depicting the industrial environment and juxtaposing such 'incompatible' realities as heavy drinking, KGB, militia, pornography, shabby toilets, empty and abandoned streets, etc. Both in Rabin's paintings and in Kabakov's albums, boredom appears as the only form of existence in Soviet society.

Yet the most notable works on the subject of boredom were created by the Ukrainian photographer Boris Mikhailov. As early as the 1960s he was photographing dreary and run-down cityscapes on the outskirts of Kharkov and emphasising boredom rather than masking it behind action or expressive rendering. In their discussions of Mikhailov's photographs, Russian researchers and critics emphasize his interest in the discrepancy between image and reality, but do not draw attention to boredom. The reason for this is, perhaps, the fact that in the Soviet Union boredom was a normal condition and it would have seemed banal to talk about it, while the new ideas concerning photography as language that were coming from the West were an intriguing subject. However, Western researchers view social boredom as the most important subject of the early photographs by Mikhailov, for instance Gilda Williams has written about 'the tiresome, endless pageantry to the glory of the Revolution', 'the unsmiling faces of bored citizens forced to march gaily in a parade; the dull, militaristic public display of agricultural machinery'.[7] Boredom was conspicuous to them also, perhaps, due to the fact that the reality recorded by Mikhailov was radically different from the dynamic environment which to which people are accustomed in Western societies.

In *Unfinished Dissertation* (1985) Mikhailov himself mentions boredom. But even more than words, this state of mind is suggested by the photographs pasted on the underside of the dissertation, which he found, thrown out in a rubbish bin. Kharkov, as photographed in winter 1982, looks monotonous and boring. [...] Mikhailov emphasizes the meaninglessness of all actions (the unfinishedness of the dissertation adds to this) and the experience of the emptiness of existence. *Unfinished Dissertation* presents a narrative in which the narrator has assembled the insignificant details of his own life gathered over an extended period of time, that 'almost nothing', as if trying to grasp the traces of authentic being in the emptiness of a deteriorating social life. He expects the spectator to recognize those traces as his or her own experiences (aided by the photography 'that has been') and this is especially relevant to the spectator who belongs to the same context. Here we see the spectator merging with the subject of enunciation, which makes not only aesthesis, but also reflection possible: a reflection on the spectator's boredom lived as a normal part of everyday routine. [...]

Mikhailov's social boredom also has its equivalents within a foreign context: the photography of Robert Frank and Walker Evans, who recorded the same emptiness in the faces of people living in a seemingly very different society. Moreover, their faces are also contrasted with the pompous character of the political leaders, flags and slogans that mark the environment. Ideological signs in Mikhailov's photographs perform the same function as advertisements do in the American photographs: their aggressive design and straightforward meaning is juxtaposed against faces that say nothing, faces that represent a society devoid of all meaning. Mikhailov, however, treats the signs of ideology differently from Frank or Evans: he sometimes highlights them with red, and sometimes subdues them by pushing them into the darkened distance. The first case falsifies an ironic compliance with Soviet ideals (the red colour was the colour of revolution and dominated the political scene); in the second case as the ideological signs merge with the dreary environment, they lose their power and significance. Thus, the signs of Soviet propaganda are simply objects of irony and mockery in Mikhailov's photographs. This indicates the weakening grip of ideology in the 1980s, which leaves only emptiness in terms of values, leading to permanent boredom. […]

1 [footnote 251 in source] Orrin Klapp, *Overload and Boredom: Essays on the Quality of Life in the Information Society* (Westport, Connecticut: Greenwood Press, 1986) 23.
2 [252] Patricia Spacks, *Boredom: The Literary History of a State of Mind* (Chicago: University of Chicago Press, 1995) 264.
3 [253] Komar & Melamid, 'The Barren Flowers of Evil', in *Primary Documents: A Sourcebook for Eastern and Central European Art since the 1950s* (New York: The Museum of Modern Art, 2002) 270.
4 [254] 'Operacija Nr. 1', a letter by P. Slavinskas, 'Kalta monotonija', *Jaunimo gretos* (December 1979) 24.
5 [256] Alfonsas Andriuskevicius, *Lietuviuu dailé: 1975–1995* (Vilnius: Vilnius dailees akademijos leidykla, 1997) 74.
6 [262] Jean Baudrillard, *The Consumer Society: Myths and Structures* (London: Sage Publications, 1999) 183.
7 [265] Editor's introduction, *Boris Mikhailov*, ed. Gilda Williams (London and New York: Phaidon Press, 2001) 8.

Agne Narusyte, extract from *The Aesthetics of Boredom: Lithuanian Photography 1980–1990* (Vilnius: Vilnius dailes akademijos leidykla, 2010) 129–35.

Alla Efimova
Photographic Ethics in the Work of Boris Mikhailov//1994

[…] Boris Mikhailov became fascinated with the sea of visual anonymity that flowed through his hands every day. He began selecting the most memorable and perhaps most grotesque specimens of the *luriki* [types of black and white family photograph that he then hand-tinted in traditional style] which gave his new series its name. After the outright transgression of his female nudes and the open suggestiveness of the *Nalozhenie*, the images from *Luriki* are ambiguous, as if escaping interpretation. Are they mocking the popular taste, or revelling in it? Are they critical of the sweetness of kitsch by making it almost palatable with the pastel (or sugary pastille) coloured faces of someone's loved ones: oddly posed young soldiers, cherubic children, men and women awkwardly and naïvely staring into the camera? Or do they find comfort in this sweetness, the comfort of innocence and predictability? Whatever the case may be, Mikhailov put his finger on the pulse of this monstrous yet living and breathing visual culture, felt its palpitations and transmitted it to others with honesty and perhaps a touch of compassion. *Luriki* offered a truth that was collective or national, transcending any individual artist, and Mikhailov cast himself in the role of its conduit. But most important, *Luriki* made use of the photographic codes that, although stereotyped in their own way, survived beyond and outside state-propagated ethics and aesthetics. In this they can be considered, if not anti-Soviet, then at least a-Soviet.

By the end of the 1970s the rigidly congealed space of Soviet society appeared to show signs of dissolving. Emigration, dissent and widespread cynicism highlighted the growing incongruity between the social ideal and the discrepant reality. This incongruity became more and more visible, saturating the landscape: the contrast between the weary, tired faces of the passers-by and the monuments exuding great enthusiasm, between the pathetic, dilapidated interiors and the grandiose façades, between the greyness and blandness of everyday life and the crimson banners that stretched along the streets. The specifically Soviet elements of culture no longer seemed integrated into life but stood out like deeply familiar yet alien oddities.

The visual essence of this newly disintegrating space became the subject of Mikhailov's series *Sots Art I* and *Sots Art II*. At this time the artists of the Moscow conceptualist circle pursued the analysis of Soviet visual symbolism in paintings, installations and performances, producing a body of work later called Sots Art. Represented by such artists as Vitaly Komar and Alexander Melamid, Erik Bulatov and Ilya Kabakov, the movement has by now been well publicized and exhibited in the United States and Europe. Mikhailov became the photographer of Sots Art, which was perhaps a role potentially more explosive than that of a painter. He did not rely on allegory or conceptualist abstraction – just his own black and white photographs of everyday scenes, which he coloured to draw attention to parlicular elements. There were photographs of gloomy men and women forced to march in a political demonstration; of awkwardly shaped middle-aged women in an amateur gymnastics club, strangely at odds with the world's image of perfect Soviet super-athletes; of a pudgy, bundled-up woman selling pastries in front of a monument to Maxim Gorky that soars into the sky. The last image, with its unstated contrast of sweetness (the neatly laid-out pastries) and bitterness (Gorky translates literally as 'bitter'), epitomizes for me the sense of discomfort created in Mikhailov's *Sots Art* series, the sense that becomes even more pronounced in his later work. It has a feeling of irreparable scission, an overflowing sadness, a schizophrenia that threatens to set in for good. A political critique on the one hand, it is also a record of a state of mind common to millions. […]

Alla Efimova, extract from 'Photographic Ethics in the Work of Boris Mikhailov', *Art Journal*, no. 53 (Summer 1994) 66–7.

Ilya Kabakov
On Emptiness//1990

[…] Here I would like to discuss a possible topographical form of residence in emptiness. Topographically this form is expressed and exists in the principally insular character of the settlement of emptiness. We can speak directly of a distinctive Ocean, of an archipelago of small and large settlements, lost and scattered about the expanse of emptiness resembling some sort of Philippines, but these are not islands in a warm ocean, but in an ocean of uncertainty, an ocean of emptiness. Here, in our case, the shape, the essence of emptiness shallows itself. The very dimensions of the territory – its invisibility, endlessness, uncloseability, immeasurability – are not simply a large space, which one could calculate, comprehend and assimilate, but rather a groundless, interminable blending-together with emptiness, a moving over into emptiness. These islands of habitation contract and huddle together unto themselves, protecting and preserving themselves from the surrounding emptiness. This applies to both the configuration of villages and hamlets, where houses are pressed up against one another, as well as the gigantic cities, the very dimension of which speaks of the multitude of people gathered and crowded within them, running and saving themselves from emptiness.

As is the custom in insular culture, these islands of habitation are unified with one another by systems of communication, bridges across emptiness. But these communications, all of these roads, paths, highways, rivers and railroads, belong to a somewhat different form of emptiness, and are in a certain sense the opposite of the life of the islands, but we shall discuss that a little later. Just now I would like to emphasize the peculiar state of mind of the residents of these islands which inheres in the special knowledge that emptiness and non-existence begin immediately beyond the border of the island, past its final home. Let us move to an examination of an island itself, of that place in which the 'colonists of emptiness' are crowded – its permanent residents, islanders for many generations. What does this community, this fellowship of people 'swimming in emptiness', this 'society in a canoe', constitute? Does this community present a certain unity and continuity, in short, a single, interacting human social body in the face of emptiness?

Nothing of the sort.

Scrutinizing an island on which there are from a hundred to a thousand people as in villages, or from one to seven million as in enormous cities, that which is most important in them comes to light: a man on this island, in this village, city or large city conducts himself JUST AS HE WOULD IN EMPTINESS, not noticing the tens, hundreds and millions crowded alongside him, resembling him. The feeling, the terror of the experience of emptiness within him is so great that he and those around him see and endure it as emptiness. The sea of people around him does not lead to the formation of links between him and others, to benevolent harmony with the other. Everything around him is equally indistinguishable and inimical. Everything is equally the other's – the streets, houses, today's tasks and yesterday's, the things surrounding him – all is void-like. Everything incarnates emptiness. Inside the island salvation from emptiness is the very same emptiness, and thus for each denizen of this island all that is outside and inside the island, without exception, is nothing, emptiness.

Let us move to the next level of the topography, topography inside the island.

All the inhabitants of the islands feeling themselves to be surrounded by emptiness take refuge in BURROWS.

These burrows constitute the most important cell, the basic atom perhaps in the atomistic construction of the island. The burrow is the sole place of residence of the inhabitant of emptiness, a relatively hopeful refuge from emptiness and its bearer – Man. And as the island itself is an asylum from the emptiness of space, so the ever so similar burrow is the asylum of the individual man from the other inhabitants of the island. This structure is principally non-social and antisocial, as it should be, since emptiness is the arena where all of this takes place. It is ubiquitous, acts in every cage, penetrates everything which is arranged on it. The other inhabitants surrounding the 'burrow man' present a potential danger for him, they are inimical or, in the best case, neutral, harmless and homogenous. The movements of the 'burrow man' reproduce the communicational structure of the insular culture as a whole. In the same general way, he moves about the island as through emptiness, shifting to a different burrow, that of one of the few residents close to him, for whom he feels trust, trying as he can to pass and traverse the dangerous zone between the two burrows, the zone located immediately behind the line of his entrance into the burrow, the line where his security ends and emptiness begins. All of the streets, roads and sidewalks of these islands, these villages, cities and settlements are filled with thousands of these 'burrow residents' rushing from one burrow to another, who neither see nor notice anyone and fear all while outside their burrows, although they shove and collide with many similar to themselves.

There is almost no interaction or interrelation of the inhabitants of one burrow with those of other burrows except among acquaintances. And there is less garrulity here than among animals living in the forest, where there are spatial zones of influence of every form, an autonomy of particular paths, and a regulated spatial stratification of being.

Earlier we talked of the personification and denomination of this feeling by the denizens of these islands. This denomination is connected with the conception of 'stateness' for the residents of the burrows. This conception is located in one sequence with such conceptions of our place as emptiness, island, communication and burrow.

The stateness in the topography of this place is that which belongs to an unseen impersonality, the element of space, in short all that serves as an embodiment of emptiness, combines with it and expresses it. A metaphor comes closest of all to a definition of that stateness: the image of wind blowing interminably alongside and between houses, blowing through everything by itself, an icy wind sowing cold and destruction, howling and crushing with one unchangeable composition.

In precisely the same way as the wind's aim and meaning and the constant pressure of the stateness are incomprehensible for the burrow dwellers, its terrible fits, changes of direction, its movement, are all equally incomprehensible. The constant, ferocious pressure, the menacing, terrifying fits directly behind the door of the burrow inspire horror in the soul of the person sequestered within, filling him constantly. And for nought. In these fits, in these claps and blows of thunder, in this implacable, irrepressible movement inaccessible to either comprehension or entreaties, the timid resident of these places recognizes the voice of emptiness. The stateness is emptiness itself, not materially or substantially given to the denizen of these regions, but all the while instilling terror, fear, and appearing as his punishment. Above all, the stateness, an operation incomprehensible to this man, is opposed and inaccessible to him by meaning. It demands from him the execution of its own 'governmental aims', known only to it, which are fixed, promising only mercy in return. What sort of goals does this wind, this stateness, set for itself, if they exist at all? These goals always bear in mind the mastery of the scope of all territory occupied by emptiness as a SINGLE WHOLE. The inhabitants of this place are cast into this sweeping stream, themselves becoming powerless elements of the whirlwind.

For just this reason authentically governmental acts often have to do with superhuman, megalithic projects and constructions: Peter the Great's canals, flowing across the entire country from North to South; the regular militarization of the cantons along the entire border of Nicholas the First's empire; Stalin's forest-protecting zones, his razing of mountains and changing the flow of rivers; the passage of skiers from Khabarovsk to Moscow and back; Krushchev's development of virgin soil and space flights: *and other acts possessing governmental significance*. But all these constructions and projects, replacing one another like terrifying fits of wind, changed nothing either in the territory itself of this place, nor in the situation and state of mind of the inhabitants of these burrows, although all of them were realized by the power of those residents. The residents always feel themselves cast into these dislocations, fits and great deeds, sensing them as gloom, violence, or as senseless intoxication. [...]

Ilya Kabakov, extract from 'O pustote' (On Emptiness), trans. Clark Troy, in *Between Spring and Summer: Soviet Conceptual Art in the Era of Late Communism*, ed. David A. Ross (Cambridge, Massachusetts: The MIT Press/Tacoma: Tacoma Art Museum/Boston: Institute of Contemporary Art, 1990) 56–8.

Mikhail Epstein
Negative Emptiness//1999

What is the significance of emptiness for Kabakov? Why does he seek to impart cultural forms to it and imprison it in the clutches of words and images? In trying to answer these questions, we shall turn to Kabakov's own contradictory stance on the subject, with his two opposing views about the nature of emptiness.

One of these views has been expounded by Kabakov in his theoretical piece entitled 'On Emptiness'. 'First we must say something of the psychic constitution, the psychological condition of the people who were born in the void and live there.'[1] This is how Kabakov describes the essence of his native Soviet-Russian world as he experienced it against the backdrop of his first trip abroad, to Czechoslovakia in 1981. The Soviet world appeared to him as a giant reservoir of emptiness, which could not be filled by any imaginable human effort. In Europe, emptiness is still a vacant space, not yet cultivated, waiting to be conquered and husbanded, requiring active human intervention, care and work. In Russia, emptiness itself is an active principle, a frenzied vacuum that sucks all human initiative and endeavour into nothingness, all history, tradition and culture into its whirlpool-like sieve. It is a commonplace saying that 'nature does not tolerate a vacuum', but it is equally true that a vacuum 'does not tolerate nature'.[2] Instead, it swallows nature, devastates forests and fields, devours and dissolves all positive value and every constructive principle. Such a vampire-like emptiness cannot remain alive for a single instant without drawing the living blood out of its inhabitants, without implanting in them a gnawing feeling of nausea and mortal self-destruction: '… things are begotten of nothing, nothing is connected with anything else, nothing signifies anything, everything is suspended in and disappears into the void blown away on the icy wind of the void.'[3] Kabakov's perception of Russia as a 'negative lesson' to the world is similar to Chaadaev's.[4] But it is tinged with even deeper despair because, over the century and a half since Chaadaev, this void that was then perceived only by a few refined minds has managed to grow into a terrible Eurasian abyss, whose edges are rimmed by a widening landslide. The adjacent European and Asian countries could all be sucked into it, without hope of ever extricating themselves. Russia has thus become the black hole of humanity. If emptiness in Europe were represented by a table-top, awaiting the serving of dishes on its surface, then in Russia someone is sitting under the table, constantly pulling off the tablecloth, so that everything on the table is immediately thrown off and disappears into the void. Such is Kabakov's nightmarish and panic-stricken vision of his homeland: a metaphysical abyss.

What can an artist accomplish in such conditions? Following Kabakov's logic, it is patently clear that there is no possibility of filling this emptiness or covering it up with cultural constructions. This kind of emptiness is not susceptible to order, structure or hierarchization. Under such circumstances, one could imagine the following model of collaboration between artist and emptiness: since emptiness cannot be overcome or vanquished, the artist can only adopt it and transform it into a stylistic device. Since art cannot fill this emptiness, it itself comes to be filled by it. The artist, absorbing the emptiness around him, has but one alternative: allow emptiness to become part of the structure of his own works. By turning its flanks the artist delineates the boundaries of emptiness, although in itself it remains limitless. Art thus becomes a rite of circumnavigating emptiness, of slow, cautious and deliberate capitulation. It is Kutuzov's,[5] not Napoleon's, tactics of encountering emptiness: instead of attacking it with militant cultural projects, one retreats, ceding a place to it where emptiness least expects to find a place – at the heart of the artist's creation. In order to prevent emptiness from swallowing up this creation, depriving it of meaning from the outside, it is made to curl up inside it, like a quiet, well-fed, docile wild animal in a cage.

These are the tactics chosen by Kabakov to combat emptiness. Unlike many of his contemporaries, Kabakov does not attempt to apply a supercharged weapon of rationality or create a super-abundant structure of meaning in the texture of his canvases. On the contrary, he cuts through the texture, manufacturing a kind of trap which is able to capture an *en-O-rmous* emptiness. To catch this emptiness, speaking metaphorically, two nets are used. Both can be sprung with the same string. One is a net of words, the other a net of images. What has flown into one net can not fly out the other. What has slipped through the invisible net of images is captured in words. What has disappeared through the transparent net of words is reclaimed through lines and colours. Thus a concept demonstrates the emptiness of reality, while reality shows up the emptiness of the concept.

Casting such nets into the 'ocean of emptiness', as Kabakov calls the Russian world, he is able to catch the larger emptiness in its smaller image, which, although encompassing only the several-metres width of the artist's canvas, is virtually equivalent to the whole of Russia. Kabakov skimps neither on material nor on the labour required for the preparatory work – and then he leaves the work unfinished, just as God did with Russia, endowing her with a huge territory and natural resources, only to leave all this material unprocessed.

Kabakov's studio contains huge stands, displaying a minimum of artefacts, whitewashed like the map of an uncharted continent or the ice-clad Antarctic, to which he compares Russia in his essay 'On Emptiness'. Elsewhere in the studio are piles of rubbish, distributed amongst a host of boxes and files that are labelled and classified. There are albums made up of useless receipts, tickets and scraps of paper, all with captions and explanations. Rubbish is another form of emptiness, its static material manifestation. When emptiness penetrates the very structure of objects, eroding them from the inside, when it thrusts inner spaces onto the surface, when it reveals the wretched side of things, their futility and neglect, then out of emptiness *rubbish* emerges into the light of day, becoming Kabakov's second most favoured object of contemplation and artistic device.

At a cursory glance, this may appear to be nothing more than a form of artistic laziness. Instead of mastering chaos, the artist lets it overwhelm him, filling his folios and albums with all sorts of trivia and garbage, leaving yards and yards of unused, blank space on his giant billboards and stands. However, Kutuzov was also a 'lazy' general, but even Napoleon recognized in him 'an old Russian fox', suspecting cunning at work in Kutuzov's compliant tactics. Similarly, Kabakov plays a cunning fox's game with emptiness, covering the cracks of his artistic intention, adopting a posture of weakness, absence of resolve, a yearning for rest. He appears to say: 'I've drawn five columns and I've filled one with writing – that's enough …' Emptiness, for its part, which is always lurking somewhere nearby, ready to attack and devour any kind of superstructure or rationally drawn plan, settles down peacefully in the remaining four empty columns, enclosed in boundaries, caught in the frame of the empty-looking stand. Emptiness caught by such cunning means has been turned into a device.

Certainly, one still feels uncomfortable looking at an ice-clad continent, at an expanse covered by unanswered questions like 'Where is Yefim Borisovich?', at the transparent and disappearing wings beyond the window of Arkhipov's hospital. Nevertheless, the artist has succeeded in transporting this emptiness onto paper: one can look at it even if one cannot see it. Kabakov's entire universe is just such a porous body, whose function is to allow emptiness in and then enclose it within the limits of a work of art. [...]

1   [footnote 25 in source] Ilya Kabakov, 'O Pustote' (On Emptiness), in Ilya Kabakov, *The Life of Flies* (Cologne, 1992) 233.
2   [26] Ibid., 232.
3   [27] Ibid., 236.
4   [28] Petr Iakovlevich Chaadaev (1794–1856) was Russia's first important thinker to express bitter disappointment at Russia's failure to contribute creatively to Western civilization. [...]
5   [29] Mikhail Kutuzov (1745–1813) – field marshall; commander-in-chief of the Russian army that defeated Napoleon's troops in 1812 using the tactic of calculated retreat. [...]

Mikhail Epstein, extract from 'Emptiness as a Technique', in Epstein, Alexander A. Genis and Slobodanka M. Vladiv-Glover, *Russian Postmodernism*, ed. Vladiv-Glover (New York and Oxford: Berghahn Books, 1999) 324–7.

Boris Groys
Comrades of Time//2009

[...] One of the slogans of the Soviet era was 'Time, forward!' Ilf and Petrov, two Soviet novelists of the 1920s, aptly parodied this modern feeling with the slogan 'Comrades, sleep faster!' Indeed, in those times one actually would have preferred to sleep through the present – to fall asleep in the past and to wake up at the endpoint of progress, after the arrival of the radiant future.

But when we begin to question our projects, to doubt or reformulate them, the present, the contemporary, becomes important, even central for us. This is because the contemporary is actually constituted by doubt, hesitation, uncertainty, indecision – by the need for prolonged reflection, for a delay. We want to postpone our decisions and actions in order to have more time for analysis, reflection and consideration. And that is precisely what the contemporary is – a prolonged, even potentially infinite period of delay. Søren Kierkegaard famously asked what it would mean to be a contemporary of Christ, to which his answer was: It would mean to hesitate in accepting Christ as Saviour.[1] The acceptance of Christianity necessarily leaves Christ in the past. In fact, Descartes already defined the present as a time of doubt – of doubt that is expected eventually to open a future full of clear and distinct, evident thoughts.

Now, one can argue that we are at this historical moment in precisely such a situation, because ours is a time in which we reconsider – not abandon, not reject, but analyse and reconsider – the modern projects. The most immediate reason for this reconsideration is, of course, the abandonment of the Communist project in Russia and Eastern Europe. Politically and culturally, the Communist project dominated the twentieth century. There was the Cold War, there were Communist parties in the West, dissident movements in the East, progressive revolutions, conservative revolutions, discussions about pure and engaged art – in most cases these projects, programmes and movements were interconnected by their opposition to each other. But now they can and should be reconsidered in their entirety. Thus contemporary art can be seen as art that is involved in the reconsideration of the modern projects. One can say that we now live in a time of indecision, of delay – a boring time. Now, Martin Heidegger has interpreted boredom precisely as a precondition for our ability to experience the presence of the present – to experience the world as a whole by being bored equally by all its aspects, by not being captivated by this specific goal or that one, such as was the case in the context of the modern projects.[2]

Hesitation with regard to the modern projects mainly has to do with a growing disbelief in their promises. Classical modernity believed in the ability of the future to realize the promises of past and present – even after the death of God, even after the loss of faith in the immortality of the soul. The notion of a permanent art collection says it all: archive, library and museum promised secular permanency, a material infinitude that substituted the religious promise of resurrection and eternal life. During the period of modernity, the 'body of work' replaced the soul as the potentially immortal part of the Self. Foucault famously called such modern sites in which time was accumulated rather than simply being lost, heterotopias.[3] Politically, we can speak about modern utopias as post-historical spaces of accumulated time, in which the finiteness of the present was seen as being potentially compensated for by the infinite time of the realized project: that of an artwork, or a political utopia. Of course, this realization obliterates time invested in this realization, in the production of a certain product – when the final product is realized, the time that was used for its production disappears. However, the time lost in realizing the product was compensated for in modernity by a historical narrative that somehow restored it – being a narrative that glorified the lives of the artists, scientists or revolutionaries that worked for the future.

But today, this promise of an infinite future holding the results of our work has lost its plausibility. Museums have become the sites of temporary exhibitions rather than spaces for permanent collections. The future is ever newly planned – the permanent change of cultural trends and fashions makes any promise of a stable future for an artwork or a political project improbable. And the past is also permanently rewritten – names and events appear, disappear, reappear and disappear again. The present has ceased to be a point of transition from the past to the future, becoming instead a site of the permanent rewriting of both past and future – of constant proliferations of historical narratives beyond any individual grasp or control. The only thing that we can be certain about in our present is that these historical narratives will proliferate tomorrow as they are proliferating now – and that we will react to them with the same sense of disbelief. Today, we are stuck in the present as it reproduces itself without leading to any future. We simply lose our time, without being able to invest it securely, to accumulate it, whether utopically or heterotopically. The loss of the infinite historical perspective generates the phenomenon of unproductive, wasted time. However, one can also interpret this wasted time more positively, as excessive time – as time that attests to our life as pure being-in-time, beyond its use within the framework of modern economic and political projects.

Now, if we look at the current art scene, it seems to me that a certain kind of so-called time-based art best reflects this contemporary condition. It does so because it thematizes the non-productive, wasted, non-historical, excessive time – a suspended time, *stehende Zeit*, to use a Heideggerian notion. It captures and demonstrates activities that take place in time, but do not lead to the creation of any definite product. Even if these activities do lead to such a product, they are presented as being separated from their result, as not completely invested in the product, absorbed by it. We find exemplifications of excessive time, that has not been completely absorbed by the historical process.

As an example let us consider the animation by Francis Alÿs, *Song for Lupita* (1998). In this work, we find an activity with no beginning and no end, no definite result or product: a woman pouring water from one vessel to another, and then back. We are confronted with a pure and repetitive ritual of wasting time – a secular ritual beyond any claim of magical power, beyond any religious tradition or cultural convention.

One is reminded here of Camus' Sisyphus, a proto-contemporary-artist whose aimless, senseless task of repeatedly rolling a boulder up a hill can be seen as a prototype for contemporary time-based art. This non-productive practice, this excess of time caught in a non-historical pattern of eternal repetition constitutes for Camus the true image of what we call 'lifetime' – a period irreducible to any 'meaning of life', any 'life achievement', any historical relevance. The notion of repetition here becomes central. The inherent repetitiveness of contemporary time-based art distinguishes it sharply from happenings and performances of the 1960s. A documented activity is not any more a unique, isolated performance – an individual, authentic, original event that takes place in the here-and-now. Rather, this activity is itself repetitive – even before it was documented by, let us say, a video running in a loop. Thus, the repetitive gesture designed by Alÿs functions as a programmatically impersonal one – it can be repeated by anyone, recorded, then repeated again. Here, the living human being loses its difference from its media image. The opposition between living organism and dead mechanism is made irrelevant by the originally mechanical, repetitive and purposeless character of the documented gesture.

Francis Alÿs characterizes such a wasted, non-teleological time that does not lead to any result, any endpoint, any climax, as the time of rehearsal. An example he offers – his video *Politics of Rehearsal* (2007), which centres on a striptease rehearsal – is in some sense a rehearsal of a rehearsal, in so far as the sexual desire provoked by the striptease remains unfulfilled even in the case of a 'true' striptease. In the video, the rehearsal is accompanied by a commentary by the artist, who interprets the scenario as the model of modernity, always leaving its promise unfulfilled. For the artist, the time of modernity is the time of permanent modernization, never really achieving its goals of becoming truly modern and never satisfying the desire that it has provoked. In this sense, the process of modernization begins to be seen as wasted, excessive time that can and should be documented – precisely because it never led to any real result. In another work, Alÿs presents the labour of a shoe cleaner as an example of a kind of work that does not produce any value in the Marxist sense of the term, because the time spent cleaning shoes cannot result in any kind of final product as required by Marx's theory of value.

But it is precisely because such a wasted, suspended, non-historical time cannot be accumulated and absorbed by its product that it can be repeated – impersonally and potentially infinitely. Already Nietzsche has stated that the only possibility for imagining the infinite after the death of God, after the end of transcendence, is to be found in the eternal return of the same. And Georges Bataille thematized the repetitive excess of time, the unproductive waste of time, as the only possibility of escape from the modern ideology of progress. Certainly, both Nietzsche and Bataille perceived repetition as something naturally given. But in his book *Difference and Repetition* (1968) Gilles Deleuze speaks of literal repetition as being radically artificial and, in this sense, in conflict with everything natural, living, changing, and developing, including natural law and moral law.[4] Hence, practising literal repetition can be seen as initiating a rupture in the continuity of life by creating a non-historical excess of time through art. And this is the point at which art can indeed become truly contemporary. [...]

1   [footnote 3 in source] See Søren Kierkegaard, *Training in Christianity* (1850) (New York: Vintage, 2004).

2 [4] See Martin Heidegger, 'What is Metaphysics?' (1929), in *Existence and Being*, ed. W. Brock (Chicago: Henry Regnery Co., 1949) 325–49.
3 [5] See Michel Foucault, 'Of Other Spaces' (1969), *Diacritics*, no. 16 (Spring 1986) 22–7.
4 [6] See Gilles Deleuze, *Difference and Repetition* (1968); trans. Paul Patton (London and New York: Continuum, 2004).

Boris Groys, extract from 'Comrades of Time', *e-flux journal*, no. 11/12 (December 2009). (www.e-flux.com)

TAGLINES OF CRITICAL THOUGHT FLOAT IN THE VACUOUS SPACE OF THE GALLERY A PASSIVE-AGGRESSIVE PERFORMANCE WHOSE VIEWERS DEFINE THEMSELVES THROUGH THEIR RESPONSES

Chris Kraus on Stefan Brüggemann, in *Where Art Belongs*, 2011

DISENGAGE!

Critical Art Ensemble
Case History and Clinical Report on the Pastiche of Boredom//1992

Throughout the nineteenth century and into the early years of the twentieth century, a reasonably exhaustive study of boredom progressed in the West. As the study became more cynical after the collapse of romanticism and the failure of the 1848 revolutions, the pure pessimism of Schopenhauer came into vogue. This philosophy put forth the idea that human suffering oscillated along a continuum between anxiety/privation and boredom/satiety. The former, though of interest to Realists, carried a connotation of commonality, a quality abhorrent to post-romantic thought, while the latter had more of a connotation of nobility. Boredom became a last gasp exploration into the psyche of a declining aristocracy. The decay of this economic or cultural elite into the impending doom of bourgeois mundanity came to define the cultural moment of understimulation settled in the overstimulating excess of the aristocratic environment. *À Rebours*, J.K. Huysmans' chronicle of aristocratic-aesthetic collapse, offers a final monument to boredom as the end of nobility. It is, in part, this connection between boredom and the aristocratic ideology of nobility that places the topic under historic erasure. The privileged narrative of boredom disappears in its own nihilism, never to resurface in its post-romantic state as a separate and pure narrative.

By flipping over the coin of boredom, the modern aesthetic takes the narrative in the other direction. Rather than having the connotation of nobility, boredom became an attack on the mundane aspects of fragmentation and redundancy found in the modern division of labour. It became a democratic affliction that affected everyone, from the factory worker caught in the repetition of h/er specialized task, to the bureaucrat filling out forms in triplicate. Everyday life increasingly became less a problem due to shortages of production (privation), than it was a problem of the monotony of production itself. Emerging from the ruins of boredom/nobility came alienation/commonality – a quality no longer to be savoured in the poetic moment.

The expansion of boredom under the rubric of alienation breaks the boundary of the nineteenth-century narrative that separated boredom/satiety and anxiety/privation. There is a high velocity crash, and the two once separate qualities are twisted together in an inseparable entwinement. There is a simultaneous suffering of both anxiety and boredom. One cannot exist without the other. The Western postmodern becomes a Bergman film, standing still for an insufferable duration (hyper-inertia), and yet moving along in painful disquieting spasms (hyper-speed). We fidget in our understimulation, and yawn at our overstimulation. But the postmodern aesthetic never lets an exploitable narrative die; a night of championship wrestling is convincing evidence. Boredom, like all narratives of mythic proportion, has been appropriated, reinvented, and is living in the realm of Disney simulation. Boredom, with all its connotation of nobility, repeats itself in the spectacular image. Turn the pages of a fashion magazine and witness the perfect calm of boredom in the environment of excess. The legacy of Des Esseintes [Huysmans' protagonist] lives on the in the fashion shows of Claude Montana.

Sublime dilettante. Electronic toys. Gunshot wound to the head. A woman of fashion with real gifts, real abulia. Mental illness and hebetude, suicide, the powers to imagine without the drive to focus them. Material comfort and the squandering thereof. The enigma of sexual attraction, while the rational shakes its head. Convinced of ability, ignorant of its control. Treats PDR like the phone book. Distrust of any medical treatment. You cannot call the evil by its name. Sexual jealousy, the collapsing dialectic, never resting, never letting you rest.

Critical Art Ensemble, 'Case History and Clinical Report on the Pastiche of Boredom', *Documents*, no. 1–2 (Fall/Winter 1992) 90–91.

David Foster Wallace
The Pale King//2011

Lane Dean Jr. with his green rubber pinkie finger sat at his Tingle table in his Chalk's row in the Rotes Group's wiggle room and did two more returns, then another one, then flexed his buttocks and held to a count of ten and imagined a warm pretty beach with mellow surf as instructed in orientation the previous month. Then he did two more returns, checked the clock real quick, then two more, then bore down and did three in a row, then flexed and visualized and bore way down and did four without looking up once except to put the completed files and memos in the two Out trays side by side up in the top tier of trays where the cart boys could get them when they came by. After just an hour the beach was a winter beach, cold and grey and the dead kelp like the hair of the drowned, and it stayed that way despite all attempts. Then three more, including one 1040A where the deductions for AGI were added wrong and the Martinsburg print-out hadn't caught it and had to be amended on one of the Form 020-Cs in the lower left tray and then a lot of the same information filled out on the regular 20 you still had to do even if it was just a correspondence audit and the file going to Joliet instead of the District, each code for which had to be looked up on the pull-out thing he had to scoot the chair awkwardly over to pull out all the way. Then another one, then a plummeting inside of him as the wall clock showed that what he'd thought was another hour had not been. Not even close. 17 May 1985. Lord Jesus Christ have mercy on me a poor sinner. Crosschecking W-2s for the return's Line 7 off the place in the Martinsburg print-out where the perforation if you wanted to separate the thing's sheets went right through the data and you had to hold it up against the light and almost sometimes guess, which his Chalk Leader said was a chronic bug with Systems but the wiggler was still accountable. The joke this week was how was an IRS rote examiner like a mushroom? Both kept in the dark and fed horseshit. He didn't know how mushrooms even worked, if it was true that you scooped waste on them. Sheri's cooking wasn't what you would call at the level of adding mushrooms. Then another return. The rule was, the more you looked at the clock the slower the time went. None of the wigglers wore a watch, except he saw that some kept them in their pockets for breaks. Clocks on Tingles were not allowed, nor coffee or pop. Try as he might he could not this last week help envisioning the inward lives of the older men to either side of him, doing this day after day. Getting up on a Monday and chewing their toast and putting their hats and coats on knowing what they were going out the door to come back to for eight hours. This was boredom beyond any boredom he'd ever felt. [...]

Drinion is *happy*. Ability to pay attention. It turns out that bliss – a second-by-second joy + gratitude at the gift of being alive, conscious – lies on the other side of crushing, crushing boredom. Pay close attention to the most tedious thing you can find (tax returns, televised golf), and, in waves, a boredom like you've never known will wash over you and just about kill you. Ride these out, and it's like stepping from black and white into colour. Like water after days in the desert. Constant bliss in every atom. [...]

David Foster Wallace, extracts from *The Pale King* (New York: Little, Brown, 2011) 376–7, 546.

Sianne Ngai
Stuplimity//2005

[...] As Gertrude Stein acknowledges in *The Making of Americans*, 'Listening to repeating is often irritating, listening to repeating can be dulling'. Yet in that book, which presents a taxonomy or system for the making of human 'kinds', repeating is also the dynamic force by which new beginnings, histories and genres are produced and organized. As Lacan similarly suggests, 'repetition demands the new', including new ways of understanding its dulling and irritating effects.[1] It thus comes as no surprise that many of the most 'shocking', innovative and transformative cultural productions in history have also been deliberately tedious ones. In the twentieth century, systematically recursive works by Andy Warhol, Robert Ryman, Jasper Johns, John Cage and Philip Glass bear witness to the prominence of tedium as an aesthetic strategy in avant-garde practices; one also thinks of the 'fatiguing repetitiveness of Sade's books'[2] and the permutative logics at work in the writings of Samuel Beckett, Raymond Roussel, Georges Perec, Alain Robbe-Grillet, Jackson Mac Low and of course Stein. This strange partnership between enervation and shock in the invention of new genres is not limited to the avant-garde. It can likewise be found in the contemporary slasher film, which by continually using a limited number of trademark motifs replicates the serial logic of the serial killer (while also, of course, producing thrills), and in the pulsating, highly energized, yet exhaustively durational electronic music known as techno, which generated new musical subcultures in the 1980s.

Though repetition, permutation and seriality figure prominently as devices in aesthetic uses of tedium, practitioners have achieved the same effect through a strategy of agglutination – the mass adhesion or coagulation of data particles or signifying units. Here tedium resides not so much in the syntactic overdetermination of a minimalist lexicon, as in Robert Ryman's white paintings, but in the stupendous proliferation of discrete quanta held together by a fairly simple syntax or organizing principle. This logic, less mosaic than congealaic, is frequently emphasized by sculptor Ann Hamilton in her installations, which have included 16,000 teeth arranged on an examination table, 750,000 pennies immobilized in honey, 800 men's shirts pressed into a thick wedge, and floors covered by vast spreads of linotype pieces and animal hair.[3] A similar effect is achieved by Gerhard Richter's installation *Atlas* (1997), which confronts the spectator with 643 sheets displaying more than 7,000 items – snapshots, newspaper cuttings, sketches, colour fields – arranged on white rectangular panels.[4] While here the organization of material is primarily taxonomic rather than compressive, like Hamilton's, the accumulation of visual 'data' induces a similar strain on the observer's capacities for conceptually synthesizing or metabolizing information. The fatigue of the viewer's responsivity approaches the kind of exhaustion involved in the attempt to read a dictionary.

This mode of tedium is specifically foregrounded in Janet Zweig's computer/printer installations, where rhetorical bits and scraps are automatically produced in enormous quantities, then stacked, piled, enumerated, weighed on scales, or otherwise quantified. To make *Her Recursive Apology* (1993), for example, four computers, each hooked up to a dot-matrix printer, were programmed to randomly generate apologies 'in the smallest possible type' on continuously fed paper. As Zweig notes, 'The printer apologized for two weeks, day and night. Whenever a box of paper ran out, the computer displayed the number of times it had apologized. Because the apologies were randomly chosen by the computer, no two sheets of paper are alike. I arranged the pages in a recursive spiral structure, each stack one sheet larger than the next.'[5] Pushing the boundary between the emotive and the mechanical, and ironically commenting on the feminization of apologetic speech acts, *Her Recursive Apology* stages the convergence of gendered subject and machine not via a fashionable cyborg figure but through a surprisingly 'flat' or boring display of text, its materiality and iterability foregrounded by the piles of its consolidation. Zweig's work calls attention to language as the site where subject and system intersect, as Stein similarly demonstrates through her own vast combinatory of human types – a text in which new 'kinds' or models of humans are made through the rhetorically staged acts of enumerating, 'grouping', 'mixing' and above all repeating. For both Stein and Zweig, where system and subject converge is more specifically where language piles up and becomes 'dense'.

Like the massive *Making of Americans*, the large-scale installations of Zweig, Hamilton and Richter register as at once exciting and enervating, astonishing yet tedious. Inviting further comparison with Stein's human taxonomy is the fact that each of these installations functions as an information-processing system – a way of classifying and ordering seemingly banal bits of stuff: newspaper clippings, snapshots, teeth, words and phrases, repetitions. To encounter the vastness of Stein's system is to encounter the vast combinatory of language, where particulars 'thicken' to produce new individualities. As an ordering of visual data on a similar scale, what Richter's *Atlas* suggests through its staggering agglomeration of material is not so much the sublimity of information, but the sublimity of its ability to thicken and heap up.

But sublimity does not really seem the right concept to use here, despite its early role in making emotion – negative emotion, in particular – central to aesthetic experience. As noted in this book's introduction, the sublime might be thought of as the first 'ugly feeling', in the sense of being explicitly contrasted with the feelings or qualities associated with the beautiful. It thus comes as no surprise that the sublime, conscripted to theorize an observer's response to things in nature of great or infinite magnitude (what Kant calls the mathematically sublime) or of terrifying might (Kant's dynamical sublime),[6] has had a revitalized cachet in what Arthur C. Danto describes as the twentieth-century avant-garde's attempt to separate the concepts of art and beauty.[7] Though the dynamical sublime is characterized in particular by 'astonishment that borders upon terror' or by a kind of 'holy awe' coupled with 'dread',[8] both sublimes involve an initial experience of being overwhelmed in a confrontation with totality that makes the observer painfully aware of her limitations – or at least at first. There is a sense in which astonishingly massive and totalizing works like Kenneth Goldsmith's *No. III 2.7.93–10.20.96* and Richter's *Atlas*, which reveal the limited reach of our perceptual and cognitive faculties, would seem to do the same. But Kantian sublimity remains the wrong aesthetic concept, as well as the wrong concept of feeling, to appeal to in describing the effects of works like *No. III*, *Atlas* and *The Making of Americans* on the reader or viewer. And its interesting failure to account for the affects summoned by works like these stems from reasons more complex than the ones detailed explicitly within the *Critique of Judgement* (1790), such as the fact that Kant limits his concept of the sublime to 'rude nature', and explicitly bars it from being applied to products of art 'where human purpose determines the form and the size'.[9] [...]

More specifically, the sublime cannot be properly mobilized to account for the affective response elicited by enormous, agglutinative works like *Atlas* or *Americans*, since here the initial experience of being aesthetically overwhelmed involves not terror or pain (eventually superseded by tranquility), but *something much closer to an ordinary fatigue* – and one that cannot be neutralized, like the sublime's terror, by a competing affect. In the case of Stein's colossal novel, a dysphoric affect is similarly summoned in which the reader's or observer's faculties become strained to their limits in the effort to comprehend the work as a whole, but the revelation of this failure is conspicuously less dramatic – and does not, in the end, confirm the self's sense of superiority over the overwhelming or intimidating object.

Our encounters with astonishing but also fatiguing works like *Americans* thus call for a different way of thinking what it means to be aesthetically overpowered – a new way of characterizing an affective relationship to enormous, stupefying objects that may seem similar to, but ultimately does not fall within the scope of, either the Kantian or the popular sublime. One strategy for calling attention to the difference between the mixture of shock and exhaustion produced and sustained by a text like *Americans*, and the 'dread' and 'holy awe' eventually superseded by disinterested pleasure that are particular to the sublime, is to refer to the aesthetic experience in which astonishment is paradoxically united with boredom as *stuplimity*. This term allows us to invoke the sublime – albeit negatively, since we infuse it with thickness or even stupidity – while detaching it from its spiritual and transcendent connotations and its close affiliation with Romanticism. For whereas contemporary criticism depends on and repeatedly returns to make use of older aesthetic categories, even in its engagement with radically different forms of cultural production, these different forms call for new modes of critical response and thus for new terms designating our ways of responding to them. […] [F]or now I will briefly describe it as a concatenation of boredom and astonishment – a bringing together of what 'dulls' and what 'irritates' or agitates; of sharp, sudden excitation and prolonged desensitization, exhaustion or fatigue. While the Kantian sublime stages a competition between opposing affects, in which one eventually supersedes and *replaces* the other (as Paul de Man notes, 'The victory of the sublime over nature is the victory of one emotion [tranquillity] over another emotion, such as fear'),[10] stuplimity is a tension that holds opposing affects together. And while the sublime traditionally finds a home in the serious modes of the lyrical, elegiac or tragic, stuplimity could be said to belong more properly to the dirtier environments of what Stein calls 'bottom humour'.

Stuplimity reveals the limits of our ability to comprehend a vastly extended form as a totality, as does Kant's mathematical sublime, yet not through an encounter with the infinite but with finite bits and scraps of material in repetition. […]

1 [footnote 21 in source] Jacques Lacan, *The Four Fundamental Concepts of Psychoanalysis*, ed. Jacques-Alain Miller, trans. Alan Sheridan (New York: W.W. Norton, 1981) 61.
2 [22] Susan Sontag, 'The Pornographic Imagination', in idem, *Styles of Radical Will* (New York: Farrar, Straus & Giroux, 1966) 62.
3 [23] Neville Wakefield, 'Ann Hamilton: Between Words and Things', *Ann Hamilton: Mneme* (Liverpool: Tate Liverpool, 1994) 10.
4 [24] Gerhard Richter, *Atlas* (Cologne: Verlag der Buchhandlung Walther König, 1997).
5 [25] Janet Zweig, *Her Recursive Apology* (1993) (a work consisting of 4,386,375 apologies), paper, 2 x 9 x 9 ft. Janet Zweig, note on *Her Recursive Apology*, in *Chain*, no. 2 ('Documentary') (1995) 248–9.
6 [26] Immanuel Kant, *Critique of Judgement* (1790); trans. J.H. Bernard (New York: Hafner, 1951).
7 [27] Arthur C. Danto, *The Abuse of Beauty: Aesthetics and the Concept of Art* (Chicago: Open Court, 2003).
8 [28] Alan J. Isaacs, 'The Ironic Sublime', dissertation, Stanford University, 1993, 40.
9 [29] Ben Watson, *Art, Class and Cleavage* (London: Quartet, 1998) 233.
10 [32] Paul de Man, 'Phenomenology and Materiality in Kant', in idem, *Aesthetic Ideology* (Minneapolis: University of Minnesota Press, 1996) 123.

Sianne Ngai, extracts from Ugly Feelings (Cambridge, Massachusetts: Harvard University Press, 2005) 262–3, 264–5, 270–71.

Christine Ross
The Performance-Management Model of Performative Subjectivity//2006

When depressive disorders are envisaged as emerging not from loss (as first theorized by Freud in 'Mourning and Melancholia', in 1917) but from one's maladaptive coping style, and when a person's life story is reduced to the development of a negative cognitive view of the self, the world and the future, depression ceases to be an integral part of the psychoanalytical subject defined in terms of lack, conflict and repression. It becomes instead […] the disavowing counterpart of entrepreneurial subjectivity, a disease of performance to be cured by the restoration of adaptive coping strategies. […] It discloses depression (showing it without obviously criticizing it or providing an alternative) as an integral constituent of the neoliberal entrepreneurial perspective of subjectivity.

But what does one mean exactly by 'entrepreneurial subjectivity'? I adopt here new media theoretician Jon McKenzie's definition of performance management as a paradigm of organizational theory and practice that has shaped management in the United States and worldwide (through American economic and political hegemony) at least since World War II. Displacing rather than replacing Taylorism, it is a model that seeks efficiency through decentralized and flexible styles of management instead of highly centralized bureaucracies with a top-down management philosophy; 'styles that, rather than controlling workers, empower them with information and training so that they may contribute to decision-making processes'.[1] Historically, Frederick W. Taylor's scientific management of industrial work, applied at the beginning of the twentieth century as much by Henry Ford for the mass production of automobiles through carefully orchestrated assembly lines as by the Soviet Union for the industrialization of its own economy, promoted, for the sake of maximum production, the optimal use of tools. This was a task-oriented approach to production defending strict specialization, centralized planning and the suppression of useless motion. Although this machine-like model is still present today in certain sectors of the economy, it soon became apparent that, in most sectors, efficiency was better maximized with less centralized bureaucracy and heightened organization flexibility so as to accommodate a growing informational society. Human-relations theorist Douglas McGregor describes well the contrast I wish to highlight between scientific and performance management. He keenly observes that scientific management is a process in which managers direct the efforts of the employees, 'motivating them, controlling their actions, modifying their behaviour to fit the needs of the organization', whereas in the performance-oriented model, employees are motivated to be creative and independent so that they may direct their own performance toward desired goals. Clearly taking sides with performance management because of its privileging of the creative potential of the employees, McGregor writes, 'The essential task of management is to arrange organizational conditions and methods of operation so that people can achieve their own goals *best* by directing their *own* efforts toward organizational objectives.' Management must, moreover, 'involve the individual in setting "targets" or objectives for *himself* and in a self-evaluation of performance annually or semi-annually'.[2]

The paradigm of performance management regroups a variety of discourses, practices and conceptual models (including human relations, systems theory, organizational development, information processing and decision making, and peak performance) that articulate different ways of generating, developing, measuring and evaluating performances for the sake of efficiency.[3] But these different models converge in their promotion of a type of management that aims at empowering workers instead of controlling them, promoting participatory interactions between employees and managers, and delegating information processing and decision making to everyone. The key concepts of such organizational models are diversity, innovation, invention, sense of initiative, responsibility, creativity, self-evaluation, self-transformation and supportive feedback (the manager's means to measure and evaluate performance). Although this organizational model can be seen as an improvement over the more machinist-oriented perspective of Taylorism, it normatively enforces the view of the independent subject who is required to be inventive, creative, full of initiative and self-transformational. In his assessment of the performance paradigm, McKenzie thus concludes that whereas, as Foucault's writings have shown, power regimes of modernity were once modelled on an epistemology of discipline (based on the juxtaposition of the discourses of penal law and the architectural mechanisms of surveillance embodied in Bentham's panoptic prison), they are now modelled on an epistemology of performance, which is simultaneously organizational, cultural and technological.

[…] [I]sn't it the case then that depression is the failure to keep up with the performance-management demands of constant self-creation and self-actualization? In other words, isn't depression a pathology of performance management, a pathology of adaptability, flexibility, responsibility and, most importantly, reiterated self-creation?

It is useful here to refer briefly to *Mr Pickup* (2000), a three-monitor video installation by John Pilson, which establishes a similar association of depression, deficient coping style and performance-management philosophy. […] *Mr Pickup* constructs its own laboratory of subjectivity so as to create a behavioural-cognitivist viewer whose main task is to observe the collapse of a professional unable to cope with the performance requirements of the business world. The installation features a single seventeen-minute take of a lawyer in the process of picking up files before an important meeting. About to close an important deal, he attempts to gather the required folders, but this simple action becomes a sheer impossibility. As soon as he picks up a file, another one falls. When he picks up the contents of one file sprawled on the floor, the rest slip away. As he succeeds in organizing a pile, it is sure to break apart and collapse on the floor. Sweating, he removes his jacket to gather the papers anew but fails again. He calls for help, but nobody answers. These gestures are repeated until (without the files!) he finally leaves the room in a state of chaotic mess. Crucial here is the way in which the monitors have been installed. Arranged side by side at eye level, they enable the viewer to observe the coping style of the individual by comparing the different images. The three monitors present the same sequence but with a slight discrepancy. After looking at one monitor, the viewer is thus invited to look at another so as to either anticipate what is to come or reflect on what has just happened. This is to say that the setting of the monitors allows us to identify the chain of action-reaction of the subject whose behaviour is under observation, to measure the time length of these reactions, to elaborate hypotheses about the causes of dysfunctionality, to diagnose the pathology (is this depression?), and to predict what, how and why this dysfunctionality has come about. We have become behavioural-cognitivist viewers. Moreover, we evaluate the coping skills of the subject according to the performance-management values of flexibility, adaptability, responsibility, decision making and problem-solving ability. But, as the installation exposes these values and shows us the lawyer in a state of collapse, it also opens up the hypothesis that mental disorder here emerges precisely from the lawyer's failure to meet the values according to which we have been evaluating him.

This complexified view of depression resonates with the findings of Alain Ehrenberg, whose *Fatigue d'être soi* (1998) shows that depression emerged as a leading mental illness in the 1970s, a period of decline of norms of socialization based on discipline, obedience and prohibition and the concomitant rise of norms of independence based on generalized individual initiative (personified by the model of the entrepreneur) and pluralism of values (exemplified by the dictum 'It's my choice').[4] With its valorization of the creation and assumption of responsibility of the self, the culture of individualized independence is at the root of performance-management philosophy. In such a culture, constraints still pressure subjectivity, but the imperative is to initiate one's own identity instead of being disciplined to do so. Discipline has been replaced by the highly mediatized idea that one has the right (even the duty) to *choose* one's own life: to liberate the self from prohibiting laws, to prioritize personal blooming, even to share one's intimate problems publicly (notably, on television reality shows). Norms of independence are also supported by the judicial system, notably through the legalization of abortion, the facilitation of divorce and the legislation of euthanasia and genetic engineering – domains that consolidate the right to choose one's life and to dispose of one's body. What these norms do is incite the individual to be the sole agent of his or her subjectivity, to be the subject of himself or herself. This also means, however, that the individual will be affected by troubles of the self.[5] 'Depression', writes Ehrenberg, 'is the counterpart of the democratization of the exceptional, of this quest to only be oneself',[6] in societies where 'no moral law, no tradition shows from the outside who we have to be and how to conduct ourselves'.[7] Psycho- and pharmacotherapy thus become the motor by which the main characteristics of depression – inhibition, fatigue, the diminution of cognitive activity – are treated so as to reinstate the independence of the individual. Depressive disorders are not so much a failure to perform as a failure to perform the self in a culture whose norms of socialization are based on self-creation.

1 [footnote 137 in source] Jon McKenzie, *Perform or Else: From Discipline to Performance* (London and New York: Routledge, 2001) 6.
2 [138] *Leadership and Motivation: Essays of Douglas McGregor*, ed. Warren G. Bennis and Edgar H. Schein, with the collaboration of Caroline McGregor (Cambridge, Massachusetts: The MIT Press, 1966) 15, 19.
3 [139] McKenzie, *Perform or Else*, op. cit., 56.
4 [140] Alain Ehrenberg, *La Fatigue d'être soi* (Paris: Éditions Odile Jacob, 1998) 10; and idem, 'Des troubles du désir au malaise identitaire', *Magazine littéraire*, no. 411 (July/August 2002) 24 (all quotations my translation). [...]
5 [141] Ehrenberg, 'Des troubles du désir ', op. cit., 26.
6 [142] Ibid.
7 [143] Ehrenberg, *La Fatigue d'être soi*, op. cit., 14.

Christine Ross, extract ('The Performance-Management Model of Performative Subjectivity'), from *The Aesthetics of Disengagement* (Minneapolis: University of Minnesota Press, 2006) 88–93.

Dominic Fox
The Cold World//2009

Sadness does something to the way we see the world. In the experience of deep sadness, the world itself seems altered in some way: coloured by sadness, or disfigured by it. Rather than living inside us, as our normal passions do, our sadness seems to envelop everything: we live inside it, as if it were a cocoon or a prison. At such times we seem particularly aware of the world *as* a world, as a place where we have to live. This awareness can become artistic or political: *artistic*, when the world made strange by our own detachment and dissociation presents itself as an object of fascination; *political* when the difficulty of going on living in such a world begins to reveal its causes in the impersonal circumstances of our personal sorrows.

Both kinds of awareness have their origins in desolation, in the sense that the world is frozen and that nothing new is possible. Both can lead to terrible paroxysms of destruction, attempts to shatter the carapace of reality and release the authentic self trapped within; but both can also lead away from the self altogether, towards new worldly commitments that recognize the urgent need to develop another logic of existence, another way of going on. […]

[W]e will call this frozen constellation the 'cold world': the world voided of both human warmth and metaphysical comfort. This cold world is the world made strange, a world that has ceased to be the 'lifeworld' in which we are usually immersed and instead stands before us in a kind of lopsided objectivity. It is a world between worlds, a disfigured world. […]

The cold world is the world in abeyance, in withdrawal […]. It is the vitalist world fallen into inert matter, the animist world deserted by its presiding spirits, the heroic world overtaken by bourgeois commercialism – which, Marx claimed, 'drowns the most heavenly ecstasies of religious fervour, of chivalrous enthusiasm, of philistine sentimentalism, in the icy water of egotistical calculation'. Finally, it is the world of amorous occlusion, of love's failure or exhaustion. […]

The cold world imposes itself as final, terminal, because it is the termination of a world, its metaphorical freezing or blackening. Just as a given 'life-world' is endowed with resources and qualities which make it possible to live well within it, so the experience of the cold world (or 'unlife-world') is the experience of the exhaustion of these resources and the extinction of these qualities. This experience places in question the value of 'the world', and with it the opposition between the mundane and the exceptional, the worldly and the unworldly. 'The' world, thus disenchanted, is revealed as 'a' world, a world among possible worlds; but it is also estranged from its conditions of possibility, to the extent that it seems scarcely credible that such a world could ever have existed at all. […]

Let us now revisit our earlier assertion that the experience of the cold world brings the opposition between the worldly and the unworldly into question. In that experience, the world appears before us in a kind of disfigured objectivity. We are no longer fully immersed in it, or engaged with it; indeed, our habitual satisfactions and modes of engagement are suspended, placed beyond reach. It is at this moment, however, that the 'mechanisms of power' truly become accessible to understanding. The experience of the cold world is one of dislocation, of eviction; of being eased or jiggled or jolted out of one's place in the world. One possible, and politically significant, consequence of this is that one's former position in the scheme of things may become apparent as a meeting-place of forces: one is separated, more or less forcefully, from what one had previously assumed and defended as one's 'interests'. […]

The rhetoric of worldliness emphasizes the immediately situated character of political decision-making and action, against abstract or other-worldly considerations of principle. It inveighs against abstract moralism, utopianism and fantastic dreaming, the solipsistic cinema of revolt that plays endlessly in the private inner theatres of privileged would-be radicals. But a political situation is seldom immediately graspable in its concrete reality; it is rather 'enworlded', materialized through a relational order of appearances, and it is with these appearances that – whatever the real stakes of the conflict – the actors in a political situation are often largely concerned.

Let us fix this 'seldom' and this 'often' to a condition: only at certain very rare moments, moments of profound disruption and severity, do mundane and quotidian calculations of interest, reckoning with the present world-order of values and appearances, give way to concrete decisions in the subjective path of a truth. Worldly realism knows nothing of truth; it is wholly absorbed in deliberating between greater and lesser 'evils', which is to say that it moves entirely within corruption, employing corrupt means in the pursuit of corrupt ends. Such are the 'mechanisms of power' with which we are encouraged to acquaint ourselves. The cold world is the world in which these mechanisms are shown to be incapable of upholding a truth, but to operate rather through a kind of generalized power of falsity. It is not the world is at really is, but the un-world in which 'the thing which is not' stands exposed in its lack of being.

It is the inhabitant of the cold world, evicted from all home comforts and pressed 'sheathe-and-shelterless' against the emptiness of being, who like the poet Gerard Manley Hopkins must find a way to recommence his existence, a new way to go on:

NOT, I'll not, carrion comfort, Despair, not feast on thee; / Not untwist – slack they may be – these last strands of man / In me ór, most weary, cry *I can no more*. I can; / Can something, hope, wish day come, not choose not to be.

Dominic Fox, extracts from 'The Cold World', *Cold World: The Aesthetics of Dejection and the Politics of Militant Dysphori*a (Alresford, England, and Washington, DC: Zero Books, 2009) 1, 4, 7, 12–14.

Bernadette Corporation
Bedrooms Boredoms (Short Escapes in New York City)//2004

Two lands, two territories, whose borders overlap. Bedrooms are the site of intimacy. What is more intimate, when shared, than boredom. Boredom is the site of lassitude. Where is there more lassitude than in a bedroom. We at Bernadette Corporation love bedrooms, and we love boredoms. We love couples. We discuss them in our boardroom. Couples are a machine. Most cars are made for couples. The best looking ones are. Even bicycles are, really. So are bodies I guess, but let's not talk about that. Sometimes the less said the better about bodies. Are they metaphors, are they real, are they everything, are they death, is mine yours. Let's be quiet and just shove off with our paddles.

B	B
E	O
D	R
R	E
O	D
O	O
M	M
S	S

Two canoes. Two seats in one canoe.

> B is for boredom
> E is for enthusiasm
> O is for orgasm
> D is for drugged

R is for retarded
M is for money
S is for shopping

To Begin:

Experience #1. (Boredom to Boredom).
Boredoms: When you enter into deep conflict between two or more things to do, realize you made a very wrong choice in going to one thing over another. Resign yourself to ennui. No matter your choice, you'll wish you were somewhere else. Which is ennui. Get to it before it gets to you. Boredom like stupidity contains its own treasures. A state of grace providing zero payoff. You'll recognize it. Ignore any path that would seem to give you advantage, in terms of amusement or some kind of good use of the time. Ignore the bong for once. Take your companion outside into the too bright sun. Each of you try to want what the other wants. You'll soon reach an impossible state. Look to the left. Find it tedious. Proceed to the right with the sun assaulting your pates. In consideration for each other, fail to decide what to eat. Immediately on changing the subject of conversation, run out of energy. Understand your partner's agony. Don't give in to understanding. Let the day drag on. [...]

Experience #8. (Shopping to Shopping).
You are standing in line with your sisters in the discount store. You have a handful of nylon-laced g-strings in candy colours and try to convince the clerk to give you your money back, saying you bought them just 10 minutes ago and have the timed register slip to prove it. 'So why did you buy them?', the clerk asks, 'if you didn't want them?' You must have just acted on an impulse and you cry for the manager because there is always a manager behind such impulsive moments. You can't explain where the impulse came from and it feels stupid to try. You want to see the manager.

What were the things you always wanted and for what? There was something but it is not of interest anymore. You feel exceptionally weird. You want no-things. It is your state of mind now, for a moment. All exists in undifferentiated potential. The 'endless world' that is of and in the most starkest contrast to the creatures of the 21st century. You got the sudden desire to make one last purchase, a golden hat. Then no longer feeling a distinction between the agent and the product of its action you decide you will become gamblers, betting on bets, money for money, shopping for your shopping.

Bernadette Corporation, extracts from *Reena Spaulings* (Los Angeles: Semiotext[e], 2004) 84-5, 91-2.

Claire Fontaine
Dear R.//2007

Dear R.,
It's been too long since we've spoken of anything besides the daily grind.

Since we last saw each other, the weight of things has slightly shifted and I don't know why I can no longer really look at people in the streets with indulgence.

I also have the impression that I am not the only one in this disturbing situation.

It is as if grace has permanently deserted the encounters between the glances of strangers in this city. The bodies of the passers-by hold no beauty and no silent dialogue of desire unites them.

Yes, it's burning again, there are shards of glass on the sidewalks and taxi drivers often refuse to take the shortest route between two places. But those things aren't the reasons for the change in the gravity of the real I am referring to – they are only its symptoms. The relationship between cause and effect has been afflicted by a dire illness for some time now, and nothing can ever be said as being the direct consequence of something else. So, as soon as there is an urgent need to put an end to injustice or to resolve a problem, we cannot find the ones responsible, there are no doors to knock on, or to be kicked or to throw stones at. All that's left is our solitude and our questions without addressees.

None of this is new, you will tell me, and I grant you that, however not so long ago I have seen power trembling like a lit match with my own eyes, and order coming to protect it from the wind of the revolts.

This morning we, the passers-by, all looked like culprits illegitimately freed, and the cars and the shop windows and the whole public space showed their teeth as only prisons do with inmates. We were part of a vicious circle we had not even contributed to forming.

The police populated our fields of vision in an incongruous way, like a profusion of trash covering a vacant lot. And if the streets are in such need of being defended – we were thinking to ourselves – then our deep and confused impression must be right.

If our footsteps are to this extent deprived of pleasure, it's because the fabric binding things and images has become unravelled; because something constantly disrupts our happiness to be alive and to be walking one morning, our feet on the pavement, amongst strangers. I keep feeling tempted to name this something and I stop, because words of philosophers interfere with my conjectures and they are not the appropriate ones.

Words themselves in any case have changed place and shifted their weight and that's surely why for children reading and writing has become increasingly complicated. But that's another story.

There is also the difficulty of taming the idea that the pleasure of a few lies in causing the suffering of others.

We've had class and gender struggle, racial unrest, generational conflict, but what's coming now is a war without a name. Whatever they call it – terrorism, insecurity – they speak of this war without being able to discern it. At present, what burns and what breaks does so as an object participating in a world contaminated by the lack of meaning, relieved of all signification. Innocence and impunity are now so intimate that it's impossible to distinguish them. Fear reigns sovereign under these conditions and the sirens that cleave through the traffic fuel it. The world and its inhabitants have begun to embody the plausible targets of a violence so logical that it has become universally shareable.

But we still call certain acts of destruction 'violence' and there are no words for the harm that has been done to our capacity to love each other, to give ourselves to each other, to fight and to share. No words for the cruelty of the smiling faces pasted on all the walls, inviting us, without saying it, to remain silent and forget.

Money divides us, of course, but it is also – as you say – what keeps us alive. And it's precisely this idea of 'life' that I can no longer bring myself to share. Beyond the fossils of contestation from another cycle of capitalism and another cycle of anger and despair, we are completely deprived of gestures and words to proclaim our need for joy and freedom, our need to crush everything that degrades the basic force of the bodies moving together without a guide and without constraint. This new poverty is also a nascent force we are not yet sure how to use, although power apprehensively spies on it.

I sometimes stop writing to you because I wonder if you really want these words of doubt, if they sound like words of defeat but, I can reassure you, they aren't.

It's not my strength and the strength of our friendship that has unravelled and been emptied – they remain intact and have even been reinforced – but it is the fabric of the world. Wherever there are public transportation, shops, offices, neighbourhoods, schools, there used to be networks of solidarity, of affects, of complicities, poised to stop at any moment, to close up on themselves for protection whenever necessary.

And when we passed through these places, these fluxes, we felt different intensities, odours, tastes, which gave meaning to the simple fact of being there and not somewhere else at a given moment. Passing through life meant passing through these unicities because one doesn't love, doesn't sleep, doesn't eat in the same way within the different magnetic fields of the present. We were our potentiality of sharing at each instant, in each encounter, we were a possibility that called to others.

Now we coexist in a present of the colonized, we are subjected to the time and space of an Other that has different faces: reassuring, artificial, ignorant of pleasure, of affection and of illness. Monstrous faces that we often think we recognize in people's traits and expressions.

Truce, you'll say, respite from these considerations, which are true, but which bring us nothing, which are fair, but which do not help us to live simpler lives. Truce.

That's what everyone is asking for and yet it's this truce that has produced the new war. The war in which one mustn't choose one's camp by going toward others, one must descend into the depths of the self and recommence the interrupted conversation with the most uncanny host. This situation will not resolve itself without violence, no matter what we wish, because at this stage our desires are worthless. Yet the revolt that we will know is not going to be corporatist, it will no longer speak the language of work and its procession of social identifications. The change that is coming, that is already here, will be a change of ourselves, a strike of the most rooted and persistent habits, beginning with the nostalgia for the past and for what hasn't happened and what the past carried away. This will be what I call a human strike.

Dear R., you know we could become beings without regrets and forget any fear, if only we understood the extent to which we are already deprived of destiny. But this letter is already much too long and I know how much work you have at the moment, so I'll finish here and we'll see each other soon.

Best, Claire

Claire Fontaine, 'Dear R' (Paris, 8 May 2007).

The Invisible Committee
The Coming Insurrection//2007

[…] The injunction, everywhere, to 'be someone' maintains the pathological state that makes this society necessary. The injunction to be strong produces the very weakness by which it maintains itself, so that *everything seems to take on a therapeutic character*, even working, even love. All those 'How's it goings?' that we exchange give the impression of a society composed of patients taking each other's temperature. Sociability is now made up of a thousand little niches, a thousand little refuges where you can take shelter. Where it's always better than the bitter cold outside. Where everything's false, since it's all just a pretext for getting warmed up. Where nothing can happen since we're all too busy shivering silently together. Soon this society will only be held together by the mere tension of all the social atoms straining towards an illusory cure. It's a power plant that runs its turbines on a gigantic reservoir of unwept tears, always on the verge of spilling over.

'I AM WHAT I AM.' Never has domination found such an innocent-sounding slogan. The maintenance of the self in a permanent state of deterioration, in a chronic state of near-collapse, is the best-kept secret of the present order of things. The weak, depressed, self-critical, virtual self is essentially that endlessly adaptable subject required by the ceaseless innovation of production, the accelerated obsolescence of technologies, the constant overturning of social norms, and generalized flexibility. It is at the same time the most voracious consumer and, paradoxically, the *most productive self*, the one that will most eagerly and energetically throw itself into the slightest *project*, only to return later to its original larval state.

'WHAT AM I', then? Since childhood, I've been involved with flows of milk, smells, stories, sounds, emotions, nursery rhymes, substances, gestures, ideas, impressions, gazes, songs and foods. What am I? Tied in every way to places, sufferings, ancestors, friends, loves, events, languages, memories, to all kinds of things that obviously *are not me*. Everything that attaches me to the world, all the links that constitute me, all the forces that compose me don't form an identity, a thing displayable on cue, but a singular, shared, living *existence*, from which emerges – at certain times and places – that being which says 'I'. Our feeling of inconsistency is simply the consequence of this foolish belief in the permanence of the self and of the little care we give to what makes us what we are.

It's dizzying to see Reebok's 'I AM WHAT I AM' enthroned atop a Shanghai skyscraper. The West everywhere rolls out its favourite Trojan horse: the exasperating antimony between the self and the world, the individual and the group, between attachment and freedom. Freedom isn't the act of shedding our attachments, but the *practical* capacity to work on them, to move around in their space, to form or dissolve them. The family only exists as a family, that is, as a hell, for those who've quit trying to alter its debilitating mechanisms, or don't know how to. The freedom *to uproot oneself* has always been a phantasmic freedom. We can't rid ourselves of what binds us without at the same time losing the very thing to which our forces would be applied.

'I AM WHAT I AM', then, is not simply a lie, a simple advertising campaign, but a *military* campaign, a war cry directed against everything that exists *between* beings, against everything that circulates indistinctly, everything that invisibly links them, everything that prevents complete desolation, against everything that makes us *exist*, and ensures that the whole world doesn't everywhere have the look and feel of a highway, an amusement park or a new town: pure boredom, passionless but well ordered, empty, frozen space, where nothing moves apart from registered bodies, molecular automobiles and ideal commodities.

France wouldn't be the land of anxiety pills that it's become, the paradise of anti-depressants, the Mecca of neurosis, if it weren't also the European champion of hourly productivity. Sickness, fatigue, depression, can be seen as the *individual* symptoms of what needs to be cured. They contribute to the maintenance of the existing order, to my docile adjustment to idiotic norms, and to the modernization of my crutches. They specify the selection of my opportune, compliant and productive tendencies, as well as those that must be gently discarded. 'It's never too late to change, you know.' But taken as *facts*, my failings can also lead to the dismantling of the hypothesis of the self. They then become acts of resistance in the current war. They become a rebellion and a force against everything that conspires to normalize us, to amputate us. *The self is not some thing within us that is in a state of crisis; it is the form they mean to stamp upon us.* They want to make our self something sharply defined, separate, assessable in terms of qualities, controllable, when in fact we are creatures among creatures, singularities among similars, living flesh weaving the flesh of the world. Contrary to what has been repeated to us since childhood, intelligence doesn't mean knowing how to adapt – or if that is a kind of intelligence, it's the intelligence of slaves. *Our inadaptability*, our fatigue, are only *problems* from the standpoint of what aims to subjugate us. They indicate rather a starting point, a meeting point, for new complicities. They reveal a landscape more damaged but infinitely more sharable than all the fantasy lands this society maintains for its purposes.

We are not depressed; we're on strike. For those who refuse to manage themselves, 'depression' is not a state but a passage, a bowing out, a sidestep towards a *political* disaffiliation. From then on medication and the police are the only possible forms of conciliation. This is why the present society doesn't hesitate to impose Ritalin on its overactive children, or to strap people into lifelong dependence on pharmaceuticals, and why it claims to be able to detect 'behavioural disorders' at age three. Because everywhere the hypothesis of the self is beginning to crack.

The Invisible Committee, extract from *The Coming Insurrection* (Los Angeles: Semiotext[e], 2009) 31–4.

Sven Lütticken
Lazy Labour: Chronopolitical Remarks//2014/16

[…] Sleep and laziness have long been associated; while offering respite from dulling labor, sleep could also be the apogee and fulfilment of laziness. Now that indolence has become a near impossibility in our networked neo-productivism, we see an ideologization of sleep as the last refuge of laziness.

In his book *24/7: Late Capitalism and the Ends of Sleep* (2013), Jonathan Crary notes the gradual erosion of the average time of sleep per day during the twentieth century (from ten hours to less than seven), and argues that sleep 'is a ubiquitous reminder of a premodernity that has never been fully exceeded, of the agricultural universe that began vanishing 400 years ago. The scandal of sleep is the embeddedness in our lives of the rhythmic oscillations of solar light and darkness, activity and rest, of work and recuperation, that have been eradicated or neutralized elsewhere.' (11) Crary reminds us that industrial temporality still had its zones of exception, its archaic pockets; industrial time was imposed only gradually, triumphing finally in the post-war consumer society, ready to morph into the post-Fordist 24/7 time of permanent performance, permanent readiness. In this 24/7 regime, Crary 'dreams of sleep' in order to begin to imagine a future beyond capitalism, to imagine 'a shared world whose fate is not terminal, a world without billionaires, which has a future other than barbarism or the post-human, and in which history can take other forms than reified nightmares of catastrophe'. (128)

If idling – being lazy – is a kind of waking sleep, it has its twin in boredom. Like sleep and laziness, boredom is seen as being in decline and under attack. If, among the waking equivalents of sleep, boredom had the worst reputation, today's popular discourse revalorizes the experience (now facing extinction): 'It's sad to think kids of this generation won't be able to experience boredom like we have. Consider how boredom was handled at a younger age, as though it was a matter of solving a problem. Do children really need to worry about that, or can they just boot up their iPad? […] Instead of embracing boredom and using it as a creative application, we choose to replace it with some "busy" activity. Instead of sitting in thought, we impulsively pull out our phones.' [Zack Katz, 'Boredom Leads to Productivity', *Spectator*, 27 February 2013] However, relearning how to be bored is not a Craryesque exercise in imagining a different future beyond catastrophe, but rather an attempt at improving one's performance: 'It probably sounds a little counter-intuitive to suggest to anyone that they start slacking off, but in reality it's about as important to your brain's health as sleeping is. Being bored, procrastinating, and embracing distraction all help your brain function. In turn, you understand decisions better. You learn easier.' [Thorin Klosowski, 'The Holy Trinity of Inactivity: How Boredom, Distraction and Procrastination are Vital to Healthy Living', *Lifehacker*, 19 September 2012]

Boredom is a modern concept – which obviously does not mean that pre-modern people never experienced states that we would now characterize as boredom. Rather, it means that boredom 'in the modern sense that combines an existential and a temporal connotation' only became a theoretical concept and a problem in the late eighteenth century – in fact, the English term *boredom* emerged in the late eighteenth century, under the combined impact of the Enlightenment and the Industrial revolution. As Elizabeth Goodstein puts it [in *Experience without Qualities*, 2005], boredom 'epitomizes the dilemma of the autonomous modern subject', linking 'existential questions' to 'a peculiarly modern experience of empty, meaningless time'. (3) Boredom became a crucial notion for the 1960s avant-garde in different ways. On the one hand, the Cagean neo-avant-garde (Fluxus) embraced boredom as a productive strategy; on the other hand, the Situationist International attacked boredom as a disastrous symptom of capitalism.

In the late 1960s, Situationist and pro-situ slogans such as 'Boredom is always counter-revolutionary' and 'There's nothing they won't do to raise the standard of boredom' made the term a battle cry, though it is not particularly prominent in Debord's writings. Boredom for the SI was a symptom of the inhuman nature of capitalism. As Raoul Vaneigem put it: 'We do not want a world in which the guarantee that we will not die of starvation is bought by accepting the risk of dying of boredom.' [*The Revolution of Everyday Life*, 1967] Boredom is a kind of byproduct of industrial labour that creates new markets for entertainment, for while boredom during working hours is unavoidable and can only be alleviated in part by half-hearted measures (playing music to the workers), boredom also infects 'free time', where various leisure activities and the products of the entertainment industry are ready to help – if only, as the slogan has it, to 'raise the standard of boredom'.

In fact, 'raising the standard of boredom' could be taken for a tongue-in-cheek description of some Cage-inspired aesthetic practices of the early 1960s, particularly in the context of Fluxus. The theorist of the role of boredom in Fluxus is Dick Higgins. 'The use, in Fluxus format works, of boredom became not so much a structural factor as an implicit factor, as, for example, when Jackson Mac Low proposed a project, a film which for financial reasons was not executed (but which was widely published). The film was to be made of a tree on which the camera would be trained from the start of light to the end of light in the course of a single day. This film would clearly have been more environmental than entertaining, cinematic, or educational. One would relate to it in direct proportion to the ability to look with concentration at it. Boring? Of course; if one were to ignore the more intense activity involved, which one might call super-boring, and which took one beyond the initial level of simple boredom.' ['Boredom and Danger', 1966] The Mac Low film of course immediately recalls some of Warhol's cinematic work from the 1960s, such as *Sleep* or *Empire* – and in fact Maciunas pointed out Warhol's 'plagiarism' in 1969.

It is significant that Warhol's *Sleep* was incorporated into installations by younger artists during the 1990s, in the context of 'relational' practice. Pierre Huyghe's *Sleeptalking* (1998) projected the film in one room, while an adjacent room (with a window through which one could see the film) contained an audio monologue by John Giorno, who was Warhol's 'actor' in that film, reminiscing about the 1960s. The other piece, Bik Van der Pol's *Sleep With Me* (1997), is an installation in which people can lie down on mattresses and watch the film or sleep with/through it. In this case, the circle has in a sense been completed: sleep produces a boring or 'super-boring' viewing experience, which is in turn transmuted into more sleep. Furthermore, this sleep, like Giorno's but on a more collective basis, has been made productive: it is part of an art event and as such an exemplary manifestation of the time of continuous performance.

While sleep, according to Crary, is under attack because it is a reservation of unproductive life that is subjected to various forms of biopolitical primitive accumulation, various expert and non-expert authors argue that boredom can actually be productive – and important for kids' development. 'Some experts say that people tune things out for good reasons, and that over time boredom becomes a tool for sorting information – an increasingly sensitive spam filter. In various fields including neuroscience and education, research suggests that falling into a numbed trance allows the brain to recast the outside world in ways that can be productive and creative at least as often as they are disruptive.' [Benedict Carey, 'You're Bored, But Your Mind is Tuned in', *The New York Times*, 5 August 2008] It would no doubt be possible to make a similar case for sleep. In fact, Franco 'Bifo' Berardi appears to do as much in a gloss on the Italian Autonomists' version of the Lafargian motif, with their 'refusal of work' rhetoric: 'Refusal of work means quite simply: I don't want to go to work because I prefer to sleep. But this laziness is the source of intelligence, of technology, of progress. Autonomy is the self-regulation of the social body in its independence and in its interaction with the disciplinary norm.' [What is the Meaning of Autonomy Today?', 2003]

Here, laziness and sleep are in fact seen as productive forces; for Crary, of course, of forms of psychic productivism, and he proposes a kind of anachronic resistance on the basis of survivals of pre-modern behaviour patterns. In this respect, his stance is quite traditional. However, one should be careful to distinguish Berardi's version of 'intelligence, technology and progress' from their perverted, 'actually existing' incarnation in contemporary hyper-capitalism – in which sleep has not only been made productive in the traditional manner, by restoring body and mind, but in innovative ways. The 'album' *Sleepify* (2014) by the band Vulfpeck consists of soundless tracks that can be put on repeat on Spotify at night; in this way, fans can make their sleep productive by making a few bucks for the band.

In light of the productive turn of sleep, laziness and boredom, does the radical tradition that provided our starting point still have any value? Already in 1973, Jean Baudrillard attacked the habitual glorification of laziness and non-work for ultimately turning non-work into 'the repressive desublimation of labour power – the antithesis that acts as an alternative'. Baudrillard claimed that even if 'one does not immediately confuse [the sphere of non-work] with that of leisure', it remains ensnared in a cult of freedom and self-production of the individual, positing 'the ideality of time and of the individual as an empty form, to be filled in the end by his freedom'. In other words, according to Baudrillard's full-frontal attack, 'The finality of value is always there. It is no longer inscribed in *determined* contents as in the sphere of productive activity; henceforth it is a *pure form*, though no less determining. Exactly as the pure institutional form of painting, art and theatre shines, emptied of its contents, in anti-painting, anti-art, anti-theatre – non-work shines in the pure form of labour.' ['The Mirror of Production', 1972]

For Baudrillard, any immanent dialectical engagement with(in) the prevailing conditions, any historical praxis, was fundamentally compromised; only terrorism still appeared to be a viable form of action. One might agree with Baudrillard that the pervasive reality of labour shines forth in the theory of non-labour, but without regarding this as a complete disqualification. Conceptualizations of laziness, of boredom, of sleep are all marked by the fundamental antinomies of industrial and post-industrial capitalism, and in their negation of productiveness, they do indeed tend to substitute other, 'purified' forms of human productivity and self-creation. These are, indeed, historical theories. Some remain trapped within a specific historical moment, while others manage to push the articulation of these contradictions to a point where they explode and light up in an illuminating constellation. Such is the case with Paul Lafargue's text [*The Right to Be Lazy*, 1883], for instance. If this text appears once more to be highly contemporary, it is perhaps most of all because of its articulation of capitalism's contradictions in a manner that is itself profoundly quizzical, and points both in the direction of a radical negation of work and toward an instrumentalization of non-work, of consumption. […]

Sven Lütticken, extract from essay first published as 'Liberation Through Laziness: Some Chronopolitical Remarks', *Mousse Magazine*, no. 42 (2014). (http://moussemagazine.it); retitled and revised by the author, 2016 [footnotes not included].

Peter Osborne
Art Time//2013

[…] Art distracts and art compels attention, art bores and art produces distraction. Today, perhaps more than ever before, art is received in distraction. For Walter Benjamin, in the 1930s, 'reception in distraction' was already 'the sort of reception which is increasingly noticeable in all areas of art and is a symptom of profound changes in apperception'. Indeed, 'the sort of distraction that is provided by art' represented for him 'a covert measure of the extent to which it has become possible to perform new tasks of apperception'; that of a 'distracted examination' in particular, an 'evaluating attitude' that requires 'no attention'. Historically, it has been architecture that offered the prototype of an artwork that is 'received in a state of distraction', but Benjamin took the 'training ground' of distracted reception in his day to be film; or rather cinema, as a particular architectural space and social use of the temporal qualities of film.[1] By the 1960s the cultural training ground of distracted reception had changed location, from cinema to television. Commercial cinema remained a distraction, but as a routinized narrative spectacle that absorbed the viewer, it set few new tasks of apperception, leading to a revival of that 'ancient lament that the masses seek distraction', from which Benjamin (following Kracauer) had so decisively distanced himself.[2] Today, with the digitally based convergence of audio-visual communication technologies, the training ground of distracted reception has moved again, from television to the multiplying sites and social functions of the interactive, liquid crystal computer-display screen: smartphones and tablet computers, in particular. We are experiencing a new, much more spatially diffuse 'cult of distraction' of the Internet, the social and economic – but not yet the artistic – significance of which is clear.[3]

This is the context of a renewed – and newly historical – interest in film and video in art spaces, in which 'the sort of distraction provided by art', and 'the new tasks of apperception' to which it attests, are at issue once more. As the economic logic of the cultural industries imposes itself on art institutions, subsuming them into its cycles of reproduction, the question of what modes of experience are specific to art, at any particular historical moment, finds itself enlivened once again by technology. […]

Time-based technologies of representation construct their own forms of temporal continuity out of their own technologically specific temporal differentiations (twenty-four frames per second, for example). And the temporality of reception will be a product of this temporality of the work and the other temporalities at play in the field of the viewer (the viewer as field) –

temporalities that are embodied articulations of spatial relations. Each work makes its own time, in relation to its space, and hence to other times; but it can only succeed in doing so by taking account of the spatio-temporal conditions – the dialectics of attention, boredom and distraction – characteristic of its prevailing reception. It is through the spatial articulations of temporal relations that time is socialized. The temporal dialectic of distracted reception, into which art film and video intervene, is a socio-spatial as well as a psychological one. Indeed, when Benjamin wrote of reception 'in a state of distraction', he identified it with reception 'through the collective' – that is, with a certain public use.³ (Distraction, one might say, is the sociality of attention.) This raises the question of the character of the collectivity at work in the distracted reception of contemporary film and video art; and through it, the question of the broader, historical time within which it is inscribed and upon which it draws. There is a complex overlay of rhythms condensed into the casual act of viewing a work of art. One criterion of judgement of a work – one new task of apperception – might be the extent to which it opens up this network of temporal connections (psychic, social, historical) to reflective and transfigurative view.

Large-scale quasi-cinematic video installation, for example, is a staple of contemporary art. The sort of distraction it provides is in some respects not unlike that of early cinema, in that it acknowledges its spatial conditions as part of the viewing experience, albeit usually only negatively, by enclosing itself off from the rest of the gallery, but only for a relatively short while in the viewer's tour. But the form of collectivity here is very far from that of the cinematic masses of Kracauer's picture palaces; it is a privatized, serial, small group affair. The work has only a short time to engage, and immobilize, the sampling viewer, by imposing its image and rhythm – although once captured the cinematic conditions of blackout will help to keep the viewer lingering, before they move off and out to the next distraction. A work displayed on a monitor, perhaps, standing ignored in a gallery corner. What this points to, I think, is a deepening of distracted perception, psychic attention in dispersal, not as a barrier to, but more simply, as a condition of reception. At their best, contemporary galleries reproduce the antagonistic multiplicity of the social image-space in such a way as to impose new reflective rhythms of absorption, distraction and boredom, new articulations of duration, interruption, beginning, ending, repetition and delay. The non-places of informational cities are their context; digital technologies are the basis of their operational techniques; and increasingly, the philosophy of time holds the key to understanding the possibilities inherent in the experience of the works on display. [...]

1 [footnote 41 in source] Walter Benjamin, 'The Work of Art in the Age of Its Mechanical

Reproducibility' (3rd version), in *Selected Writings* (Cambridge, Massachusetts: Harvard University Press, 1996), vol. 4, 268–9. […]
2   [42] Ibid., 268. […]
3   [50] Ibid.

Peter Osborne, extracts from 'Art Time', *Anywhere or Not At All* (London and New York: Verso, 2013) 184–5, 189–90.

Stefan Brüggemann
In Conversation with Malcolm McLaren//2006

Malcolm McLaren What is this?

Stefan Brüggemann These are scribbles – a double negation. So I scribble then I double scribble and then there's different colours, a few, it's a very aggressive work that's very nihilistic; it's about negation and about the capacity of not writing and then having it in a form that's about seduction and celebration. And I think light …

McLaren So neon was the way to do it?

Brüggemann Yes, and light and also colour. I normally don't use colour.

McLaren But basically the neon has colour …

Brüggemann … combinations. So for me, it was like having contradictions all the time between writing and non writing, visual and non visual, pop commodity and punk nihilism, on-no, black and white, expression and non expression; things that confront each other. This *Obliteration* series is very musical – it produces mental sounds.

McLaren Really? I'm confused!

Brüggemann There is also a type of emptiness in my work.

McLaren What do you mean?

Brüggemann Like I'm very obsessed lately about capitalism and failure.

McLaren How?

Brüggemann Well … it's not about criticizing it but more about just celebrating, but then that's very empty, but I kind of get attracted to that.

McLaren It's difficult for me, always, to think as a visual artist. Simply because I've been so much outside of that game that I tend to think … in less abstract terms and in more obvious political, social, economic and more literary, and maybe more practical terms. But that doesn't necessarily mean I don't appreciate it. I do. It's just that I've been through so many doors since I was at art school that I can't remember, any longer, how to think in a purely visual way.

Brüggemann Yeah, but for instance, I think, I think […] that now the role of the artist is very questionable.

McLaren That is true.

Brüggemann And I've always been doing lots of other things, like I'm doing a movie now, I'm doing hotels.

McLaren But nevertheless, still the same critique applies. If an artist builds a hotel, it's going to look an awful lot different to a hotel by an architect. When you're directing a movie, it's going to look very different to a movie director directing a movie simply because you're an artist. If you compare movies made by artists to movies made by movie directors, trained as part of the movie genre with certain ground rules, they are different, because artists try not to tell stories but destroy them. Artists generally don't behave.

Brüggemann Of course. It's about finding a new way of communication and experimentation and not always using the same medium; each medium has its own language and it is very exciting to find new mediums that form part of your own language.

McLaren So when you say NO CONTENT in that neon, I think that's interesting. It suggests the Next Big Thing. I want to know what happens with no content. Where does that go? Where does that lead me? I think it leads me to say no sex! No show?

Brüggemann No.

McLaren And … no logo.

Brüggemann Yes.

Stefan Brüggemann and Malcolm McLaren, extract from 'Conversation between Malcolm McLaren and Stefan Brüggemeann' (2006, Paris). (www.stefanbruggemann.com)

Chris Kraus
Twelve Words, Nine Days//2011

1.
Punta Banda, Baja California North
July 18, 2007

    boredom …

I'm very obsessed lately about capitalism and failure', the conceptual artist Stefan Brüggemann remarked to Malcolm McLaren. 'How's that?' asked the *eminence grise* of punk nihilism. 'Well it's not about criticizing it, but more about just celebrating, but then that's very empty, but I kind of get attracted to that', replied Brüggemann.

What struck me about McLaren's part of this dialogue was that he was extremely specific. As if he's spent most of his time since punk's demise acquiring and refining information, i.e. becoming a thinker. It is possible for someone to be highly intelligent and yet have no information. This condition – usually associated with youth or prolonged adolescence – results often in *boredom*, the existential progenitor of nearly every significant art and cultural movement. I'm thinking dada–surrealism–*dérive*–Guy Debord–East Village punk–mid 90s grunge/heroin chic–late 90s Los Angeles. Boredom, a brilliant and brazen stupidity, is dazzlingly preemptive. When the bored youth is no longer young, he/she generally either enacts his/her own early demise, or devotes him/herself to acquiring information. Specificity preempts boredom. Like the incandescence of *pop*, boredom cannot be sustained indefinitely. The *seduction* of pop is to render everything nascent, just on the verge of becoming.

No No No NO, Brüggemann asserts in one of his pieces. Let critics ponder the presence or absence of irony in his use of this two-letter word, is it an homage to Bruce Nauman? In *Obliteration*, Brüggemann's graceful and casual scratches of nothing freeze on the wall as halations. Boredom is pop's weighted corollary, but it can't be sustained once someone acquires an interest in details.

A Brüggeman show entitled 'Shallow' featured boxes of Nothing, conjoined with the subtitle of Gilles Deleuze and Félix Guattari's *A Thousand Plateaus* reduced or expanded to giant Styrofoam letters alongside an M&M warehouse in Puerto Rico, *Capitalism and Schizophrenia* ... is there another place in the world where this concept would have more and less resonance? *I'll be your mirror*. Taglines of critical thought float in the vacuous space of the gallery, a passive-aggressive performance whose viewers define themselves through their responses.

I think Stefan's real work is to act as a catalyst.

2.
Punta Banda, Baja California North
July 19, 2007

    capitalism ...

Chilly morning, grey coastal fog rolls in across the peninsula. I can't shake this feeling of abandonment, sadness – it's like those years in East Hampton when mornings began with a *weight*. A political scientist from Ottawa, Canada, writes about globalization in terms of *extreme loneliness*, and this is a radical thing, to imagine anyone outside the privileged West even having a subjectivity. Contemporary fiction takes this one step further: only upper-middle class domestic life is worth considering. My Grandmother's Cancer, My Divorce, My Subjectivity. And they could be right. The Polish theatre director Tadeusz Kantor once staged a play in which a cast of elderly men and women sat at long benches and desks in an old-fashioned primary schoolroom – the modernist nightmare of constant return and repetition.

    I CAN'T EXPLAIN
    AND
    I WON'T EVEN TRY
    (Brüggemann – white neon, 2003) [...]

Chris Kraus, extracts from 'Twelve Words, Nine Days', *Where Art Belongs* (Los Angeles: Semiotext[e], 2011) 155–8, 164–5.

Biographical Notes

Simone de Beauvoir (1908–86) was a French philosopher, feminist and novelist.

Walter Benjamin (1892–1940) was a German Jewish critical and cultural theorist.

Bernadette Corporation is an artist collective based in New York and Paris, founded in 1994. Its members include Bernadette Van-Huy, John Kelsey and Antek Walczak.

Maurice Blanchot (1907–2003) was a French philosopher, writer and literary critic.

Ina Blom is an art historian and critic and Professor at the University of Oslo.

Nicolas Bourriaud is a curator and critic, and Director of La Panacée/Centre de culture contemporaine, Montpellier.

Stefan Brüggemann is a Mexican-born artist based in London and Mexico City.

John Cage (1912–92) was an American composer, artist and writer.

Ivan Chtcheglov (1933–98) was a French theorist, activist and writer.

Critical Art Ensemble is a critical media collective formed in Tallahassee, Florida, in 1987. Its core members have included Steve Kurtz, Steve Barnes, Dorian Burr, Beverly Schlee and Hope Kurtz.

Jennifer Doyle is Professor of English, University of California at Riverside.

Alla Efimova is an art historian and curator, and Principal of KunstWorks, Berkeley.

Mikhail Epstein is S.C. Dobbs Professor of Cultural Theory and Russian Literature, Emory University.

Peter Fischli is a Swiss artist based in Zurich.

Jonathan Flatley is Associate Professor of English, Wayne State University.

Claire Fontaine is a French artist collective based in Paris.

Dominic Fox is a British writer, poet and musician based in London.

Betty Friedan (1921–2006) was an American writer, feminist and activist.

Elizabeth S. Goodstein is Professor of English and the Liberal Arts, Emory University.

Dan Graham is an American artist based in New York.

Boris Groys is Global Distinguished Professor of Russian and Slavic Studies, New York University.

Julian Jason Haladyn is an art historian, curator and professor at OCAD University, Toronto.

Dick Hebdige is Professor of Film & Media Studies and Art, University of California at Santa Barbara.

Richard Hell is an American musician and writer based in New York.

Dick Higgins (1938–98) was an American artist, musician and composer based in New York.

The Invisible Committee is an anonymous French revolutionary collective.

Ilya Kabakov is a Soviet-born artist based in New York.

Jonathan D. Katz is Director of the doctoral program, Visual Culture Studies, State University of New York.

Siegfried Kracauer (1889–1966) was a German theorist of society, culture and cinema.

Chris Kraus is an American writer and artist based in Los Angeles.

Henri Lefebvre (1901–91) was a French philosopher and sociologist.

Tan Lin is an American poet, writer and filmmaker based in New Jersey.

Sven Lütticken is an art historian and theorist who teaches at the Vrije Universiteit, Amsterdam.

Greil Marcus is an American cultural critic and author based in California.

Ivone Margulies is Professor of Theatre, The Graduate Center, City University of New York.

Jonas Mekas is a Lithuanian-born American artist and filmmaker based in New York.

John Miller is an American artist and writer based in New York and Berlin.

Robert Morris is an American artist based in New York.

Agne Narusyte is an art historian, critic and curator, and Associate Professor, Vilnius Academy of Arts.

Sianne Ngai is a professor of American Literature, Stanford University.

Peter Osborne is Professor of Modern European Philosophy, Kingston University, London.

Georges Perec (1936–82) was a French writer and filmmaker based in Paris.

Patrice Petro is Professor of Film and Media Studies, University of California at Santa Barbara.

Sadie Plant is an independent cultural theorist and writer based in Switzerland.

Yvonne Rainer is an American choreographer, filmmaker and writer based in Los Angeles.

Barbara Rose is an American art historian, critic, filmmaker and curator.

Christine Ross is Professor of Contemporary Art History, McGill University.

Moira Roth is Trefethen Professor of Art History, Mills College, Oakland.

Jon Savage is a British writer, music journalist and broadcaster.

The Situationist International was a European revolutionary movement centred on Paris that included artists, theorists and activists, active from its emergence from Surrealism and Lettrism in 1957 to its official dissolution in 1972.

Valerie Solanas (1936–88) was a dramatist and radical thinker based in New York.

Susan Sontag (1933–2004) was an American critic, writer, activist and filmmaker.

Georges Teyssot is Professor in the School of Architecture, Laval University, Quebec.

Mierle Laderman Ukeles is an American artist based in New York.

Raoul Vaneigem is a Belgian writer and member of the Situationist International from 1961 to 1970.

Geoff Waite is Professor, Department of German Studies, Cornell University.

David Foster Wallace (1962–2008) was an American novelist and writer.

Andy Warhol was an American artist based in New York.

Faith Wilding is a Paraguayan-born American artist and activist, and Professor Emerita of Performance Art, School of the Art Institute of Chicago.

Aleksandr Zinoviev (1922–2006) was a Russian logician, sociologist and writer.

Bibliography

This selection focuses on further reading and does not repeat all of the bibliographic references for writings included in the anthology. Please also see the citations at the end of each text.

Ackerman, Chantal, 'Jeanne Dielman, 23 Quai du Commerce, 1080 Bruxelles', *Camera Obscura*, vol. 1, no. 2 (Fall 1977) 115–121

Atack, Margaret, *May 68 in French Fiction and Film: Rethinking Society, Rethinking Representation* (Oxford and New York: Oxford University Press, 1999)

Bataille, Georges, *Blue of Noon*, trans. Harry Mathews (New York: Urizen Books, 1978)

Baudrillard, Jean, *The Consumer Society: Myths and Structures* (London and Thousand Oaks, California: Sage, 1998)

Beckett, Samuel, *Waiting for Godot: Tragicomedy in Two Acts* (New York: Grove Weidenfeld, 1956)

Benjamin, Walter. 'The Storyteller: Reflections on the Works of Nikolai Leskov', in *Illuminations*, ed. Hannah Arendt, trans. Harry Zohn (New York: Harcourt, Brace & World, 1968) 83–110

Berg, Gretchen, 'Nothing to Lose: An Interview with Andy Warhol', in *Andy Warhol Film Factory, 54–61*, ed. Michael O'Pray (London: BFI Publishing, 1989)

Bergstrom, Janet, 'Chantal Akerman: Splitting', in *Endless Night: Cinema and Psychoanalysis, Parallel Histories*, ed. Janet Bergstrom (Berkeley and Los Angeles: University of California Press, 1999) 273–90

Boym, Svetlana, 'Ilya Kabakov: The Soviet Toilet and the Palace of Utopias', *ARTMargins* (31 December 1999). Accessible at http://www.artmargins.com/index.php/3-exhibitions/435-ilya-kabakov-the-soviet-toilet-and-the-palace-of-utopias

Buck-Morss, Susan, *The Dialectics of Seeing: Walter Benjamin and the Arcades Project* (Cambridge, Massachusetts: The MIT Press, 1989)

Carroll, Mary Ellen, Jonathan Flatley, and Hamza Walker, *MEC* (Göttingen: Steidl, 2010)

Charney, Leo, *Empty Moments* (Durham, North Carolina: Duke University Press, 1998)

Chatelet, Gilles, *To Live and Think Like Pigs: The Incitement of Envy and Boredom in Market Democracies*, trans. Robin Mackay (Falmouth, England: Urbanomic/New York: Sequence Press, 2014)

Colpitt, Frances, 'The Issue of Boredom: Is It Interesting?', *The Journal of Aesthetics and Art Criticism*, vol. 43, no. 4 (Summer 1985) 359–65

Crangle, Sara, *Prosaic Desires: Modernist Knowledge, Boredom, Laughter and Anticipation* (Edinburgh: Edinburgh University Press, 2010)

Cvetkovich, Ann, *Depression: A Public Feeling* (Durham, North Carolina: Duke University Press, 2012)

de Olivera, Nicolas, 'I'm saying nothing and I'm saying it …', in *Stefan Brüggemann* (Zurich: JRP/Ringier, 2008)

—— and Nicola Oxley. 'We Were Never Being Boring: Between Concentration and Inattention', in *Habitus in Habitat II: Other Sides of Cognition*, ed. Sabine Flach and Jan Söffner (Bern: Peter Lang, 2010) 75–88

Debord, Guy, *The Society of the Spectacle*, trans. Donald Nicholson-Smith (New York: Zone Books, 1995)

Doyle, Jennifer, 'The Trouble with Men, or, Sex, Boredom and the Work of Vaginal Davis', in *After Criticism*, ed. Gavin Butt (Malden, Massachusetts/Oxford: Blackwell, 2005) 81–100

Duffy, Nikolai, 'Reading the Unreadable: Kenneth Goldsmith, Conceptual Writing and the Art of Boredom', *Journal of American Studies*, vol. 50, no. 3 (August 2016) 679–8

Elkins, James, 'Are Artists Bored by Their Work?', *Huffington Post* (15 December 2010). Accessible at http://www.huffingtonpost.com/james-elkins/are-artists-bored-by-thei_b_792913.html

Essays on Boredom and Modernity, Critical Studies series, no. 31, ed. Barbara Dalle Pezze and Carlo Salzani (Amsterdam and New York: Rodopi, 2009)

Flaubert, Gustave, *Madame Bovary: Provincial Manners*, trans. Margaret Mauldon (Oxford and New York: Oxford University Press, 2004)

Gardiner, Michael E, 'Henri Lefebvre and the "Sociology of Boredom"', *Theory, Culture & Society*, vol. 29, no. 2 (2012) 37–62

—— *Critiques of Everyday Life* (London and New York: Routledge, 2005)

Gavin, Francesca, 'Bernadette Corporation: Club Kid Collective', *Dazed* (October 2012). Accessible at http://www.dazeddigital.com/artsandculture/article/14640/1/bernadette-corporation-club-kid-collective.

Gilbertson, Leanne, 'Andy Warhol's *Beauty #2*: Demystifying and Reabstracting the Feminine Mystique, Obliquely', *Art Journal*, vol. 62, no. 1 (Spring 2003) 24–33

Goldsmith, Kenneth, 'Being Boring' (2004). Accessible at http://epc.buffalo.edu/authors/goldsmith/goldsmith_boring.html

Goodstein, Elizabeth S., *Experience without Qualities: Boredom and Modernity* (Stanford: Stanford University Press, 2005)

Groys, Boris, 'The Speed of Art', in *Peter Fischli David Weiss*, ed. Urs Staub (Bern: Bundesamt für Kultur/Baden: Verlag Lars Müller, 1995) 53–61

—— *History Becomes Form* (Cambridge, Massachusetts: The MIT Press, 2010)

Haladyn, Julian Jason, *Boredom and Art: Passions of the Will to Boredom* (Winchester, England, and Washington: Zero Books, 2015)

Healy, Seán Desmond, *Boredom, Self and Culture* (Rutherford, New Jersey: Fairleigh Dickinson University Press, 1984)

Heidegger, Martin, *The Fundamental Concepts of Metaphysics: World, Finitude, Solitude*, trans. William McNeill and Nicholas Walker (Bloomington: Indiana University Press, 1995)

Highmore, Ben, *Everyday Life and Cultural Theory: An Introduction* (London and New York: Routledge, 2002)

Houellebecq, Michel, *Whatever: A Novel*, trans. Paul Hammond (London: Serpent's Tail, 1999)

Jameson, Fredric, *Postmodernism, or, The Cultural Logic of Late Capitalism* (Durham, North Carolina: Duke University Press, 1991)

Klapp, Orin E., *Overload and Boredom* (New York and Westport, Connecticut: Greenwood Press, 1986)

Komar & Melamid, 'The Barren Flowers of Evil', in *Primary Documents: A Sourcebook for Eastern and Central European Art since the 1950s*, ed. Laura Hoptman and Tomás Pospiszyl (New York: The Museum of Modern Art, 2002) 258–71

Kuhn, Reinhard Clifford, *The Demon of Noontide: Ennui in Western Literature* (Princeton: Princeton University Press, 1976)

Langbauer, Laurie, 'The City, the Everyday and Boredom: The Case of Sherlock Holmes', *differences: A Journal of Feminist Cultural Studies*, vol. 5, no. 3 (Fall 1993) 80–102

Lefebvre, Henri, *Everyday Life in the Modern World*, trans. Sacha Rabinovitch (New Brunswick: Transaction, 2007)

Legge, Elizabeth, 'Boredom', *Public: An Interdisciplinary Journal of Art, Culture and Ideas*, vol. 19, no. 1 (Spring 2000) 19–20

Lin, Tao, *Shoplifting from American Apparel* (New York: Melville House, 2009)

Marcel Broodthaers: Collected Writings, ed. Gloria Moure (Barcelona: Ediciones Polígrafa, 2012)

McBride, Rita, and Koenraad Dedobbeleer, *Tight: Repeating Boredom / Hall / Privaat* (Dijon: Les Presses du réel, 2009)

McNeil, Legs, *Please Kill Me: The Uncensored Oral History of Punk* (New York: Grove Press, 1996)

Martin, Angela, 'Chantal Akerman's Films: A Dossier', *Feminist Review*, no. 3 (1979) 24–47

Mavor, Carol, 'The Writerly Artist: Beautiful, Boring and Blue', in *A Companion to Contemporary Art Since 1945*, ed. Amelia Jones (Malden, Massachusetts and Oxford: Blackwell, 2006) 271–95

Meno, Joe, *Office Girl: A Novel* (New York: Akashic Books, 2012)

Moran, Joe, 'Benjamin and Boredom', *Critical Quarterly*, vol. 45, no. 1–2 (July 2003) 168–81

Moravia, Alberto, *Boredom*, trans. Angus Davidson (New York: NYRB Classics, 2004)

Narusyte, Agne, *The Aesthetics of Boredom: Lithuanian Photography 1980–1990* (Vilnius: Vilniaus dailes akademija, 2010)

Ngai, Sianne, *Ugly Feelings* (Cambridge, Massachusetts: Harvard University Press, 2005)

Nuur, Navid: *Navid Nuur: Bored at the Museum, Bored at the Studio* (Milan: Mousse Publishing, 2011)

Parr, Martin, *Boring Postcards* (London and New York: Phaidon, 1999)

Pease, Allison, *Modernism, Feminism and the Culture of Boredom* (Cambridge and New York: Cambridge University Press, 2012)

Pelbart, Peter Pál, *Cartography of Exhaustion: Nihilism Inside Out* (Minneapolis: University of Minnesota Press, 2015)

Pessoa, Fernando, *The Book of Disquiet*, ed. and trans. Richard Zenith (London and New York: Penguin, 2002)

Petro, Patrice, 'Historical Ennui, Feminist Boredom', in *The Persistence of History: Cinema, Television and the Modern Event*, ed. Vivian Sobchack (London and New York: Routledge, 1996)

Pettman, Dominic, *After the Orgy: Toward a Politics of Exhaustion* (Albany: State University of New York Press, 2002)

Phillips, Adam, *On Kissing, Tickling and Being Bored: Psychoanalytic Essays on the Unexamined Life* (Cambridge, Massachusetts: Harvard University Press, 1998)

Price, Peter, and Tyler Burba, *On Becoming-Music: Between Boredom and Ecstasy* (New York: Atropos Press, 2010)

Priest, Eldritch, 'Listening to Nothing in Particular: Boredom and Contemporary Experimental Music', *Postmodern Culture*, vol. 21, no. 2 (January 2011)

―― *Boring Formless Nonsense: Experimental Music and the Aesthetics of Failure* (London and New York: Bloomsbury, 2013)

Ramos, Filipa, 'Ragnar Kjartansson', *Domus* (December 2013). Accessible at http://www.domusweb.it/en/art/2013/12/10/ragnar_kjartansson.html

Rehberg, Vivian Sky, 'Tant qu'il est encore temps / While There Is Still Time', in *Chantal Akerman: Too Far, Too Close*, ed. Dieter Roelstraete and Anders Kreuger (Antwerp: Ludion, 2012) 51–9

Sadler, Simon, *The Situationist City* (Cambridge, Massachusetts: The MIT Press, 1999)

Sartre, Jean-Paul, *Nausea*, trans. Lloyd Alexander (New York: New Directions, 1964)

Schivelbusch, Wolfgang, *The Railway Journey: The Industrialization and Perception of Time and Space*, trans. Anselm Hollo (Malden, Massachusetts and Oxford: Blackwell, 1980)

Sheringham, Michael, *Everyday Life: Theories and Practices from Surrealism to the Present* (Oxford and New York: Oxford University Press, 2006)

Sholette, Gregory, *Dark Matter: Art and Politics in the Age of Enterprise Culture* (London and New York: Pluto Press, 2011)

Situationist International Anthology, ed. and trans. Ken Knabb (Berkeley: Bureau of Public Secrets, 1981)

Spacks, Patricia Meyer, *Boredom: The Literary History of a State of Mind* (Chicago: University of Chicago Press, 1995)

Strickland, Edward, *Minimalism – Origins* (Bloomington: Indiana University Press, 1993)

Svendsen, Lars, *A Philosophy of Boredom*, trans. John Irons (London: Reaktion, 2005)

Toohey, Peter, *Boredom: A Lively History* (New Haven and London: Yale University Press, 2011)

Vanhaelen, Angela, 'Boredom's Threshold: Dutch Realism', in *The Erotics of Looking: Early Modern Netherlandish Art*, ed. Vanhaelen and Bronwen Wilson (Chichester, England: Wiley-Blackwell, 2013)

Warhol, Andy and Pat Hackett, *POPism: The Warhol '60s* (New York: Harcourt, Brace & World, 1980)

Wittmann, Marc, *Felt Time: The Psychology of How We Perceive Time*, trans. Erik Butler (Cambridge, Massachusetts: The MIT Press, 2016)

Woo, Jung-Ah, 'On Kawara's Date Paintings: Series of Horror and Boredom', *Art Journal*, vol. 69, no. 3 (2010) 62–72

Index

Adorno, Theodor W. 117n7, 170n5
Akerman, Chantal 18, 136-8, 142, 143
Alÿs, Francis 191-2
Andersen, Eric 83, 84
Andre, Carl 101
Andress, Ursula 90
Andriuskevicius, Alfonsas 178, 181n5
Aristotle 116, 168, 169
Armleder, John 111
Armstrong, Carol 13, 21n5
Artaud, Antonin 103, 118
Augé, Marc 12, 21n2

Baldessari, John 118-23
Bannard, Walter Darby 99
Barthes, Roland 159
Bataille, Georges 111, 192
Baudelaire, Charles 13, 27, 114, 115, 117n8
Baudrillard, Jean 20, 22-23n25-6, 179, 181n6, 219
Beaton, Cecil 123
Beauvoir, Simone de 17, 129
Beckett, Samuel 102, 199
Beethoven, Ludwig van 126, 129
Bellow, Saul 177
Bengston, Billy Al 101
Benjamin, Walter 14, 21n6, 28-30, 31, 33, 41-2, 43n4, n6, n7, 115, 117n15, 142, 220, 221n1, 222n2-3
Berardi, Franco ('Bifo') 218
Bergman, Ingmar 105, 196
Bernadette Corporation 209-10
'Bike Boy' (Joe Spencer) 138
Bik Van der Pol (Liesbeth Bik, Jos van der Pol) 218
Blanchot, Maurice 15, 16, 22n10, 53-7, 139, 143n4
Blom, Ina 84-6

Boon, Richard 149
Boone, Pat 127
Bourriaud, Nicolas 110-11
Brecht, George 82-3
Breton, André 159
Brown, Denise Scott 21n1
Brüggemann, Stefan 222-5
Büchner, Georg 57
Buck-Morss, Susan 22n7
Burroughs, William 109
Buzzcocks 148, 149-50

Cage, John 16, 17, 72, 73, 74, 75, 76, 76n2-3, 77, 78, 79, 80, 80n1, 81n5, 82, 85, 102, 104, 105, 108, 109, 111, 120, 199, 217
Camus, Albert 191
Carey, Benedict 218
Chaadaev, Petr Iakovlevich 187, 189n4
Chambers, Ross 79, 80n3
Chekhov, Anton 53
Childs, Lucinda 95
Christ (Jesus of Nazareth) 189, 198
Chtcheglov, Ivan ('Gilles Ivain') 15, 22n8, 46-7
Clark, T.J. 13, 21n4, 123n2
Clash, The 18, 169, 170n13-14, 171n15
Cohn, Roy M. 76
Collective Actions 179
Crary, Jonathan 121, 123n1, 216
Critical Art Ensemble 196-7
Csikszentmihalyi, Mihaly 39, 40n7
Cunningham, Merce 73, 74, 98, 99, 101

Danto, Arthur C. 202n7
Davis, Gene 101
Dean, James 152
Debord, Guy 15, 22n9, 64-7, 69n3-5, n7-17, n19, 217, 224
Deleuze, Gilles 23n27, 193n4, 225
D'Emilio, John 80n2
de Man, Paul 202, 202n10

Derrida, Jacques 79-80
Descartes, René 189
Devoto, Howard 149
Doyle, Jennifer 138-44
Duchamp, Marcel 73, 74, 75, 76n1, 77, 78, 102, 104, 111
Dunn, Judith 95
Dunn, Robert 101
Duve, Thierry de 137, 138n1

Edison, Thomas 121
Efimova, Alla 181-3
Ehrenberg, Alain 205, 206, 206n4-7
Eisenstein, Sergei 121, 122
Elizabeth I of England 126
Engels, Friedrich 29, 68, 69n18
Epstein, Brian 150-51
Epstein, Mikhail 186-9
Evans, Walker 180

Feldman, Morton 103
Fenichel, Otto 39, 40n5-6
Ferenczi, Sandor 39
Fischli, Peter 148
Flatley, Jonathan 112-17
Flaubert, Gustave 13
Flavin, Dan 101
Fontaine, Claire (collective) 211-13
Ford, Henry 203
Foster, Hal 22n20
Foucault, Michel 193n3
Fournel, Victor 30
Fox, Dominic 207-9
Frank, Robert 180
Freed, Alan 150-51, 152
Freud, Sigmund 203
Friedan, Betty 17, 114, 115, 117n10, 126-8

Gasché, Rodolphe 33, 34n5
Geldzahler, Henry 16, 22n13

Gelmis, Joseph 87-8
Gide, André 29
Gilman, Charlotte Perkins 13
Ginsberg, Allen 73
Giorno, John 218
Glass, Philip 199
Godard, Jean-Luc 151
Godfrey, Mark 148
Goffman, Erving 143n2
Goldman, Peter 89, 89n1
Goldmann, Lucien 22n21, 57n1
Goldsmith, Kenneth 201
Goncharov, Ivan 39
Goodstein, Elizabeth S. 22n14, 26-8, 30, 31, 33n2-3, 217
Gordon, Kim 153
Gorky, Maxim 182
Goya, Francisco de 110
Graham, Dan 150-52
Gramsci, Antonio 165, 166, 168, 170n8, n10
Grimm, Jacob and Wilhelm 155
Gross, Sally 95
Groys, Boris 20, 22n23-24, 189-93
Guattari, Félix 225

Haladyn, Julian Jason 30-34
Hamilton, Ann 199, 200
Harris, Ed 123
Hay, Deborah 95
Hebdige, Dick 19, 22n19, 157-60
Heidegger, Martin 190, 191, 193n2
Hell, Richard 151, 157, 161-2
Higgins, Dick 81-4, 84-6, 86n1, n3-7, 217-18
Ho Chi Minh 156
Hoffman, Abbie 141, 151
Holder, Tony 95
Hölderlin, Friedrich 103
Hopkins, Gerard Manley 208
Horkheimer, Max 170n5
Huyghe, Pierre 218

Huysmans, Joris Karl 196, 197

Ilf, Ilya 189
Invisible Committee, The 213-15
Isaacs, Alan J. 202n8
Izenour, Steven 21n1

Jameson, Fredric 19, 22n22, 112, 117n3
Jankélévitch, Vladimir 37, 38, 39, 40n1-2
Jarman, Derek 158
Jay, Gregory 43n8
Jerphagnon, Lucien 178
Johns, Jasper 73, 74, 75, 78, 99, 109, 111, 199
Jones, Steve 19
Jordan (Westwood/McLaren model and actor) 158
Joselit, David 141, 143n10
Judd, Donald 101, 112-17, 117n1

Kabakov, Ilya 20, 179, 183-9, 189n1-3
Kafka, Franz 53
Kandinsky, Wassily 81
Kant, Immanuel 201, 202, 202n6
Kantor, Tadeusz 225
Kaplan, Cara 139, 143n2, n8
Kaprow, Allan 118
Katz, Jonathan D. 77-81
Katz, Zack 216
Kaufman, Eleanor 139, 143n3-6
Keats, John 106
Kennedy, Jackie 91
Kerouac, Jack 73
Kierkegaard, Søren 13, 189, 192n1
Klapp, Orrin E. 39, 40n8, 177, 181n1
Kleist, Heinrich von 103
Klosowski, Thorin 217
Komar & Melamid (Vitaly Komar, Alexander Melamid) 177, 181n3
Kooning, Willem de 99, 111
Kostelanetz, Richard 76n2-3

Kracauer, Siegfried 27, 28n2, 34-7, 41-2, 43n2, 43n5, 115, 117n14, n16, 140-41, 142, 143n9, 144n13, 220
Kraus, Chris 224-5
Kristall, Hilly 161
Kuhn, Reinhard 33n1
Kutuzov, Mikhail 187, 189n5

Lacan, Jacques 199, 202n1
Lafargue, Paul 218, 219
'Lautréamont, Comte de' (Isidore Ducasse) 103
Lears, Jackson 117n6
Led Zeppelin 153
Lefebvre, Henri 12, 15, 21n3, 22n16, 49-52, 56, 57
Lefevre, Mike 163-4, 165, 166, 168, 170n3
Lenin, Vladimir 168
Leopardi, Giacomo 38, 40n4
Lepenies, Wolf 114, 117n13
Levine, Sherrie 111
LeWitt, Sol 110
Lichtenstein, Roy 110
Lin, Tan 90-91
Linton, Ralph 102
Lohan, Lindsay 161
Lukács, Georg 22n21, 57n1, 64
Lütticken, Sven 216-19
Lydon, John ('Johnny Rotten') 19, 151, 156, 163, 170n2
Lyotard, Jean-François 43, 43n9

McCarthy, Joseph 17, 73, 74, 75, 76
McDonough, Tom 12-23
McGregor, Douglas 204, 206n2
Maciunas, George 218
McKenzie, Jon 203, 204, 206n1, n3
McLaren, Malcolm 18, 19, 150-52, 162, 167, 168, 169, 222-4
Mac Low, Jackson 83, 199, 217, 218
McLuhan, Marshall 73, 106

Mallarmé, Stéphane 107
Malraux, André 110
Manet, Édouard 13, 111
Mannoni, Octave 170n6
Marcus, Greil 152-7, 162-3, 167, 168, 169, 170n1, n4, n11
Margulies, Ivone 22n17, 136-8
Marley, Bob 160
Marx, Harpo 105
Marx, Karl 13, 29, 64, 65, 66, 68, 69n6, n18, 121, 151, 155, 165, 166, 168, 169, 170n7, n9, 207
Mayakovsky, Vladimir 61
Meek, Joe 150
Mekas, Jonas 88-9
Melville, Herman 21
Meyer, James 117n5
Mikhailov, Boris 20, 179-80, 181n7, 181-3
Miller, John 118-23
Mills, C. Wright 114, 115, 117n11-12
Monroe, Marilyn 91
Monteverdi, Claudio 129
Morris, Robert 94, 95, 96, 97-8, 101
Mulvey, Laura 141, 142, 143n11, 144n12

Namuth, Hans 122-3
Napoleon Bonaparte 187, 188
Narusyte, Agne 177-81
Nauman, Bruce 225
New York Dolls 19, 151, 153, 162
Newman, Barnett 97, 99
Ngai, Sianne 199-203
Nietzsche, Friedrich 192

Oldenburg, Claes 120
Oldham, Andrew Loog 150
Orton, Fred 80, 80n4
Osborne, Peter 220-22
Ouspensky, Pyotr Demianovich 149

Paxton, Steve 96

Perec, Georges 58-60, 199
Petro, Patrice 40-43
Petrov, Yevgeni 189
Phillips, Adam 142
Phillips, Sam 153
Pilson, John 205
Plant, Sadie 64-9
Plato 169
Poe, Edgar Allan 73
Polke, Sigmar 111, 148
Pollock, Jackson 101, 122-3
Ponge, Francis 108
Poons, Larry 101
Pop, Iggy 168
Potts, Alex 117n4
Public Image 163

Rabin, Oskar 179
Rainer, Yvonne 94-7, 101
Ramones 18, 151
Rauschenberg, Robert 73, 74, 77, 78, 79, 80, 96, 98, 111
Reid, Jamie 18, 163
Reinhardt, Ad 98
Richter, Gerhard 199, 200, 201, 202n4
Rilke, Rainer Maria 107-8, 109
Riesman, David 73, 114
Robbe-Grillet, Alain 100, 108, 199
Rose, Barbara 16, 22n11, 98-103
Rosenquist, James 110
Ross, Christine 203-6
Ross, Kristin 17, 22n15
Roth, Moira 73-6, 77, 78
Rothko, Mark 123
Rotten, Johnny: see Lydon, John
Roussel, Raymond 108, 199
Ryazanov, Eldar 177
Ryman, Robert 199

Sade, D.A.F., Marquis de 110, 199

Satie, Erik 81-2, 84, 101, 102, 103
Savage, Jon 149-50, 169
Schiller, Friedrich 26, 27n1
Schine, G. David 76
Schlichter, Joseph 96
Schlüpmann, Heide 41, 43n3
Schoenberg, Arnold 81
Schopenhauer, Arthur 32, 34n4, 37, 40n1, 196
Schor, Naomi 139, 143n1
Sedgwick, Edie 90
Seidenberg, Robert 170n2
Sex Pistols 18, 22n18, 151, 153, 156, 163, 164, 169
Shattuck, Roger 100, 102, 103
Shelley, Pete 149-50
Simmel, Georg 40, 41, 43, 43n1
Situationist International 47-8, 64-9 passim., 69n1, 151, 155, 167-8, 170n12, 217
Smith, Patti 151
Solanas, Valerie 143, 144n14, 144-5
Sonic Youth 153
Sontag, Susan 16, 22n12, 103-10, 202n2
Spacks, Patricia 181n2
Stein, Gertrude 100, 101, 120, 199, 200, 201, 202
Stella, Frank 97
Stemrich, Gregor 118
Stewart, Rod 153
Superstar, Ingrid 138-44

Tannen, Deborah 140
Tardieu, Émile 28, 38, 40n3
Taussig, Michael 121
Taylor, Frederick W. 203
Terkel, Studs 163-4, 170n3
Teyssot, Georges 27-40
Tiqqun (collective) 21, 23n28
Truman, Harry S. 74

Ukeles, Mierle Laderman 18, 129-32

Vaneigem, Raoul 60-63, 64, 69n2, 217
Veblen, Thorstein 118
Velvet Underground 141
Venturi, Robert 21n1
Veuillot, Louis 28
Vicious, Sid 151
Vogler, Candace 139-40, 143n7
von Gall, Ferdinand 29
Vulfpeck 219

Waite, Geoff 162-71
Wakefield, Neville 202n3
Wallace, David Foster 197-8
Wallace, George 164
Warhol, Andy 16, 87-91, 101, 102, 108, 110, 112-17, 117n2, n9, 119, 121, 122, 138-44, 151, 199, 218
Watson, Ben 202n9
Westmoreland, William 156
Who, The 153
Whyte, William H. 114
Wilding, Faith 18, 133-6
Williams, Emmett 83, 84
Williams, Gilda 180, 181n7
Wilson, Edmund 156

Young, LaMonte 83, 101
Young, Neil 168-9

Zinoviev, Aleksandr 19, 174-6
Zizek, Slavoj 170n6
Zox, Larry 99
Zweig, Janet 200, 202n5

ACKNOWLEDGEMENTS

Editor's acknowledgements
I would like to thank Iwona Blazwick, OBE, Director of the Whitechapel Gallery, for first proposing that I take on this project, and Ian Farr, who as commissioning editor of this series guided this book toward completion in ways both practical and intellectual. Conversations with several colleagues provided key suggestions and invaluable advice; among them are Suzanne Cotter, Mark Godfrey, Jen Kennedy, Lolita Jablonskiene, Nadja Millner-Larsen, Christian Rattemeyer, Kitty Scott and Brian Wall.

Publisher's acknowledgements
Whitechapel Gallery is grateful to all those who gave their generous permission to reproduce the listed material. Every effort has been made to secure all permissions and we apologize for any inadvertent errors or omissions. If notified, we will endeavour to correct these at the earliest opportunity. We would like to express our thanks to all who contributed to the making of this volume: Ina Blom, Nicolas Bourriaud, Stefan Brüggemann, Claire Fontaine, Critical Art Ensemble, Jennifer Doyle, Alla Efimova, Mikhail Epstein, Jonathan Flatley, Mark Godfrey, Kenneth Goldsmith, Elizabeth Goodstein, Dan Graham, Boris Groys, Julian Jason Haladyn, Dick Hebdige, Ilya Kabakov, Jonathan D. Katz, Tan Lin, Sven Lütticken, Ivone Margulies, Jonas Mekas, John Miller, Agne Narusyte, Sianne Ngai, Peter Osborne, Patrice Petro, Sadie Plant, Yvonne Rainer, Christine Ross, Moira Roth, Jon Savage, Georges Teyssot, Mierle Laderman Ukeles, Catie Heitz and Megan Paetzhold, Geoff Waite, Faith Wilding.

We also gratefully acknowledge the cooperation of AK Press, Counterpoint Press, Duke University Press, Faber & Faber, David R. Godine, Harvard University Press, The Estate of Dick Higgins, Hill Nadell Literary Agency, John Hunt Publishing, Lisson Gallery, University of Minnesota Press, MIT Press, MIT Press Journals, PM Press, Rutgers University Press, Semiotext[e], Stanford University Press, Tate Etc., Verso, Wesleyan University Press, Yale French Studies, Zero Books.

Whitechapel Gallery

whitechapelgallery.org